RESURRECTING THE CROSS

How Embracing the Way of the Cross Frees us
to Grow in Love and Truth Through the Spirit

The Cross is:

The Way of Truth   The Way of Restoration

The Way of Overcoming Evil   The Way of Freedom
& Purpose

The Way of Forgiveness   The Way of Love

ERNEST RANDOLPH

Trilogy Christian Publishers
A Wholly Owned Subsidiary of Trinity Broadcasting Network
2442 Michelle Drive
Tustin, CA 92780

For information, address Trilogy Christian Publishing
Rights Department, 2442 Michelle Drive, Tustin, Ca 92780.
First Trilogy Christian Publishing hardcover edition May 2018
Trilogy Christian Publishing/ TBN and colophon are trademarks of
Trinity Broadcasting Network.
For information about special discounts for bulk purchases, please
contact Trilogy Christian Publishing.
Manufactured in the United States of America

10 9 8 7 6 5 4 3 2 1
Library of Congress Cataloging-in-Publication Data is available.
ISBN 978-1-68556-020-1
ISBN 978-1-68556-021-8 (ebook)

THESIS

THE IMPORTANCE OF UNDERSTANDING THE TRUE
TRANSFORMATION OF THE CROSS WHICH ENDS
THE LAW IN THE BELIEVER'S LIFE, REPLACING
IT WITH SANCTIFICATION SOLELY BY THE SPIRIT
WHO TEACHES US THE TRUTHS OF OUR SALVATION
AND TEACHES US TO EMULATE THE LOVE JESUS
DEMONSTRATED ON THE CROSS

Support the Ministry of Ernest Randolph

If you have a hard copy of this book, it might mean that you were given a copy. Ernest is happy to give his book away, but he asks, if you like the book, that you would buy an online digital copy to support the distribution of more books. While you're there, please leave a review.

In addition, Ernest would be happy to speak at your church or event. Please feel free to email him your request at: ernestrandolph@msn.com. Or, visit his website at www.GraceTalk.net.

TABLE OF CONTENTS

APPENDIX   288

BIBLIOGRAPHY   319

PREFACE

For the message of the cross is foolishness to those who are perishing, but to us who are being saved it is the power of God.

1 Corinthians 1:18 (NKJV)

Jesus brought a paradigm shift to the whole world by modeling an entirely new way of life through His loving, sacrificial death on the cross. He possessed more power and wisdom than anyone who ever lived, yet He did not use it to rule the world; instead, He suffered in order to have a relationship with humanity. Understanding this reason-defying act from a new perspective greatly enhances our sense of how Jesus changes our lives and defines our purpose as His followers in this seemingly confusing world we live in. The work of Christ on the cross frees us to live by the Spirit and opens up for us a whole new life. The Apostle Paul wrote that this freedom is not the old life of living by the "law of sin and death;" it is a new life lived by the "law of the Spirit."[1] The Apostle John explained how to live by the "law of the Spirit" when he wrote: "If we love one another, God abides in us, and His love is perfected in us" (1 John 4:12, NASB). The essence of the new life paradigm is that we emulate the love of Jesus through the power of the

---

1 Romans 8:2 (NASB)

11

Spirit.

Of course, our transformation begins with following Jesus as Lord, but the richness of understanding the cross promotes real, lasting change in us. In light of this truth, I made a great effort to explain and simplify the gospel and also have attempted to demonstrate how the Christian life is lived out at the foot of the cross. In some respects, this book might be looked at as an existential guide to the Christian life.

As we journey through this life, there are a number of influences that affect who we are becoming. From the earliest part of our lives, we are shaped by the people around us. They teach us how to think and how to relate to others. As we mature, we begin to think for ourselves, but we carry the influence of our early years with us. We also experience heartache, shame, regret, and suffering, sometimes far too early in life. These experiences combine with our inherent personalities, our physical makeup, strengths, weaknesses, likes, and dislikes to make us who we are.

All of our experiences in life affect our journey, influencing how we see our world, what we believe is true, and how we act based upon what we believe. I am not asking you to throw away any of these experiences and any of the opinions that make you who you are today. I am simply hoping that this book can help you along in your journey, and Lord willing, that I can influence you to move closer to Jesus and closer to a life of living by His love.

The insight I am sharing may stretch what you have previously believed about Christianity. Because of the differences I am presenting, I have strived to keep every claim I make within the bounds of scripture using multiple references. Knowing how entrenched and complicated our belief systems can be, I understand how hard it is to consider, what seems to be strange, ideas that may be a little different. There will be a few key concepts in this book that will challenge the conservative and the not-so-conservative Christian. I also hope to offer the non-Christian some compelling reasons to follow Jesus. Because of my strong desire that all people experience the transforming power of salvation as I believe God intended it, I am urging you to look at salvation and sanctification from this slightly different perspective.

Understanding what life in the Spirit looked like from a new perspective was not easy for me. It took me forty-five years to listen to what the Spirit was trying to teach me all my life. He was imploring me to embrace the love and sacrifice that Jesus demonstrated on the cross—where He took away my sins, freed me from the law, and transformed me by teaching me to love! He was showing me that this life is not about becoming righteous by following rules. Rather, this life is a process of the Spirit perfecting His children in heavenly love. I believe God has unending truths to teach me no matter how long it takes, and He is faithful in teaching me through His Spirit. Hopefully, I have received a glimpse of His truth regarding salvation and the cross and am able to share it with you so that, by reading this book, you will grow closer to knowing Jesus from the perspective of the cross.

INTRODUCTION

And we know that in all things God works for the good of those who love him, who have been called according to his purpose.

Romans 8:28 (NIV)

From the very moment we are born, it seems we begin creating our kingdom. Our first servants are our mother and father. They do everything for us at our beck and call. We may add in a brother, a sister, extended family, a babysitter, and others to our court. All must be approved by us. We scream and cry at the ones we don't like and smile at the ones we do.

As you know, our power begins to fade quickly. Tables turn, and we are now being corrected or ignored when we are mean or demanding. We are disciplined when we hurt someone else. We don't get everything we want. Some people decide they don't like us. The building of our kingdom gets exponentially more complicated with each passing day.

Soon it is time to enter school. We now learn that kingdom building is highly competitive, with thousands of other kids on the same journey. In America, we are told that if you do everything right, you can become anything you want, maybe even the president. We have to decide what we must learn and who to become in order to achieve our desired kingdom.

As we get older, we are faced with the very difficult question of higher education. Greater learning is expensive and difficult. One must be convinced that it will be a good building stone.

The prospect of obtaining a spouse, a life partner to join us on this journey weighs heavily on everyone. Desires to not have to continually struggle for companionship and wanting someone permanent to give and receive love with can be overwhelming. We may have the desire to have children and build a family, much like the family we had, except improved, of course.

At different stages of this building project, most of us will stumble on the prospect of the existence of a higher power, and we must decide if that higher power has a place in our kingdom. I'm sure you logically assume that this book is going to be about including Jesus in your kingdom as that higher power. If that is what you thought, you are close. It is not only about including Him but allowing Him to transform your entire kingdom.

Please allow me to share some of my personal journey with God that led me to the place of writing this book. By my eighteenth year, I fully embraced the need for Jesus in my life, but it was not an easy road to get there. My interaction with Christianity started very young, and my personal Christian struggle emerged in my heart around the age of twelve. I grew up in a small town in the West as a backsliding, conservative Christian, living in a chaotic and dysfunctional family of two brothers and five sisters. The turmoil of my childhood and the hypocrisy of my father's faith led me to have multiple questions about what I wanted God's role to be in my kingdom. My father would wear out Bibles, reading them every night, and have us in church on Sunday, but he brutally fought with my mother every Sunday afternoon. To solve some of these incongruencies of their Christianity, I found myself seeking some explanation beyond the over-simplified and superficial Christian explanations. The standard answers I had encountered were not adequately explaining my situation, and I found myself becoming quite rebellious toward my family and God. Throughout my waywardness, Jesus continued to pursue me, and at sixteen, I began to see His importance in my life.

I drew closer to Jesus, but I struggled with knowing Him and experiencing the freedom and love that was promised. I knew plenty of commendable Christian people for whom the Christian religion of rules and confession worked to inspire them to live somewhat honorable lives, especially on the outside, but it did not work for me. On the inside, my hate, anger, and judgment ran deep and would continue to plague me up until recently; there was no religious cure. I had not been shown by my family how to behave. I was under control enough to be acceptable but usually not exceptional, and I made some great mistakes that hurt others dearly. There was no Bible verse or repenting of sins that could fix me. There was no list that I could follow, commitment I could make, or self-punishment I could inflict to change my behavior. Christianity had been a part of my life since day one, and it had not cured me of my problems. How could something so true not transform my kingdom in the way that I thought it should? Was I looking at it all wrong?

The route that led me to understand God's solution to my problems started in high school. As a senior in high school, I had a revival in my Christian life and made a plan to conquer my sin. I went through the New Testament and made a list of all the bad behaviors not to do and all the good actions I need to perform. Wow! Now that was a great list. There are few propositions that we encounter in life that can make you feel more overwhelmed and discouraged than a list of dos and don'ts, but I was up for the challenge. I was doing well, I thought. I sought God with all my heart, avoided all the usual sins, respected my parents, loved my siblings, and even kept my actions respectable with my girlfriend. My behavior had been the opposite just a year prior, which made me feel like I was doing a great job at being a satisfactory Christian. I thought I had found an answer to including God in my kingdom.

The summer after my senior year of high school, I had the privilege to be camp counselor for six weeks. This was an amazing experience of friendship, worship, and godly teaching. At the end of the season, the director felt it edifying to do a personal evaluation of each counselor. Now came the first great blow to my legalism and self-empowered righteousness. The dean said I was "not committed to God enough." It is hard to think of a worse criticism he could have said to a young, idealistic Christian. At that moment, I broke the command not to hate. It discouraged me greatly to have a Christian leader criticize me harshly. I was shaken in my resolve. I was still committed to God, but my commitment to righteous behavior began to waiver.

During my freshman year of college at a Christian university, I was catapulted on my journey of learning truths about Christianity and life. I was shocked and enlightened as a young believer. My two favorite classes were "Developing a Christian Worldview," which helped me relate Christianity to the broader world, and "Introduction to Psychology," which helped me understand truths about my own behavior. On the not-so-positive side, in my personal life, I began to question moral boundaries with my girlfriend. In some ways, I saw her as the answer to fill the deficit of love left by my broken family. The kingdom I was building was greatly expanded.

During my sophomore year, things took a darker turn. I crossed moral lines in my dating relationship, which rocked my world. I was now a walking, living hypocrite. Not only was this against the rules of the college, but it was also tremendously mentally and morally conflicting for someone headed into ministry. I had plenty of Christian knowledge: I could describe the Christian influence on western culture, I could explain the trinity and predestination, and I knew the five points of Calvinism, but these truths did not help me control my day-to-day behavior. Something was drastically wrong, and learning more about Christianity and its rules was not solving my problems.

Without any alternative solutions to guide me, I went back to following my legal regiment and committed to behave better for the sake of my love for God and my future working in ministry. This attempt to pull me up by my bootstraps had a strong sense of legalism to it in terms of an attempt to earn God's favor by behaving well. Even though I knew God still loved me when I failed, I still thought it was my job to behave better, crashing hard when I would fail. I did not fully understand that He was in the process of changing my heart first before He changed my actions; that would follow.

In my struggle throughout my twenties, I wondered the same thoughts most people do: What is my purpose? Will I ever find a mate? Am I a fairly good person, even though I have done some awful sins in the past and still seem to fail quite often? Why is my life not easier? All of these questions and more swirled around in the back of my mind. In the stew of my conscious and subconscious mind, these questions mingled with all the emotions of loneliness, hurt, pride, disappointments, happiness, depression, and all my needs and desires. It seems our psychological health can be a mess for many of us, especially young adults. At that time, I did not understand how much I needed to rely on God's Spirit. I was doing whatever I wanted while trying to make my life better as I was building my kingdom on my own. I definitely tried to get it right, yet I was a long way from finding out what "right" was.

At twenty-two, I finished up my undergraduate program in youth ministry and was working at a church as an intern. They offered me a part-time junior high youth pastor position for $700 a month. This was not much to live on, even in 1990, so I waited tables on the side to pay the bills. Feeling a bit out of place and unappreciated, I went to my pastor for counseling and direction. He shared his opinion that I needed to go to seminary—the last place I wanted to go. I knew, subconsciously, that learning more about Christianity would not cure the confusion in my heart. Instead of staying and following the pastor's direction, I left looking for another ministry job and landed at a boy's camp in North Carolina, a Christian wilderness therapy camp for troubled teens. I spent a year there in the woods with delinquent kids, some wards of the state and some whose parents could no longer handle them. A year was all I could handle being isolated from peers at such a young age, and I quickly moved on.

I found myself back in Denver and began working as an electrician to make ends meet. I was advancing in my electrical skills, but my heart was not done with ministry. Finally, listening to my old pastor's advice, I enrolled in seminary. I initially started with two night courses the first term and needed to increase it to all-day Monday classes for the upcoming term. The prospect of working four days a week did not sit well with my electrical boss, and he demanded that I choose one or the other. I chose to drop seminary. My real boss, God, did not agree with that decision.

As I drove to work on the day that seminary registration was to take place, a song blared on the Christian radio station with lyrics to the effect of "How can you turn your back on me after what I've done for you?" I was a little disconcerted with how applicable the song felt to my decision not to stay in seminary. When I arrived at the job site, no supervisor was there to meet me and tell me what to do, which had never happened before. I went to a payphone and called in. I was instructed to simply wait for the supervisor to show up. Sitting at a random job site for almost two hours with nothing to do felt like God was literally "icing me." Agonizing over my decision as the time ticked away on my watch, I realized that if I left right then, it still was not too late to register. Finally, I followed God's obvious prompting, quit my job on the spot, and left to enroll in seminary. It was an exciting time where it demonstrably felt like God stepped into my life that day. I was high on the Spirit, and seminary was right where God wanted me.

It is interesting how God works in our lives, and we see it much clearer when we look back. I found that the more I sought God's will and purpose in my life, the more circumstances continued to get better for me. I met my amazing wife shortly after graduating from seminary, and we were married two years later. In time, we took a part-time junior high youth pastor position in Aurora, Colorado, for three years. At thirty-four, this was my last time working officially in a church. It was a life-changing experience, and we left with fond feelings about what we had accomplished. We then found ourselves volunteering at a church near our house on the west side of Denver, helping another youth-pastor acquaintance. I continued to love working with youth, whether paid or not. I felt very led by the Spirit at this time.

A painful experience at my next ministry led me to abandon the ways normally taught in the church in regard to what the core motivations of Christianity are. I began volunteering as a youth leader, which was enjoyable and fruitful for the first year, and the youth pastor and I became relatively close friends. In the second year, the church began to pressure him to increase numbers and morale. My wife and I began investing more time and energy to help, which proved to be a futile effort because, unfortunately, the church leadership had already made its decision about the health of the youth group. Consequently, the church chose to hire an outside consultant to evaluate his youth program and enact change. Sadly, they looked past all the progress we were accomplishing and saw only the weaknesses. Much of the blame for the failing youth group was laid on me because I was helping with quite a few aspects of the group. It was even theorized that I was trying to take over the youth pastor's job.

The consultant, who incidentally was a close friend of mine, called me up one night. He was subversively trying to confirm his suspicion that I wanted to take over the youth group. Since that was not my intention and he was getting nowhere in the conversation, he came right out and said, "Ernie, you're a washed-up youth pastor trying to take over John's job." This statement from my friend tore out all of my desire to be a part of this ministry or any ministry in the future. Even though it hurt me to the core, I could not abandon the youth. I tried to ignore the hurtful, wrong accusations and even continued to help until the church ended my friend's job, but the hurt did not go away. It ripped at my heart, and each little incident brought it back. I was completely confused as to what God wanted from me and why He would do this to me through His pastor and my friend. I felt I had failed God and was finished with the ministry, thinking, "What other sign could God give me?" This two-by-four upside the head had left its mark.

Shortly after the experience, I began to avoid reading the Bible. I knew I could barely—if at all—obey even one of the sayings or commandments in the Bible perfectly. I had studied the Bible my whole life, so I thought I already had enough scripture in my head to remind me of my inadequacy. I also knew the Bible well enough to discuss what I needed to keep up my youth group teaching. God still worked on me in the darkness. I continued to devote myself to work and to my wife and kids, feeling depressed when I failed. Since I believed I had failed God as a youth worker, I wanted to get this part of my life right. Even with all my effort, I was not always successful. I was relatively happy—except when someone expected what I could not deliver or when people were dissatisfied with my work. I tried not to let either happen.

In my time of struggle, God introduced me to a radio show done by Aaron Budjen with Living God Ministries.[2] Jesus changed my life through Aaron's teaching about the complete forgiveness given at the cross and expanded my understanding of the gospel. My eyes were slowly opened through listening to countless hours of his broadcasts. I finally understood the great forgiveness God gives us at salvation and how He gives us His Spirit and frees us from the law. What a life-changing realization! I then realized that it was God's plan for me to back off scripture so I could allow God to correct my misconceptions about salvation and His grace. I needed this time for a paradigm shift about whose kingdom I was building and how much Christ's work on the cross plays a central role in how we build our kingdoms in the fashion of His example.

I am not disappointed about my ministry path because I can look back and see the journey God was taking me on and how I needed to change my understanding of salvation. My small mountain church, where I attended and worked with the youth during this time, was a perfect environment for me to process this. I did not abandon God, nor did He abandon me; we grew closer and deeper together in all my struggles.

My walk with God, including my experiences in ministry, has been amazing and transforming. As I look back, it is clear that God reached out to me at a young age and walked me through the turmoil of my childhood. I had some wonderful friends, caring siblings, and an abundance of great Christian influences in my life. God even gave me experiences that were

---

2 Aaron Budjen, www.livinggodministries.net, 2020

supernatural at times. There was plenty of good and bad, the bad mostly due to struggle with the sin of others and my own sin. On the darker side, I was often guilty of self-sabotage. It seems my efforts were rarely enough and either led to failure or underperforming, and I remember not being satisfied and wanting more. At times, the harder I tried, the harder I fell. Gratefully, God was able to take my eclectic life of good and evil and use it to help me see life from a unique perspective in regard to religion, faith, and His grace. Truth did not come easy to me because almost all I knew concerning how to live a life of love and the true gospel, had to be learned from scratch. The benefit of that is that I was forced to re-evaluate the claims of what is true about life and the way of Jesus.

Even though I came at my growth process slightly different than most, I assume that there are many who have had a similar experience when it comes to trying to understand exactly what God was doing through all of their life experiences. We can all look back and make assessments about the life we have lived and see God's hand in multiple places. Our lives are often built clumsily in the dark, especially when we are building our own kingdom without God. But we should not be without hope because we know that God takes our mistakes and shapes them into something that can be of benefit, sometimes great benefit.

I hope this book gives you insights into understanding the work that He wants to do in your life. If you can get a glimpse of our freedom from the law and take hold of the love that Jesus demonstrated on the cross, it will transform how you read scripture and transform how you interact with others. If only you could know for certain that the creator God, Jesus Christ, has chosen you, He loves you, He died for you, and He has given you an abundance of gifts, then your world would be opened up to His transformation. Jesus has shared His glory with us and has established a place for each one of us in His kingdom. When we resurrect the love of the cross in our lives and begin seeking His kingdom and not our own, it sets the Spirit free to accomplish amazing things in our lives and with our lives.

Part 1: The Cross is the Answer

CHAPTER 1

"IN THIS WORLD YOU WILL HAVE TROUBLE"[3]

Night

The midst of the night engulfs me
in the thick consequences of the day before.
I lie in the presence of the quiet hum
in awe of the fear, it brings.
Peace and serenity are all but vanquished;
terror and dread take their place.
Deep wounds bleed their debt; the blood
slowly drips into the crucible of forgiveness.
Will it all be let before my fever leaves?
I am scared, I am lonely,
I tremble at my thoughts.
Dignity and virtue,
the very things that preserve the soul,
cost so much.
And life, life is the conscious examination
of how one lives
according to the truth they know.
And sin, sin is the trickle
that will soon become the torrent,
destroying the dam.[4]

---

3 John 16:33 (NIV)
4 Ernest Randolph, 1995

I knew a kid named Mikey from the time I was fairly young. I first got acquainted with him when my mother rented his family a small house in our backyard. They were an extremely poor family of five. Mikey had three sisters and no father, although he had plenty of mom's boyfriends that pretended to be his father. In a small, square, six-inch deep hole in the backyard, I had fashioned a Matchbox car kingdom. It had tunnels, buildings, roads, and lots of fun features that I enjoyed creating. Mikey, not knowing how much it meant to me, managed to destroy the whole thing in a matter of minutes. My anger was such that I flat out refused to play with him anymore. We lost touch shortly after that, but my aunt rented to them, so I kept up on the stories about their family and Mikey; most of them were very unpleasant.

I ran into Mikey again in sixth grade. We went to the same school, and it was obvious he had no friends. He dressed in old dirty clothes, usually had smudges on his face, and wore a no-style, crew haircut. It was a hard year for me, being at a new school, struggling to make friends, and dealing with my mother having a boyfriend. Actually, it was the worst year I can remember as a child. Mikey wanted to be friends, but I could not because I knew that would end any chance of me making friends with others. Also, we didn't like each other that much. Either way, he would ruin the relationships I was trying to build. I was not going to let him destroy my kingdom like he did when we were kids. Sadly, I did not know how bad Mikey was hurting inside. It was less than a year later that he took his own life. Me protecting my kingdom at Mikey's expense was not worth it; everyone ended up hating me anyway.

It is easy to get overwhelmed as kids. Hopefully, we had adults that could rescue us. Even as adults, life can overwhelm us at times, and it can feel that our kingdom is crashing down around us. We feel we cannot bear the consequences of what we have broken or what others have destroyed. In the high times, the pleasures of life can be so great that our world is filled with happiness and smiles, yet turmoil is also a part of our journey.

Struggle and suffering can come from differing and multiple sources, including loss of a relationship, money problems, sickness, natural disaster, outside pressures, inside turmoil, family disputes, losing a loved one, or facing death itself. There usually seems to be some situation that we are dealing with that, at best, makes us uncomfortable, and at the worst, makes us suffer in agony.

We are often discouraged because we are not where we want to be in life. Maybe we have not met our goals, or maybe we have lost what we care about deeply. These events are unexpected individual trials that are unique to each of us. Some may have overwhelming fears of getting sick, getting injured, going outside, or merely talking to someone. Struggle and even suffering seem to be an integral part of being human; we are loaded with burdens as we navigate this life, building our kingdom.

Our turmoil can come from multiple directions and with different intensities, yet it can also be self-created. I have seen people suffer tremendously because the painter painted their room a slightly darker shade of the right color. Or, how about a scratch on your new vehicle? Maybe you have suffered because your steak is medium, not medium-rare, someone took your parking spot, or a driver takes a second longer at the light than you judge necessary. I am not making light of suffering, merely pointing out that some of our sufferings are a matter of perspective.

A predicament of being in a struggle, whatever the reason, can put us in a state of desperation. Our angst, while sometimes freezes us in place, more than often forces us to move, which can have beneficial or detrimental results. Turmoil leading to movement seems to constantly rear its head. Even as young children, we are looking for a way to minimize our distress or at least an easy way to avoid it.

The safest and first place we go to shelter from suffering is into our mother's arms. She is the consoler of our hunger and of our need to be loved and comforted. But mom is limited and fallible and will not be sufficient forever, if at all. What about dad? He seems to put his head down, drive forward and take on life. He may be seen as protecting, providing, correcting, and even comforting. Can he show us how to cope with our trials and tribulations? Sometimes yes, but fathers fall down and make mistakes.

As we begin to mature into young adults, parents help less and even begin to contribute to our pressure in life. They expect a level of performance from us and are not always there when we need them. We even find out that some of our parents' ideas and actions are destructive at times. Obviously, we need to move on with our own lives at some point and craft our own kingdoms. If we do not learn to grow from our struggles and keep moving forward, our struggles might possibly get bigger, overtake us, and lead to greater suffering. We can use the coping mechanisms that we are given by others, but we are also forced to come up with some of our own if we want to live healthy lives.

The obstacle that we are facing as we build our kingdom is, what are we to do to lessen or prevent our struggle, end or reduce our suffering, and obtain a comfortable and successful life? Human solutions, more specifically our solutions to life, even if they are great, seem to have low odds that they will work out in a way we predict. Multiple factors threaten our success. On the outside, disease, death, corruption, sabotage, and natural disaster can all be crouching at the door. Not only do all those threats exist, but also our best solutions can be wrong at times and bring worse results than the initial problem. Successful problem resolution, despite our best attempt, is not guaranteed.

Instead of these outside threats, it is actually our internal weaknesses that may be the biggest hindrances to our success. We may have it all together on the outside, but what is going on inside of us? There are multitudes of inner complications, including our own failures, that can derail even the simplest solutions. We are full of secret sins, depression, disappointment, anger, angst, boredom, lack of love, feelings of being out of control, and feelings of inadequacy. There is a whole labyrinth of negative emotions and thoughts going on in our hearts when we are down. Sometimes our internal motives are conflicted, and our initiatives fail to get off the ground. At other times, our plans come crashing down at different stages. Hopes and dreams are usually not fully scuttled; thankfully, they can be changed and modified. Aspirations are often salvaged, corrected, and rebuilt, etc., but it is usually not the ideal we had envisioned.

Faith in the provision of a higher power is the tool used by most people to face suffering and to keep a positive outlook. At times, when humans face suffering on their own, without faith in the provision of God, they often make what seems to be barbaric choices. One sad example of this is ending the life of unborn children through abortion. This is thought to be beneficial because it brings a better life to the mother and reduces the potential of suffering for a child. There is an understood agreement in this rationale that suffering too much is not worth it and that it is better to end the suffering before it starts, either for the mother or the child. This is not new. Ancient people would sacrifice their children to their gods. Were they doing it to appease their gods, or were they motivated by not wanting another mouth to feed? Maybe they were also willing to kill misfit children, as we are today.[5] It is hard to present our modern sanctioned practice of abortion to reduce suffering

5 April Holloway, "Accounts of Roman Infanticide and Sacrifice All Just Myth and

in a favorable light. How does abortion represent any degree of belief in God's sovereignty?

It appears humanity goes astray from love when they begin deciding on differing values and worth for individuals or people groups. The ones with the power decide what level of struggle and suffering is appropriate for those they lord over. Enslaving humans for house, farm, or factory duties was historically practiced to reduce struggle for a select group of individuals while greatly increasing the suffering and struggle of others. Countless people have been enslaved for war and pleasure in the past, and these practices still go on today. Modern regimes like Nazi Germany, Soviet Russia, and Communist China also participated in heinous acts of murder and population reduction to produce a "better" life in the future for a select group. These sacrifices of individuals were made for the collective betterment of society. I hear claims today of how evil the people of the past were and how much more enlightened we are today. It is difficult not to compare the modern embrace of abortion to other historical murderous acts since it seems to be done with similar motivation: the intention of improving one's life. This selective destruction of life is seen by some as pure evil. It demonstrates a disregard for our accountability to God and a lack of faith in His provision and providence. It also communicates a belief in humanity's ability to solve their own problems through following a pragmatic morality.

Where did this confusion about the value of life and our quest to solve our own problems begin? When God created us, we had it easy in the garden before the fall, but not without work or struggle. Have you ever tried to name thousands of animals? Have you ever tended a large

---

Legend?," Ancient Origins, September 5, 2015, https://www.ancient-origins.net/news-history-archaeology/accounts-roman-infanticide-and-sacrifice-all-just-myth-and-legend-006591

orchard? Adam and Eve had plenty of work and struggle in the garden, but it was in a relationship with God, as they grew in love and truth. Unfortunately, Adam and Eve chose to face their struggle without God and seek the "knowledge of good and evil."[6] In their rebellion, they took upon themselves the task of how to live this life correctly without God, which was sin and led to struggle, suffering, and eventually death. Adam and Eve gave up their paradise because they were tricked into thinking there was a better way. Next, they began a journey to achieve "the good life," a kingdom without God's rule. It was a journey that would take humanity to some very dark places.

How could God have allowed this to happen? Although the first humans may not have needed to make the choice of going it on their own, true freedom demanded that they have that opportunity. If we do not know evil and its consequences, it is not easy for some of us to know the greatness of God's goodness and grace. For many of us, without the knowledge of the wrong way, we could not be resolute in the conviction that we will never turn back from God. God desired to create a people who could actually choose to love Him. This choice necessitates the ability to choose not to love Him.

After the fall, Cain chose farming; it was what God instructed man to do. God commanded that man would struggle to bring fruit from the ground because of his rebellion. Cain had succeeded in reducing some of his struggles and increased his comfort with his crop. He brought his harvest to God in his pride in what he had achieved. Abel came to God in humility, willing to destroy the resource that brought him comfort, sacrificing it to God. He gave an item of great value, professing that God is the source of our life and our provider, not works I do.

---

6 Genesis 2:17 (NASB)

Cain, in prideful actions, declared that he had overcome the struggle God placed on him, overcoming God's curse. Abel, in humility, copied God's example of how his sins were covered and how he was to be made acceptable in God's sight in order to have a relationship with Him. Cain's response in murdering Abel is the earliest account of someone getting how to deal with struggle and guilt completely wrong, and it would set the stage for the future of humanity. And yes, we messed it up big time.

Humans became exceedingly wicked in their quest to build a successful kingdom, willing to abuse others and abandon God. The complete freedom God gave mankind had not resulted in the intended relationship He had hoped for, only horrible hate and destruction which had to be dealt with. God then caused a great flood to destroy His creation and all of humanity except Noah and his family.

After the flood, which was the worst suffering ever known to humanity, we entered a new era. We were still not ready as a human race to give up the struggle for success through the knowledge of good and evil. God participated in our quest to overcome evil through struggle on our own. He gave us the covenant with Noah and the law of Moses through the Jews to teach us how to love, do good, and not evil. This was probably to His regret because God knew people would depend more on the laws for salvation than Him. He foresaw laws would be a barrier to a loving relationship with Him and others in the end, yet He gave them the law because humans could not restrain their ability to cause great suffering without them.

When humanity walked away from God's plan in the beginning and then from His subsequent law, in both cases, they quickly found themselves using or sacrificing the life of other human beings for their comfort and to reduce their suffering. They practiced slavery, abortion, murder, instigated wars, and other evils in the name of reducing suffering and struggle. At times, these evils were and are justified as a means to protect and better oneself, according to humanity's knowledge of good and evil. It seems there is no end to what people are willing to do to others to keep their comfort and power, succeeding in their rebellion against God while building their kingdom and demonstrating that they can achieve a successful life without Him.

The extreme sadness and loss of the situation is that when humans walked away from God, they walked away from the source of life. They walked away from a relationship with their Father, friend, and teacher. They walked away from the one who loved them and desired the best for them and an everlasting deep and meaningful relationship. Suffering and death entered the world, something they thought they were fixing. From the very beginning, God wanted them back and to help them in their suffering. But it is a relationship between two persons, and that is not an easy proposition. This is especially hard when we are building our own kingdom, at great expense to ourselves and others. We can easily destroy our own lives and often fail to help others around us, causing plenty of suffering along with the natural suffering and human evil we all face. God wants to provide the solution to our suffering if only we have a place for Him in our kingdoms, especially as something more than just a rule giver we have to appease.

CHAPTER 2

WHAT IS ONE TO DO ABOUT SUFFERING AND EVIL?

Do not be overcome by evil, but overcome evil with good.

Romans 12:21 (NKJV)

Evil appears to run its course in this world, whether caused by humans, a supernatural force, or nature. Some are angry at God as a result and are quick to assume that He does not exist because they see evil as something God could have restrained since He is all-powerful. Yet, from our perspective, most of the time, He chooses not to intervene. It even appears that God is participating in what they would call evil. While there is no simple answer, I think it is much more complex than merely blaming God and then questioning His existence. Even with the presence of great evils, I still believe we can trust God's judgment and attempt to understand evil's necessity.

The only way I have to explain and understand the necessity of evil is the idea of free will. If humans are free agents and angels are free agents, all with the ability to choose to seek God or reject Him, then evil does and must exist. So, indirectly, God created evil and even foresaw the evil that would come as a result of entities rejecting Him. It appears He decided that the eminent evil and destruction that would come from distinct persons was worth the end result. The existence of evil was worth the real love, true justice, imaginative creativity, and friendship, which comes from the existence of a relationship with free distinct persons that could choose to love God or reject Him. Despite the existence of evil in this world, I see goodness in God's plan of creating free agents and the greatness of the end result.

Religion is sometimes presented as the answer to humanity's problems and the problem of evil. While religious systems may deal with the causes of struggle and offer ways of relief, they also seem to compound it as well. They add a considerable number of rules, rituals, and responsibilities that can give us more ways to fail. They burden and possess our attention, talents, and money that may have been put to better use elsewhere. They may distract and confuse us from the truth, and in this sense, may waste a big part of our lives. The core problem is not the sacrifice religions ask for; it is what they convince their followers to be true and righteous. Only the real truth is worth true sacrifice, the sacrifice of time and talent away from other obligations we would have devoted our lives to.

The other big purpose of religion, pertaining to suffering, is to deal with our bad behavior, which causes evil. Catholics have confession and penance. Baptists have personal confessions of the "sins" of omission and commission. Muslims seem to use submission, power, and control to overcome struggle. Jews seem to rely on self-control and tradition. Buddhists seem to deny the desires that cause the struggle, therefore eliminating the struggle in your mind and finding peace. Hindus turn to their millions of gods; there may actually be a god for our every struggle. Each religion or variation thereof has systems and practices to rid ourselves of our bad behavior and deal with the tragedies one finds ourselves in. Most are trying to help us discover a path to not repeat our self-destruction, usually by refraining from sin or other foolish behaviors. Although, it is almost impossible to accomplish their plan without heaping guilt and shame upon their followers.

In some ways, religion's quest to eliminate evil and struggle resembles all of humanity's quest to seek human flourishing. What do people need to do to bring about life with the most reward and the least pain? Originally, God intended to do that for us in the garden, and now it is up to humans to solve this problem in our rebellion. Modern humanity's creation of systems to avoid struggle is a similar quest to the one undertaken by the first humans. They set out to achieve a fulfilled life on their own without God and with their newly found knowledge of good and evil.

We face unending struggles in our lives, and surely not all are from our decisions and intentions. There are plenty of unavoidable stressful events that happen to us of which we have no control over. In praying about these struggles, some sects of Christianity are teaching a concept that if you have enough faith, God will do whatever you ask in His name to overcome these unavoidable struggles. The sad effect of this teaching is that one can get the impression that their continued suffering and struggle are the direct result of one's lack of faith. While this may be true of suffering from destructive behavior of our own doing, it is most certainly not true of suffering from disease, natural disasters, or the bad circumstances that are of no fault of our own. It is self-evident that God does not normally take away our diseases or problems. Trouble is naturally a part of all of our lives. How and when God intervenes is a mystery to us all, but it is amazing when He does. Life would teach us that our suffering is not caused by our lack of faith but is just a part of the way things are. The correlation is that our faith in Jesus should increase with our suffering.

Prayer is the main tool most religions evoke to convince their God or gods to intervene in suffering. While prayer is a somewhat universal idea, it has plenty of different meanings and ways to practice it. Unfortunately, for a lot of people, prayer is merely well-wishing and the idea of extending the combined human spirit towards a worthy cause. Religions direct their followers to prayer as a means to help with life's internal and external problems. Prayer is generally seen as a petition to God, where He is the potential intervening force helping us in our struggle. There is disagreement on the expected response from God to alleviate suffering, even when one is praying to the God of the Bible.

Christian prayer can be seen as both petitioning for help and us submitting our wills to our struggle because it is part of God's master plan. There is debate in Christian circles whether we can move God if we have enough faith and agreement among believers or if prayer only changes us because God has already determined the future. Sadly, people can veer into the idea that God needs the right people to pray the correct way to get Him to listen. Others contend that unless we are right with God, He will not listen. The truth is that when we pray as Christians, we are praying to a Father who loves us, and we know He will do the best He can with respect to the circumstances. We pray for Him to intervene, and we trust Him when He does not. Prayer helps us know who is in charge, and it gives us supernatural hope in God's love.

Including Jesus in our effort to overcome suffering is not the only promoted solution to the predicaments we find ourselves in. There are plenty of suggestions to help us, as well as inspire us to a better life, such as all the various religions, education, sports, friendship, fun outings, and companion relationships. This is only a partial list of activities we do to make our lives more inspiring. There are ways to repair us when we break, like counseling, prescription drugs, and rehabilitation. Some of us take it upon ourselves to make others' lives better through promoting social change, religious works, and involvement in politics. If one's struggle is darker, they may use alcohol, drugs, be in multiple physical relationships, have an adrenaline addiction, commit violence, commit crimes, join gangs or find other, not so admired ways to gain control over their deep struggles. With or without Jesus, one must cope in the circumstances they find themselves or flee to a perceived more hospitable environment. Hopefully, we are doing more than coping or fleeing as we build our kingdoms, aspiring to discover what constitutes a good life.

If one is not a believer in God as the giver of meaning for their life, their answer to what makes life meaningful in the face of evil may be quite different. They may refer to the blood coursing through their veins as they walk, talk, and experience this existence to its fullest. Their answer could reference the smile of a child or the thrill of youth, forgetting the drudgery of the middle years or the decay of old age. Some answers focus on moments of reward, yet this is a wanting motive because, for most human beings, these rewards are mixed in with an unfair amount of suffering. For a few, life is full of unfortunate circumstances, mistakes, suffering, and death, while for others, they find marrow around every corner. A suffering individual can only hope for a better day. No matter what positive motivation we land on, we still must face the greatest tragedy of life; living with the knowledge of our inevitable extinction. How does one find meaning in life when all that is around us can seem tainted, broken, and dying?

Without the existence of a higher power, and I would contend the Christian God, we seem to be merely a short-lived meaningless glob in a life of random good, evil, and neutral experiences. The importance of what we think, do, and believe may only be as important to the extent we impact the survival of the globs around us and, more importantly, the globs after us. If this despairing thought is true, I would find little reason to care for others or myself. Why would any of our actions and thoughts truly matter? Could not I just disappear or live entirely for my own pleasure.

A large swath of people finds truisms, in the form of believing positive thoughts about oneself and exhortations to achieve rewarding behavior, helpful in overcoming struggle. Leaders tend to come up with motivational, positive purposes like:

- Make the world a better place for the next generation.

- Do well in life and live on in the lives of the ones you have touched.

- Do not do to anyone what you would not want to be done to you.

- Be all you can be and learn all you can learn, share it with others, and in your success, you will find meaning.

- Life is about finding someone to love and share this life with.

I find these exhortations motivational as well, but also burdensome and overwhelming. As I face these and other altruisms, I feel more inadequate, and my personal struggles seem to be amplified because they seem to internally amplify my sense of failure that they try to correct. Even though loving, positive, and motivational pleas sound wonderful, why should I devote my life to them and not activities that are more immediately gratifying?

There are other more philosophical solutions to suffering. There is the fatalist who accepts their predicament, surrenders to its dictates, and does not feel compelled to change or overcome them. There is the nihilist; although they may achieve greatness, they see it all as meaningless striving and do not give any greater value to suffering than comfort. The existentialist is the nihilist who knows the meaninglessness of it all but sheds rationality and finds a meaning that transcends the implications of the meaninglessness. Ironically, one of their transcendent ideas that brings them meaning might be to devote their lives to end suffering.

In the natural, scientific-based world, on a practical level, it seems that we do plenty of actions to eliminate or prevent struggle. There are bountiful advances that have improved society like better governments with more freedom, reduced workload, plenty of leisure time, education, infrastructure, increased food production, cheap fuel, and effective healthcare. There are examples to prevent struggle resulting from negligence, like yearly well-child checks at the doctor, preventive medicine, building codes, extensive engineering, warning labels, safety protocol, etc. Some of this is beneficial, but some measures go overboard, especially when politics get involved or the threat of a lawsuit. How far will we go to protect our health, money, safety or to prevent our suffering?

There is also a dark problem with most of these solutions performed in our own strength. At some point, we will land on a spectrum of pride versus wretchedness. In facing our struggle, do we overcome it and succeed, resulting in pride, or do we succumb to its overwhelming pressure, fail in the world's eyes, our family's eyes, or even our own eyes, and become wretched? We usually are not fully one way or the other. Sometimes we feel proud of what we have overcome and moments later feel wretched about our shortcomings. Both states, pride and wretchedness, affect how we treat ourselves and others around us. Our greatest efforts can cause more internal suffering in the end. We are left asking the question, "What is the answer?"

CHAPTER 3

IS JESUS THE ANSWER?

Now may the God of hope fill you with all joy and peace as you believe in him, so that you may abound in hope by the power of the Holy Spirit.

Romans 15:13 (NET)

I have told you these things, so that in me you may have peace. In this world you will have trouble. But take heart! I have overcome the world.

John 16:33 (NIV)

Although most of us put on the facade that we have it all together, plenty of us are searching for solutions and systems to improve our lives, and some even want to improve the world around them. Many want answers to fill the longing they have inside and to understand why they are not at peace with their surroundings.

How do we measure a good, full, and peaceful life? It is as if our lives are like a bottle of wine, and we are often wondering where it all goes and how we get more? These can be hard questions to answer. Even if we believe that life is a great and precious gift, sometimes, it is not at all pretty, and most of the time, life does not seem fair.

I would like to attempt to illustrate humanity's quest to be fulfilled in a story about a fictional man named Stan:

He was a somewhat normal young man from an intact family, with no unusual problems. Still, he felt like he was born with his wine bottle already half empty. Other people appeared to get bigger portions and better wine early on in life, while all he saw was his small, somewhat empty bottle. As he started using his wine, he began to panic for fear that it would run out. He began to find little ways to replenish his supply through hard work, education, kind deeds, and religious practices, but it was never enough. There were moments when Stan assessed his bottle, only to find the level as low as ever.

Well, maybe someone else can fill my bottle, Stan thought. He found friends who shared their wine with him, and this helped for a bit. But sometimes, when Stan would share his wine with them, they took too much. He begged them to stop, but it was no use. They eventually left him almost completely dry. Fleeing for his life, he found himself alone and feeling empty, yet again.

Last week, a girl Stan knew ended her beautiful life. Some people took her bottle, abused her wine, and left her empty with a broken bottle beyond repair. They had coerced her into giving it to them with false promises of an abundance of wine. Sadly, she fell for their ruse and was left with nothing to carry her wine in. She could not bear to go on living, forced to pass from person to person begging for a drop.

Stan realized he needed to find someone who would love and cherish his wine, or else he would end up like his friend. Then it happened: He fell in love. He finally found a loving soul to give his wine to, and she intended to share her wine with him. They committed to care for one another's wine as long as they both lived.

After some years, it seemed to not be working out. They were not giving to one another as Stan had envisioned. He was trying to share as much wine as he could, and it seemed she was sharing very little. Maybe she saw it the opposite way, but Stan felt betrayed, cracked, and empty. He was running out of wine, and she would only share a dribble, leaving him barely enough to survive. He then discovered that his companion was getting wine from someone else and sharing her wine with that person. Now there was not even a drop left for him.

He barely escaped that scenario but not unscathed. Stan's bottle had developed additional cracks from the hurt and betrayal, and he was now incredibly low on wine again. He desperately needed to find a solution. In his despair, he tried alcohol and drugs to cope. Although it filled the bottle with something, it diluted and damaged the little wine that was left.

Stan then turned inwardly and tried to find more creative ways to get wine. He was not proud of some of the things he did; he hurt others and stole their wine. His ugly behavior seemed to bring only wine that soured quickly, and it added little, if any, to his bottle. To justify his behavior, he would tell himself, *I am not that bad, everyone has to live, and I took from others just as they took from me.*

As Stan looked back on his life, he saw how awful he had been to others by selfish actions that did untold damage to the very vulnerable. He wanted to change and determined that he was going to start giving more than he took. He believed that it might make up for some of his wrongs.

Stan found that if he was careful, loving, and kind, strangely enough, others would willingly share wine with him. He sought to befriend the right people. He worked, strived, meditated, exercised, laughed, and played, bringing about positive growth in his life. Stan even found a personal relationship that met his needs and connected to who he was as a person. It seemed to be working, except Stan still ran into takers and stealers. Moreover, when he was honest with himself, he knew that deep down, he was still a taker and a thief.

All the things he had been doing were not enough. Maybe they would be eventually, but he still had all those leaks from the past that he could not fix. He went to the doctor, and she showed him how to plug some of the holes, and it sort of helped. On the outside, it seemed like all was well, but on the inside, his bottle was still cracked and empty.

Then, he met a unique new friend. He shared with him an abundance of good wine and told him to come back if he needed more. Stan suspiciously thought to himself: *Where is he getting this stuff?* When he went back, he was told the source: "The Maker of Wine." *What a crazy loon, Stan thought. That guy told me that there was some supernatural maker of wine and that my empty and cracked bottle was not only the result of the foolish things I had done but also what others had done to me.* This person told Stan he was "born with cracks, and we have no choice but to steal each other's wine." This did not sit well with Stan because the guy did not know anything about his life.

Stan fumed: *His bottle was fine except for a few cracks. His new friend had been going to this winemaker since he was young. He didn't know all the other ways to fill and fix one's bottle. He thinks this winemaker of his is the only source.* Stan fled the idea and searched for another way to fill and fix his bottle to no avail. No other wine was like the drink that the Maker of Wine provided.

Finally, Stan agreed to meet this so-called winemaker; he made no promises, though. The Maker of Wine instructed Stan that he could give him wine that would never run out. Stan knew this was the answer to his cracked, empty bottle and cried out: "Please give me this wine!" The Maker of Wine said he could not unless Stan shared his bottle with him.

Trembling, Stan feared the winemaker would be like all the rest and take more wine than Stan could afford to give. But, on seeing the tender and loving demeanor of the winemaker, he slowly began to show his bottle to him. The Maker of Wine proclaimed ever so softly: "I can't put my wine in that old, cracked bottle." He motioned for Stan to hand over his bottle. *Stop! Would he give it back?* Stan feared. He had never completely let go of his bottle. *Remember what happened to the young girl who let go of hers! Remember how it didn't work out so well!* But the Maker's expression was gentle, and his new friend had told him many great things about this Maker of Wine.

Stan cautiously gave up his bottle. It felt freeing. He trusted in the Maker to fix his flawed vessel, refill it, and give it back, but the Maker of Wine did not do as he expected. He did something much better; the Maker of Wine gave him a new bottle, one that was already full and that would never run dry.

Even though the above allegory is fictional, it illustrates the transforming power of Jesus in someone's life. Jesus is the giver of the incredible lifesaving gift that humanity desperately needs. A loving relationship with Jesus brings with it incredible new freedom and empowerment that can fill us beyond measure as He grows our love for Him, others, and ourselves. Jesus is the true answer that can transform our lives in a deeply meaningful way, usually in a way that we do not expect. Jesus fills us with eternal new wine and then renews our forever relationship with Him. He enters us and becomes a part of our kingdom.

And yes, we do matter. As believers, we find a higher meaning in life than merely our current experience. Since we are created for a relationship with God, we have a supernatural purpose along with all of the natural circumstances we deal with. Every aspect of life, even natural evils, are symptoms of a bigger plan, even though they may appear to be just random occurrences of unfortunate luck. We matter to God Himself; what we do, what we say, what we think, and what we believe matters to Him, for He wants a relationship with us.

CHAPTER 4

—

THE SEA OF COMPETING BELIEFS SURROUNDING US

A group of Epicurean and Stoic philosophers began to debate with him. Some of them asked, "What is this babbler trying to say?" Others remarked, "He seems to be advocating foreign gods." They said this because Paul was preaching the good news about Jesus and the resurrection.

Acts 17:18 (NIV)

While I contend that Jesus is God and following Him is the true way to a relationship with God and the way to a full life, there are people of all walks of life and different religions who would disagree that Jesus is the answer, or at least the only answer. They most likely would promote their own beliefs or ideas as the way of solving humanity's problems. There are even differing purported ways to salvation found in major sects of Christianity. The way of salvation and the path to abundant life seems to be obscured by the muddied water of countless alternatives.

The rubber meets the road in the simple question my son asked me, "Are Mormons saved?" It is not only a question about the Mormons but a question for all who know of or believe in Jesus but do not worship Him quite as the Bible prescribes. The Koran mentions Jesus more than

Mohammad, its own prophet. Gandhi spoke fondly of Jesus. Most non-Christian religions see Jesus as a great teacher, historical figure, and some think He was a prophet or even a god. The Bahai adopt Jesus. Some Hindus and Buddhists accept Him as one of their teachers or gods. If most acknowledge Jesus, then what does one have to believe about Jesus to be a Christian or to be saved?

My goal is not to offend anyone but to present what I believe is the truth about Jesus and salvation as explained in the Bible. God is the judge of who is saved or not saved according to their belief in and understanding of Jesus. Still, drifting away from the biblical Jesus definitely confuses our understanding of the source and means of our salvation. In this book, I seek to present a clear summary of how the Bible describes Jesus and the cross as the means of salvation, and I hope that helps your understanding as a reader.

One of the main ways the nature of Jesus and the means of salvation is misunderstood is when a new teaching is added to God's Word. One prominent example, under the large umbrella of what is called Christianity, is the Church of Jesus Christ of Latter-day Saints (called the Mormon church by some). They claim to have restored the church of Jesus Christ through the prophet Joseph Smith. Smith translated the golden tablets, shown to him by an angel, into the Book of Mormon[7], which clarified some biblical principles[8]. Because the Latter-day Saints adds new teachings to the biblical revelation, many orthodox Christian

---

7 Church of Jesus Christ official website (https://www.comeuntochrist.org/beliefs/book-of-mormon/who-wrote-the-book-of-mormon).
8 Nyman, Monte S. "Why is the Book of Mormon the 'most correct book,' and how does it contain the fullness of the gospel?" Ensign 6, no. 9 (September 1976): 0-96. Accessed November 24, 2020. https://www.churchofjesuschrist.org/study/ensign/1976/09/i-have-a-question/why-is-the-book-of-mormon-the-most-correct-book?lang=eng).

traditions do not consider the Latter-day Saints to be teaching true Christianity as it is taught in the Bible.

An example outside of the Christian religion is Islam. Mohammad claimed he first met with an angel in a cave who gave him parts of the Koran, which is considered by Muslims to be the most reliable revelation of God, even over the Bible[9]. Both extra-biblical revelations of the Mormons and the Muslims were given in private situations, and the truth of their origin cannot be verified. According to adherents, their religious books correct and clarify the Bible.[10] The new revelations have led to discrepancies about the nature of Jesus and added requirements and methods to salvation beyond simple belief. The "clarifications" obscure who Jesus is and the means and results of being saved.

Muslims believe in Jesus as a prophet, but they do not believe Jesus was God nor the Son of God. Although they acknowledge that He was crucified, they deny that He died on a cross, and therefore, they do not affirm the resurrection. Does their belief in Jesus still count for salvation? Not according to the biblical text.[11] They no more have the eternal life found only in Jesus than anyone else who does not have a relationship with the Son of God.

So how does that work with Latter-day Saints? They believe in Jesus, but they also believe Jesus is only one of the many sons of God the Father and not equal to Him.[12] Does that unbiblical belief about the nature of Jesus preclude them from salvation? When they believe in the doctrine that significantly adds to the Bible and changes core beliefs

9 https://www.crossway.org/articles/the-Bible-and-islam/
10 https://www.crossway.org/articles/the-Bible-and-islam/
11 John 14:6
12 https://newsroom.churchofjesuschrist.org/article/what-mormons-believe-about-jesus-christ

about God and Jesus, are they heading in the wrong direction? Will they ever fully understand who Jesus truly is and how He has freed us to live a life of love in a relationship with God, forgiven of our sins and no longer under the law?

I can easily harp on the Mormons, but plenty of Christian denominations do not understand forgiveness and freedom from the law. Some Baptists over-emphasize sin, charismatics may focus too much on spiritual power, Messianic Jews might insist on following the law of Moses, and liturgical churches may insist too much on rituals. The father of all churches, the Catholic Church, by adding its traditions to salvation, can lose the simple understanding of the grace of Jesus, which is given freely without any works. It seems that, as humans add religion, rituals, and rules to our relationship with Jesus, we miss the simple freedom and love that Christ brought through the cross. Part of the work of the Spirit is to guide us in the truth, and people's attempts to build a religious kingdom of tradition and rules, compete with God's kingdom of grace, love, and truth.

If we think there is confusion about salvation and Jesus within Abrahamic religions and their offshoots, further confusion persists outside of them. The way to solve the dilemma of the nature of God and Jesus is not found in the solution of presumptive pluralists or universalists. I say presumptive because they make the claim that all religions are simply describing Jesus and God from a different perspective while concluding that they are all talking about the same entity. Pluralists are claiming that they are right about the universal nature of God, and others are wrong about their exclusive truth claims. The universalist's belief is contrary to the fact that most religions have clearly contradicting truth claims between core beliefs and do claim exclusivity. Ravi Zacharias put it best: "The pluralist asks: 'Aren't all religions fundamentally the same and superficially different?' No, they are fundamentally different, and at best, they are superficially similar."[13] Despite the pluralist's claims of universality, it is just not true. Different religions are far from agreeing with each other's fundamental doctrine.

Of course, one could transcend the question of the nature of God and the deity of Jesus by asserting that there is little truth in any traditional religion. Even further, atheists claim that God does not exist and religions are all merely human constructs, products of the human mind needing an explanation for the unknown. One may make the bold claim that all ideas of God, gods, and the supernatural are created by human sources, and none have in them a true way of relationship with a god if it exists, but this perceived higher thinking does not transcend the need for a relationship with God found in most humans.

Even if a person rejects traditional religious thought, they still need the means to understand their reality. There are multiple worldviews and ideologies that people knowingly or unknowingly use to interpret the world around them. In this moving away from religious belief in the traditional sense, secular religions have become more popular. Examples of secular religions include scientism, naturalism, atheism, spiritualism, and others. These Christ-denying worldviews, in the same regard as the traditional religions, are still plagued with the old temptations of power, wealth, conquest, and without question, human pride.

A religion, whether secular or based on a belief in the supernatural, spreads an ideology or worldview that helps explain the world we live in. Religions usually include a list of virtues and morals as a means to save us or at least to minimize human suffering and feelings of failure.

---

13 Ravi Zacharias, "How can we show that Christianity is the true religion?" Ravi Zacharias International Ministries April 2, 2012, https://www.youtube.com/watch?v=nWY-6xBA0Pk&feature=youtu.be

They have consequences for constituents who do not follow the rules and promote some means of redemption for repentant transgressors. Religions often enforce guilt and shame for wrong behavior and prescribe a way to find dignity, happiness, joy, love, fulfillment, and peace. Most attempt to give answers to life's most pressing questions, like: "What is the reason for it all, and what is our specific purpose?" Religious doctrine usually addresses what we want from God or our gods and what the divine wants from us. But, if a religion is not true, instead of being a solace to our soul, it can be the chains that enslave us and may even minimize one's purpose and possibilities in life.

Despite an increasingly secularized Western culture and the numerous disadvantages to religious systems, there remains an overwhelming desire for something supernatural to believe in. Magicians have mesmerized people as they appear to suspend the natural laws. The widespread success of superheroes and fantasy genres in popular culture attest to a desire to believe in something bigger than ourselves. Countless superstitions, new and old, show mankind's deep longing for a belief in an entity that is beyond this world and all-powerful—powerful enough to solve our problems. Even some atheists, who have a desire to connect with something beyond themselves, engage in religious practices like meditation, yoga, and Tai Chi.

A belief in reincarnation, karma, or an afterlife, despite the lacking scientific evidence, is another interesting phenomenon. When people die, their functioning bodily presence and their immaterial person cease to be. We have almost no verifiable proof of anything after the cessation of physical life. Yet, the belief in the supernatural afterlife is overwhelmingly present throughout human history. This belief cannot be denied. Where does it come from, and how does each individual satisfy it? I would say belief in the afterlife exists because the afterlife is a true reality that humans somehow know exists because God has "set eternity in their heart."[14]

I think we long for eternity, or at least something better than what we have and the kingdom we create for ourselves. A better existence and a connection to the eternal are not achieved through religion. The perfect ideology is not going to satisfy the longing in our hearts. I submit to you that the eternal is only found in a relationship with Jesus. Our fulfillment now and eternally is found in the restoration of our core purpose, which is to be in a loving relationship with our creator. We are saved from our dead selves and given new life in Christ for all eternity, where God's Spirit fills us, and we reside in Christ. This is an eternal condition that happens immediately. It is a new life found only in Jesus Christ. No other name, religion, or system can bring this supernatural transformation in one's life and guarantee eternal life with Jesus here on earth, and in the future[15] where we will not enter a place of suffering or even a place of waiting. In the vast sea of competing beliefs, it is only by what Jesus did on the cross that provides the necessary bridge to a relationship with the creator God. By choosing to be a disciple of Jesus at the foot of the cross, you will experience life as it was meant to be lived.

---

14 Ecclesiastes 3:11 (NASB)
15 Acts 4:12

CHAPTER 5

———

WHO IS JESUS?

He said to them, "But who do you say that I am?" Simon Peter
answered, "You are the Christ, the Son of the living God."

Matthew 16:15–16 (NET)

The core of Christianity is knowing and following Jesus. To make a
decision of this magnitude, it is essential to understand who Jesus
is.

So, what did Jesus, the one who turned water into wine, claim about
His identity, and why does He deserve our attention? He claimed to be
God on several occasions, saying, "The Father and I are one" (John
10:30, NET). This claim is most clearly shown in the discourse recorded
in John 8, ending in Jesus saying, "Before Abraham was, I am" (John
8:59, NET). He claimed the name of God that Moses had recorded as
the Lord spoke to him from the burning bush.[16] We are assured that this
statement was recognized as a claim to be God because the Jews picked
up stones to stone him.

John, one of Jesus' disciples and closest friends, wrote eloquently
about who Jesus is, calling Him the Word and the light:

---

16 Exodus 3:14

In the beginning was the Word, and the Word was with God, and the Word was God. He was with God in the beginning. Through him all things were made; without him nothing was made that has been made. In him was life, and that life was the light of all mankind. The light shines in the darkness, and the darkness has not overcome it. …The true light that gives light to everyone is coming into the world. …The Word became flesh and made his dwelling among us. We have seen his glory, the glory of the one and only Son, who came from the Father, full of grace and truth.

John 1:1–5, 9, 14 (NIV)

The Bible goes on to say much more about who Jesus is. He was and is God, the king of glory[17], the great I Am[18], the creator of the universe[19], the beginning and the end[20], the source of all knowledge[21], energy, and strength[22], the source of the very existence of life itself[23], the author of our being[24], giver of our consciousness[25], and the one whose face Moses could not even look at[26]. Even though the disciples believed that Jesus was the Messiah sent from God, I am not sure even the disciples fully comprehended that Jesus was the all-powerful creator God until after He rose from the dead.

From around 1 BC to 33 AD, God the Son was incarnate in this world

17   Psalm 24:9
18   Isaiah 48:12
19   John 1:3
20   Revelation 22:13
21   Proverbs 9:10
22   1 Chronicles 29:12
23   John 1:4
24   Genesis 1:26, Psalm 139:13
25   Genesis 2:7
26   Exodus 13:18-20

as Jesus of Nazareth, a real distinct human being. He openly identified as God, forgave sins, and cultivated relationships with people. The incarnate presence of Jesus changed history. It was at one time considered such a monumental event that Jesus' birth became the epicenter of time. All events were counted from the year He was born, labeled BC if they occurred "Before Christ" and AD—the abbreviation of the Latin phrase *Anno Domini* (the year of our Lord)—if they occurred after His birth. What made His life earth-shattering is that He changed the world, not through war or mighty governments, like Alexander the Great or Augustus Caesar, but through dying on a cross, the ultimate expression of His love.

Throughout history, Jesus has had a transformational impact on most who choose to follow Him. The early followers in Jerusalem were drastically impacted by their experience of believing and following Jesus. They changed their whole lives, sold their excess possessions, pooled their money as a church, and shared resources according to each other's needs[27]. As the salvation of individuals spread, the Spirit of Jesus began to fill the earth one heart at a time. As the Spirit transformed the new believers, major advances of love and sacrifice began to take place in those changed by following Jesus. Many of the people that the Apostle Paul shared the gospel with fully adopted Jesus as their God and subsequently sacrificed, suffered, and sometimes died for this belief in a foreign God. What kind of experience must they have had that they would be willing to lose all their worldly belongings, and sometimes even their life, in defense and support of their new God, even though they themselves had not physically met Jesus?

Each curious person must ask, who was Jesus, and how do we learn about Him today? Was He a scholar? A prophet? A great man?

---

27 Acts 2:40-47

The fulfillment of the prophecies of the Jewish Messiah? A wandering madman that claimed to be God? A revolutionary? One god of many gods? A magician or wizard? A great healer and worker of miracles?[28] A merely deep intellectual who said astonishing things that changed the paradigm in people's thoughts forever[29]? Or, was Jesus actually who He claimed to be and who the Bible claims Him to be, God incarnated, "God with us[30]?" One may find themselves tasked, on a personal level, to make up their own minds as to who He was and how they are going to respond to His call if He was and is God. To answer this question and many others, one should consult Jesus' disciples, who had physically spent around three years with Him. They wrote the only reliable, detailed, and historical accounts of Jesus, His life, and His message to us in the four gospels, Matthew, Mark, Luke, and John.

The gospels attest to the miraculous Jesus, who was God in the flesh, who eventually sacrificed Himself and rose from the dead. The writers of the gospels and Paul's doctrine of salvation seem to imply that He went to the cross to take away our sins, giving us new life, and restoring our relationship with God. Unfortunately, the only path for us to be reborn and reconnected to God was through His destruction[31], which provided for the eradication of our sin and salvation from our destruction. In doing this, Jesus was portrayed in the gospels as the fulfillment of the suffering Savior as described in Psalm 22 and Isaiah 53. He was the Savior who would heal us and free us from our transgressions, as described in these two Old Testament prophecies.

During His short ministry, Jesus proved Himself to be the fulfillment

---

28 Matthew 8:16
29 Matthew 5-7
30 Matthew 1:23 (NET)
31 John 3:3-21

of the Jewish messianic prophecies and proved Himself to be God through His new teaching, prophecies, healing, and miracles. Jesus spent His days healing the sick, giving sight to the blind[32], hearing to the deaf,[33] and raising the dead.[34] The broken came to Jesus, and all were healed.[35] Because He was the creator of all matter, He could bend it to His will, like when He performed His first miracle in the Gospel of John. He changed not a few glasses of water into sour wine but approximately 150 gallons of water into fine wine at a wedding[36]. Later, He calmed a raging storm on the Sea of Galilee[37], and He fed thousands by miraculously multiplying a few loaves of bread and a couple of fish.[38] According to the gospel accounts, He was beyond human in supernatural ways. His incarnation was the only time humanity has experienced God in the flesh, whom even the wind and the waves obeyed. His final miracle was His own resurrection, which He regularly prophesied about.[39]

Jesus embodied compassion, not only through His sacrifice on the cross but also through His daily life, resembling the healer spoken of in Isaiah 61. The gospel writers portray Jesus as loving and attentive towards the outcasts and marginalized members of society. In all His glory, He ate with sinners,[40] touched lepers,[41] spoke with women,[42] and spent time

---

32 John 1:1-38
33 Mark 7:32-35
34 John 11:43
35 Luke 4:40
36 John 3:2-11
37 Mark 4:35-41; John 6:19
38 Matthew 14:13-21, 15:32-39
39 John 18:22
40 Mark 2:16
41 Matthew 8:3
42 John 4:27

with children, giving them all equal importance. He demonstrated His compassion and love for the sick and lost[43]. His new commandment was "to love one another just as I have loved you" (John 15:12, NET). Jesus came to demonstrate sacrificial and unconditional love through His daily example and His death on the cross. He also made this love possible in us by taking away our sins, so we could receive His Spirit and be restored with God's love.

Why Was the Son of God Rejected?

Jesus came at a time when the Jews were expecting their Messiah. The Jewish concept of the Messiah was that He would be a kingly figure from the royal line of David and that He would rise up, rid Israel of their occupying enemies, restore Israel to power, and establish God's kingdom on earth. But instead of overthrowing Rome, He became a suffering servant to restore a way for humanity to come to know God. While no sign was enough for the religious rulers, common Jews praised Jesus as Lord at His triumphal entry into Jerusalem.[44] They wanted Jesus to be their Messiah and embraced Him as the king of Israel, the fulfillment of Zechariah's prophecy, as He rode into Jerusalem "on a donkey.[45]" The people shouted the messianic praise, "Blessed is he who comes in the name of the Lord" (Psalm 118:26, NKJV), and they thought Jesus would establish His earthly kingdom.[46]

It was for good reason that the people hailed Him as their king. He was the people's Messiah. He loved the poor and sinners, performed many miracles for them, and had compassion for their suffering. He

---

43 Matthew 14:14
44 John 12:13
45 Zechariah 9:9 (NKJV), John 12:15
46 Acts 1:6

valued everyone and demonstrated a desire to have a relationship with common people and show them the love of His Father. Jesus was seen by people as the prophesied Jewish Messiah, yet, even for them, He refused to set up an earthly kingdom.

The leaders had understandable reasons to reject Jesus and deem Him not qualified to be the Messiah. Born in a manger, Jesus came into the world as a lowly carpenter with no standing, one whom the kings would conscript to die for them in a war. He was a person of insignificance as far as the rulers were concerned. Being a child of a scandalous marriage from the mocked town of Nazareth with no formal education and no allegiance to any party, how could He be the ruling Messiah? Instead of joining the ruling parties and leading a physical revolution, He cleared out the temple and challenged the Pharisees' power[47], chastising them for their deception of the people[48]. He would reconcile His people to Himself through His death on the cross and lead a spiritual revolution of love through His Spirit[49]. His kingdom would be "not of this world[50]."

Even the disciples did not understand that He was not going to take an earthly throne and instead He was going to die for our salvation after a brief time on earth. On what would be His follower's last night together with Jesus, He embodied the Passover supper with His closest disciples in an upper room, explaining mysteries to them about their future with God[51]. They still thought that this was the time of His rise to power and proceeded to the Mount of Olives with Him to plot His victory, only to

---

47 Matthew 28:19
48 John 8:12-59
49 Colossians 1:20
50 John 18:36 (NKJV)
51 John 14-16

witness Jesus agonizing over His coming death.[52] On this final night of His ministry, He was betrayed by His disciples, and in the morning, He was condemned by the Jewish rulers, rejected by the common people, and crucified by the Romans.[53]

All was lost. The faithful were devastated. The disciples had believed that Jesus was the Messiah that would establish the Jewish kingdom on earth forever. How could it end this way? What were they to do? Then Jesus showed up alive again! Walking, talking, and eating with His disciples. Jesus explained how He had fulfilled the scriptures through His death and resurrection and provided a way of a relationship to God for all the world.[54] He commissioned them to take this message everywhere and to everyone.[55] He did not make His disciples high officials in a new earthly kingdom of power; instead, Jesus appointed them as humble workers to spread His kingdom of truth and love, reconciling people to God. They would go on to sacrifice their lives, spreading this great news: the message of God coming to earth to have a relationship with people[56]. Eventually, the entire world would be changed through the impact of Jesus' brief life, excruciating death on the cross, and miraculous resurrection from the dead. The message of the incarnation of God and His sacrifice to have a relationship with humanity started a fire that was—and still is being—carried to the whole world by the power of the Spirit working through His transformed followers.

(I would love to say more about Jesus in this chapter, but for brevity, I moved the rest of my introduction to Jesus into Appendix A and B.)

---

52 John 17
53 John 18-19
54 Luke 24:27
55 Acts 1:8
56 Matthew 28:19

CHAPTER 6

———

WHY DO PEOPLE NEED JESUS?

Surely He has borne our griefs And carried our sorrows; Yet we esteemed Him stricken, Smitten by God, and afflicted. But He was wounded for our transgressions, He was bruised for our iniquities; The chastisement for our peace was upon Him, And by His stripes we are healed. All we like sheep have gone astray; We have turned, every one, to his own way; And the Lord has laid on Him the iniquity of us all.

Isaiah 53:4–6 (NKJV)

You may still have your doubts as to whether Jesus is the core answer to all of our problems. Please let me begin with our need for Him in my attempt to explain why He is the true answer.

Humanity was created to have a personal relationship with God. Living life without the fulfillment of living out our true purpose leaves us with no true transcendent meaning, and we are left to scrape out meaning from what is left. In our rebellion and separation from Him, we experience even greater confusion regarding our purpose, resulting in unnecessary struggle, pain, and suffering. We are enslaved to our desires and forced to practice unloving behavior to achieve and warrant our significance. Without receiving meaning from our creator, we are left only with the value that we give ourselves and the value that others may give us. The loss of a relationship with the giver of life represents a loss of our true purpose of existence.

Much of our struggle in life is an internal struggle with how we think and feel about ourselves. Some of those internal torments are commonly expressed in the following thoughts:

- Nobody loves me.
- I am worthless.
- Nobody cares what I think.
- I am overwhelmed with anxiety, fear, and worry.
- I am depressed.
- My life is falling apart, and I need someone to make sense of it all.
- I have an empty hole in my heart.
- I feel controlled by my demons.
- I feel burdened by my failures.
- I am selfish.
- I am filled with hatred and violence.
- I feel like I have wasted my life.
- I am overwhelmed by guilt and shame.
- I am lonely.
- I struggle to give and receive love.

I may not be able to help you with your earthly purpose or give you a specific fix for what ails you, but I know without a doubt that your heavenly purpose was to be in an intimate relationship with the creator God through Jesus Christ in fellowship with the Spirit. Being reconciled to God, getting your heavenly purpose right is the first step on the road to a full life and discovering your earthly purpose. A reconciled relationship with God is the foundational cornerstone of a healthy, truthful, and loving life.

A lack of relationship with God is why many people will never be satisfied in this life. One tangible example of the type of relationship we crave with God is the desire a child has to bond with their mother. A child still continues to crave the love of their mother, even after the child can survive without constant attention. Deep down, we crave a relationship with God, our creator, just as we do with our mother. We crave guiding and loving support as we venture out on our life journey. Jesus has provided the perfect way for that relationship to become a reality. How many of us live out our lives failing to embrace this deep relationship with God given to us at such a price? We fail to embrace the amazing gift of meaning and purpose that was given to us.

Another interesting phenomenon of the human psyche is that there is an almost universal need and desire to be important, unique, loved, and special, all elements that lend to our sense of meaning. Without a creator God who loves me, I have no source of significance unless I achieve some worldly standard of influence. This does not bode well for countless numbers of people throughout the millennia, who have had horrible, or at least not so special, lives and could not find a higher meaning. I cannot accept this lack of meaning and have no reason to. It is more likely and more viable to believe that the supernatural God can provide what is needed. Jesus' sacrifice for us makes each one of us special and gives each individual meaning and purpose; in the same way, He gave His creation special purpose and beauty.

A considerable body of ancient human history and reasoned arguments by theologians and philosophers have pointed to a human need for God as an answer to remove individual guilt and consequences caused by their "sinful" behavior. Many people of atheist persuasion consider this to be a useless relic of evolution and believe that if they deny the existence of God, guilt and sin will no longer plague them. They see belief in God and moral absolutes as the source of guilt. I am right there with them agreeing that a belief in God, and an accompanying religion, will not relieve a person of their sin and guilt and may even cause more. The things that are purported to remove our guilt often create more guilt, sometimes deeper and suppressed moral angst, which can be worse in the end.

A secular practice of denial of the reality of sin and guilt can definitely makes things worse. Following a religion that gives one works to relieve our guilt is also not the answer. What is the answer is what Jesus did on the cross for us! Sadly, deception, blame, self-justification, judging, and destruction are some of the means to deal with our brokenness without the cross. We may try to fix and forget the destruction we caused and the destruction done to us, but without the cross of Jesus, its haunt will not turn away[57]. The way of the cross is the only true means to be free from sin and guilt. This grace and freedom are possible because Christ suffered the deserved consequences of our sin and therefore freed us from the bondage of sin. Without Jesus, we will go to the grave with our guilt and intensely experience the consequences of the bad we have done in the afterlife.

Blaise Pascal wrote that Jesus is the only simultaneous answer to our wretchedness and our pride[58]. The wretched either believe themselves unworthy or are so proud of their wretchedness that they will not admit

57 Romans 6:21
58 Pascal, Blaise, Pensées, pp. 63-64, trans. Honor Levi (Oxford: Oxford University Press, 1995), 63-4.

they need saving. The proud have trouble humbling themselves because of their pride in their self-sufficiency and their inability to recognize they are wrong. Through Christ's death, the wretched are lifted up, and the high are made low, for we are all sinners in need of a savior. We come to Christ realizing that in our deficiency, we need and want a relationship with Him. Our life with God starts when we acknowledge our sin and brokenness, receive His forgiveness, decide to follow His ways, and become a part of His family. God changes our lives by dwelling in us, whether that is lowering our pride or lifting our worth.

The gospel presents one of the most important meanings in life. It is the fact that our individual beliefs about who Jesus is determine where we will spend eternity. God cares utmost about what we think and believe. It is incredible how much God sees us and our beliefs as significant, especially the beliefs that affect the destiny of our lives now and in the next life.

A belief in Jesus is to embrace that all people are equal in value because of His great loving sacrifice to save each one of us. We are equal and highly valued as brothers and sisters in Christ because of the priceless worth and meaning that is given to each individual as His children. God's family has no regard for race, gender, or station in life[59]. The fact that Jesus loves each person that has lived, lives now, or will ever live, and died for every one of them, dictates equality in value that is abundantly clear. Each person we meet is someone Jesus died for.

The Bible lays out the answer to purpose and meaning for every last individual on earth. The answer is that we accept Jesus as God, believe His teachings and become His disciples. We then enter into a relationship where God's love is lavished upon us. The love of God for us is not a

---

59 Galatians 3:28

vague, peaceful feeling; it is deeply personal and begins to address our most pressing concerns. One starts on the path of learning and believing the teachings of Jesus, following Him as a disciple, and being filled with His Spirit. They then begin to learn the blessings of existing as one of God's children and begin to experience an internal transformation with Jesus walking with them through their struggles. The closer a follower comes to fully know and fully experience what Jesus did for them and the more they fellowship with His Spirit, the more Jesus will grow them in truth and love, even as they pass through their life's greatest successes and biggest dilemmas. The more they grow, the more they will experience God's love, which is the answer to what is truly missing in their lives.

CHAPTER 7

THE SIMPLE GOSPEL

And there is salvation in no one else, for there is no other name under heaven given among people by which we must be saved.

Acts 4:12 (NET)

The simple gospel is, simply put, the good news about a relationship with God made possible through Jesus and His work on the cross. The Apostle Paul gives us a clear statement of the path to salvation in his recorded reply to the Philippian jailer when he said, "Believe in the Lord Jesus, and you will be saved" (Acts 16:31, NIV). It took me forty years to be convinced that Paul's simple statement summed up the whole gospel. When I was twenty, my ten-year-old niece asked, "How does one become a Christian?" After two years of studying to be a youth pastor, I still had trouble answering that question. It did not help that her dad, who did not fully believe, was sitting next to us. I was so wrapped up in starting with the issues surrounding salvation that I skipped over the simple answer. After discussing a few peripheral issues, her interest faded.

It might help to clarify what Paul meant in his simple call to believe by taking a closer look at all the elements contained in his simple gospel presentation to the Philippian jailer. The occasion can be found recorded in the book of Acts:

About midnight Paul and Silas were praying and singing hymns to God, and the other prisoners were listening to them. Suddenly there was such a violent earthquake that the foundations of the prison were shaken. At once all the prison doors flew open, and everyone's chains came loose. The jailer woke up, and when he saw the prison doors open, he drew his sword and was about to kill himself because he thought the prisoners had escaped. But Paul shouted, "Don't harm yourself! We are all here!" The jailer called for lights, rushed in and fell trembling before Paul and Silas. He then brought them out and asked, "Sirs, what must I do to be saved?" They replied, "Believe in the Lord Jesus, and you will be saved...."

Acts 16:25–31 (NIV)

This is such a dramatic day and night in the life of a first-century Roman jailer. He was tasked with guarding these Jewish troublemakers that would not stop praying and singing, even after they were beaten. Now an earthquake and possible prison escape seem to have occurred. The only honorable thing left to do is to end his own life, yet the prisoners did not actually leave. Something supernatural is taking place, and he knows it. Paul and Silas act in kindness and love towards their enemy. The guard wants what they have and asks how to get it. "Sirs, what must I do to be saved?" I think I would have had quite a few more questions than that one, but it appears he saw, heard, and felt something that drew him into believing in a new foreign God. Paul replies, "Believe in the Lord Jesus, and you will be saved."

The first core of the simple gospel is that God wants a relationship with you so much that He sent His Son to die on the cross to facilitate it.

For God so loved the world that he gave his one and only Son, that whoever believes in him shall not perish but have eternal life.

John 3:16 (NIV)

The jailor had built his kingdom by creating a way of life for himself that had worked up to this point. It took an earthquake and a prison break to bring him to the place where he realized that his plan was not succeeding. I know we are usually impressed with the dramatic conversions such as this, but sometimes I think God is more impressed with a simple, humble decision to love Him. The reality of the simple gospel is that God wants a relationship with us. Sometimes He does do the dramatic, but usually, for most people I know, God quietly calls them to come follow Him. We make the decision to live this life in relationship with God the way it was intended to be lived and to live life for the original purpose that we were created.

When God created humanity, He created unique and special beings in His image that were capable of choosing a relationship with Him or choosing to reject Him. The volitional nature of this relationship is what makes it unique and valuable. God gave us the power to determine the reality of the relationship. I know people like to philosophize about God knowing everything, and some even claim God determines our every decision, but philosophy and reality crash together at this point. If we are a unique person and God wants to have a relationship with us, it cannot be that He is controlling all of our thoughts; that would not be a relationship. I would go so far as to say that God can be surprised by us. God wants a relationship with the unique person that you are, and He is waiting for you to open that door.

The second core of the simple gospel is that it is a simple choice to believe and enter into a relationship with God.

> For with the heart one believes and thus has righteousness and
> with the mouth one confesses and thus has salvation.

Romans 10:10 (NET)

During my undergraduate studies, I went to college with Greg Steer, a gifted evangelist of our times from Dare to Share Ministries. He would constantly tell me how simple sharing the gospel was. In his free time during college, Greg would go out and ask perfect strangers if they knew where they were going when they died. I found it hard to approach the gospel in such a direct and simple manner. I did not understand the gospel as easily as Greg did, and I constantly brought up objections to going out and evangelizing with him.

Several years later, I ran into Greg when I took my youth group to a "Dare to Share" talk. After the presentation, half of them went to the front of the room and publicly accepted Christ. I had worked with these youth for over a year and tried to present Christianity as a simple choice in my talks, but none of them publicly accepted Christ after I spoke. Why did they not choose to follow Jesus when I told them the gospel? Perhaps I made it too complicated or assumed they were already believers. God has more to do with it than Greg or myself, but what was my part? There are endless issues to talk about in youth groups that, when dealt with apart from the gospel, can muddy the waters. What they needed to hear in terms of the gospel was the simple message that Jesus loves them, forgives them, has a destiny for their lives, and all they have to do is decide to believe.

Why do some Christians, including myself, make it complicated? Is not the gospel as simple as Paul proclaimed? "Believe in the Lord Jesus, and you will be saved." Yes, it is that simple. A child can understand it, but adults have to make it complicated. I make it difficult because I want to know the whole picture. I have to ask who, what, when, where, why, and how. Sometimes, I can be a slow learner with a thick skull. How can this be so hard? Why could I not just have uttered the simple gospel message when my niece asked me about salvation instead of making it about me convincing another person to believe? Sharing the gospel is the simple task of presenting them with the choice to believe in Jesus.

The third core to the simple gospel is that when you believe, you are saved.

> I tell you the solemn truth, the one who hears my message and believes the one who sent me has eternal life and will not be condemned, but has crossed over from death to life.

> John 5:24 (NET)

It has been almost fifty years since I knelt with my mother at a Child Evangelism Fellowship Vacation Bible School and accepted Christ as my Savior. I am sure I prayed the sinner's prayer and asked Jesus into my heart that day. It seemed simple enough, but my understanding of Christianity seemed to get more complicated from there. Was I saved? Was it real? Should I do it again? In junior high, the question was, "Do I want it?" As a senior in high school, I wrote a tremendously complicated paper on salvation, inspired by books found in my family library. It was long and cumbersome because I had trouble saying what I needed to say in a few short words. I also wondered if I needed the baptism of the Holy Spirit to be saved and fully experience God. I pounded my pastor with all my hard spiritual questions during Sunday school. He became very frustrated with having to answer them all right before his sermon and quickly found someone else to teach the class. Still, I had questions that needed to be answered, so I headed off to a Christian college with the belief that it would help.

My understanding of the Christian life has come a long way since then. Not that I know it all, but I believe I have a glimpse of the big picture. Even still, when I read the Bible, some things are clear, some are deep, some take scholarly study, some are mysterious, and indeed, there are some things I still do not understand. I ask God, "Why did you not just put this in simple instructions: step one, step two, step three?" Then, I remember, "Oh yeah, we fail to read instructions." Human minds are so complicated that simple instructions are boring to us, but complicated instructions are frustrating, so we complain.

Sometimes, I wish I had an easy button, maybe a fix-it button, or how about a do-over button? I would go full speed ahead until I messed it all up and then hit the do-over button. What if Adam and Eve had a do-over button? Funny thing is, just like us, they would have messed it up again. Life in Jesus is not about having a magic do-over button; it is about growing in love, despite the decisions we make, good or bad. Our past is not an albatross but lessons in love to perfect us in God's love. As we live by the Spirit, we become more loving as we grow in the Spirit. God uses our mistakes and failures to grow us, teach us, and discipline us all for the sake of learning to love as Jesus loved.

God did give us a do-over button in the work of Christ on the cross. We do not have to fall on a sword to fix the mess we made; all we have to do is believe and enter into a relationship with Him and let Him begin to work in us—that simple decision to believe changes our whole lives, now and for eternity. We enter into a relationship with God. Similar to any relationship, it takes work and gets messy at times, but this one is more than worth it in the end. Although I have written in this book a summary of how I think our relationship with God is lived out, there are no step-by-step instructions. There is no system of knowing if we are doing it exactly right. We have to work that out on our journey with Jesus building a new kingdom with Him as the king.

CHAPTER 8

———

WHY DID JESUS GO TO THE CROSS?

But God demonstrates His own love toward us, in that while we were still sinners, Christ died for us.

Romans 5:8 (NKJV)

We would be amiss in a discussion of Jesus without attempting to understand the reason for the cross, the defining moment in His ministry and life. Christ's work on the cross brought the possibility of the end of our separation from God, the end of sin and death, and the completion of the law. His loving act on the cross is the foundational core of the gospel, and when it is emulated, the cross transforms human interaction. It was an act of love so great that it completely redefined what love is and how we are to show love for one another. Even more importantly, it was the bridge to a loving relationship with God and made possible the rebirth of our spirit to live in His presence. Through the cross, we have forgiveness of sins, and we begin a new eternal life with God. Understanding the meaning and purpose of the cross is the first core of the gospel.

The cross is the exact opposite of what humanity would expect from a savior. Our savior should ride in on a white horse and conquer our enemies. Our savior should be strong and fix all of our problems. Our savior should answer all our questions and give us solutions to the things that trouble us. Our savior should build a kingdom in the mold that we see fit. The cross did not make sense. To the Jews, it was a "stumbling block and to Gentiles, foolishness."[60] Why would a savior have to die?

To understand the cross, we must look at the past. It may seem that throughout history, God asked humans to do some strange things to facilitate a relationship with Him. One of those odd things to our modern minds, yet central to the Jewish religion, is the sacrifice of animals to cover their sins and to demonstrate their faith in God. It is hard to understand how the requirement to kill animals is logically sensible for the benefit of a relationship in today's world, although we will establish a friendship over a meal that might include meat. Christian and Jewish doctrine see the blood of an animal as representing a covenant between two parties. An example is the covenant God made with Abram in Genesis chapter fifteen, where animals were slaughtered to establish the agreement. In much the same way, Jesus referred to His blood as the new covenant between Him and His followers[61]. His blood served as a symbol of the binding agreement we are asked to enter.

Animal sacrifice can also be understood as a substitutionary death for the death we deserve for our sin[62]. We are told that the blood covers our sins and washes us clean so that we can approach God[63]. All that being said, the death of an animal through sacrifice can also represent a harsh but poignant picture of the damage we cause when we break a relationship by our evil behavior.

Another angle to see animal sacrifice is that through the killing of one's animals, faith and trust in the supernatural are demonstrated.

---

60 1 Corinthians 1:23
61 Matthew 26:28
62 Isaiah 53:6, Matthew 26:28
63 Hebrews 9:12-14

Although it is a foolish act to those who do not believe, sacrifice might demonstrate your faith and love for the Lord. Consider the strange practice of baptism for spiritual cleansing. It is meaningless in the eyes of the world yet deeply significant in the lives of God's children and in the eyes and heart of God. It is similar to the sacrifice of an animal in this way. Somehow submission to the significance of something they could not fully understand showed one's faith in, trust in, and love for the supernatural redeemer.

Does understanding animal sacrifice help us understand Jesus' sacrificial death on a cross? Although animal sacrifice was a symbol of a covenant and remission of sins,[64] could there not have been another way of salvation? In trying to fully comprehend the death of Jesus, one may contemplate that the loving, sacrificial death of God's Son is the most seemingly senseless loving act ever conceived. It does not make sense that an eternal, all-powerful God loves us so deeply and intimately that He would become a man and voluntarily suffer and die to restore a relationship with us. It might be that only what seems the most foolish act of love ever conceived could communicate the undeserved and unearned love and forgiveness that we need for salvation.[65] The other option for Jesus would have been to take power and restore order, but then how would we know such great love? How would we know that the greatest act we can do is to sacrifice ourselves for others?

This brings up the question of, How can the God of the New Testament, who loves us this much in the person of Jesus, be the same God in the Old Testament, who demonstrates His wrath? The picture of a vengeful yet loving God who makes a law of death for eating

---

64 Hebrews 9:22
65 1 Corinthians 1:18-31

a fruit seems odd[66]. But God is the source of life; without Him, we will die. Death is more of a truth about what happens without God's sustaining presence than a punishment. In the Garden, God did not say it was a punishment of death for eating the fruit; instead, He warned Adam and Eve that they would die if they turned against Him. When they did, they immediately felt guilt and shame and entered life with the knowledge of good and evil along with life under the law of sin and death and separation from God. God then gave the first humans a curse of struggle. Difficulties are not always a bad thing because they tend to be the schoolmaster to teach us what is important in life. Does it not seem that the less we struggle, the more we are tempted to not acknowledge God? We begin to see our greatness over others around us. I contend that what we call God's wrath is Him giving humans over to more struggle to reduce their sin and pride.

I do not see the Bible as a story of God's wrath but a love story of God seeking to save humanity from its self-imposed destruction and to restore the relationship humans were made to have with Him. To save humans from themselves, God allowed them to experience the consequences of their actions and continually worked with them to lead them back to Himself. What appears as God's wrath is Him turning humans over to the deserved consequences of their actions instead of continuing to pardon them. Even we as humans know that on specific occasions, allowing people to suffer the consequences is the loving thing to do with free agents. The story throughout the Bible is the true story of God's great love as He faithfully works with rebellious humans.

The story of God's love starts with Adam and Eve. They had a healthy, free, and loving relationship with God. He had Adam name all the animals. In the "cool of the day," God walked and talked with Adam

---

66 Genesis 2:17

and Eve.[67] It had to be one of those just right, loving friendships that we all crave. In love, God commanded Adam: "You must not eat from the tree of the knowledge of good and evil" (Genesis 2:17, NET). This presented a decision by Adam to trust and rely on God to teach and provide for him or to seek the knowledge of right and wrong outside of God. He gave Adam and Eve all things, except He instilled one boundary for their own protection. God knew Adam and Eve were far from ready to experience total autonomy living apart from His direction and protection. He knew it would destroy humanity because people would not yet know how to handle themselves without His guidance. Unfettered knowledge of good and evils would lead to rebellion, anger, strife, greed, lying, confusion, disobedience, destruction, murder, and much more[68].

To prevent Adam and Eve from making this horrible choice, God used the idea of death as a communication tool to demonstrate the destruction that they would bring on their lives personally and future humanity from their sin. When Adam and Eve ate the fruit, they were turned over to the outcomes of their decision to learn on their own and go it alone without God. One of the outcomes would be death, as God had informed them[69]. Graciously, on God's part, Adam and Eve did not die immediately. Eventually, they did die after an exceedingly long life. In our short lives, we see death and think, *This is not right*. Death feels inherently wrong, and it is. We were meant to live forever with Jesus in a garden. God took a lamb and slaughtered it instead of immediate death for Adam and Eve. He began the idea of substituting the death of a lamb to cover our sin.

---

67 Genesis 3:8 (NASB)

68 Genesis 6:5

69 Genesis 3:16-19

In the next chapter of Genesis, we are told that Adam's oldest son, Cain, murders his brother Abel. This was evidence that the broken relationship between God and humanity was affecting human relationships, with brother now killing brother.[70] The murder illustrated the severity of the broken relationship between God and humans. They would now build their own kingdoms by any means necessary. Humans continued to distrust God and take matters into their own hands, leading to more brokenness and pain in the world. A relationship cannot exist without trust, and all humans were now born with an inherent bent to distrust God and His goodness. Fellowship with God became more and more distant because of sin. Still, God had a plan to redeem His children and show humans His love for them.[71]

The flood now becomes the great fulfillment of His prophecy of death where God hastens the death on all of mankind, in fact, His whole creation. Humans had decided to embrace their sin and do whatever was right in their own eyes. Some even think the angels physically joined in this revelry. There are also tales of animals being exploited. It was a great corruption of God's intended purpose of creation and especially His desire for humans. It was far from the intimate companionship of a person-to-person relationship we were meant for. Humanity's corruption was incurable. Fortunately, Noah was pleasing to God, and He started over with Noah and his family. This time He would institute a covenant with mankind that said that we cannot kill one another and that we should not kill animals except for food and recognition of God's mercy. Through a story about nakedness, the writer of Genesis also illustrated the sacredness of the marriage bond and the wickedness of sexual waywardness. From this point on, God promised not to destroy

---

70 Genesis 4:8, 1 John 3:11-12
71 Genesis 12:1-3

the earth again with a flood. He did not make this promise because humans would now be righteous, but because He had the plan of the cross to restore them to their true purpose despite their failures.

The Bible then jumps forward to Abraham. God promised Abraham to use him to fulfill His plan of redemption. He promised to give Abraham numerous offspring and that, through one of his descendants, the entire world would be blessed.[72] It was a strange thing to promise to a ninety years old man who had no children. When Abraham did finally have his miracle child, Isaac, the Lord asked Abraham to take the life of his only son. Abraham loved and trusted God so deeply that he faithfully took his son Isaac to Mount Moriah with the intention to sacrifice Isaac because Abraham believed that God would raise Isaac from the dead.[73] Abraham was stopped from killing Isaac by God and was blessed for his faith and willingness to be the one to restore humanity's relationship with God.

Isaac's death would not have been sufficient to restore humanity's relationship with God because he was not a willing nor sinless sacrifice. Sinlessness is a requirement because someone already deserving of punishment cannot pay another's penalty. Only the death of the sinless Son of the heavenly Father, God Himself, could mend the break of the relationship from humans to reach God, and only the death of a sinless, earthly Son could mend the relationship from God towards humans. God gave His heavenly Son, Jesus, to repair man's rebellion against Him, and humans, unknowingly gave God their earthly Son, Jesus, to mend their guilt and shame. This reconciliation could only have been accomplished in one man, Jesus Christ, the sinless sacrifice, who was both the "Son of Man" who paid the price for humanity's sin and the

---

72 Genesis 12:1-3

73 Genesis 8:22-14, Hebrews 11:17-19

"Son of God" who gave Himself up to restore a loving relationship between God and man.[74]

It must be noted here that God did not kill Jesus, and humanity did not kill Jesus, and the end was not death but a new life[75]. It may seem that God forced Jesus to die, but Jesus was a willing participant at every moment of His life, death, and resurrection. Motivated by His great love for us and His desire to have a relationship with us, He chose His death, a horrific death, to once and for all restore the loving relationship that was lost in the garden—a mutually loving relationship extending from God toward people and from people toward God. His death was the perfect payment to appease justice, provide mercy, and pave the way for a new, loving relationship. The cross then ended the need for the law and punishment because His sacrificial death demonstrated transformation through love, and the resurrection demonstrated a result of new and greater life, free from judgment and violence.

In addition, Jesus did not go to the cross because of God's need to exercise His wrath; that is the opposite of what He was doing. God was demonstrating His love. How do we know this great love? It requires an understanding that God deeply desires a relationship with us in which He can participate in our lives as a mother, father, brother, sister, friend, king, and savior. It is important that we know that His love does not come with any stipulations to fulfill or any hoops to jump through prior to Him loving us; Jesus died for us "while we were still sinners." God put no conditions on our behavior before He would exercise His love for us. Jesus told Nicodemus, long before He was crucified, "For God so loved the world that He gave His only begotten Son, that whoever believes in Him should not perish but have everlasting life" (John 3:16, NKJV).

---

74 Matthew 18:11, John 1:49
75 John 10:17-18

Jesus came to restore eternal life in His children and repair humanity's relationship with Him. All anyone has to do to receive God's love is to believe and accept it.

In love, God forgave the sins of the whole world on the cross. The Apostle John wrote that "He Himself is the propitiation for our sins; and not for ours only, but also for those of the whole world" (1 John 2:2, HCSB). Jesus' love for us was so great that He took upon Himself all the sins of each and every human. John the Baptist exclaimed upon seeing Jesus: "Here is the Lamb of God, who takes away the sin of the world" (John 1:29, HCSB). The cross was an act of sacrificial love providing the forgiveness and atonement for all human sins to restore for every human the possibility of a relationship with God.[76] Our reconciliation was predicated on His love for the "world."[77]

One can hardly imagine the immense love Jesus demonstrated as He submitted Himself to the whipping and brutal death on a cross. At each blow, His love endured as He restrained His power to obliterate the perpetrator. Isaiah, the ancient Jewish prophet, wrote: "By His stripes we are healed" (Isaiah 53:5, NKJV). His gruesome torture and death were for an important reason. He took on the violence that we deserve for our sins, not only ours but the whole world's. In His love, Jesus literally paid the penalty and endured the destruction that our sin caused so we could be healed, freed from enslavement to destruction, and enter into a relationship with Him.

It seems Paul goes to great ends to communicate how immense and permanent the love of God is for us because of the cross:

What then are we to say about these things? If God is for us, who is

---

76 Romans 5:18
77 John 3:16

against us? He did not even spare His own Son but offered Him up for us all; how will He not also with Him grant us everything? ...Who can separate us from the love of Christ? Can affliction or anguish or persecution or famine or nakedness or danger or sword? ...No, in all these things we are more than victorious through Him who loved us. For I am persuaded that not even death or life, angels or rulers, things present or things to come, hostile powers, height or depth, or any other created thing will have the power to separate us from the love of God that is in Christ Jesus our Lord!

Romans 8:31–32, 35, 37–39 (HCSB)

The story of God's great love and sacrifice on the cross so that we might know His love and be restored to a relationship with Him is the amazing good news that should be proclaimed by all believers. It should be spoken of to a humanity who does not know God's real love and needs to be proclaimed as the desperately needed answer to what has killed our souls.

Our trust in the loving, brutal act of the cross as the means of forgiveness for our sins is the seemingly foolish act of faith that we must commit in order to change our hearts from the inside out. It was a humble sacrifice on the part of Jesus that freed us from a life of sin and death. When He died for our sin, He made it possible for the Spirit to live inside us, guiding us in His love. We are forever transformed and deeply moved by knowing of and believing in the strange act of sacrifice, where Jesus demonstrated that to love was more important than any achievement in the world's eyes, demonstrating His love was even more important than life itself. If a person is able to comprehend such a great act of love, how could they not respond positively to this love that changed so much?

God wants to bring all His children home and to love them. When a person responds to His call, they receive this love and are adopted into His family. There is nothing that can take God's love away. The following simple statement informs me and reminds me of God's great unconditional love:

> There is nothing we can do to make God love us more, and there is nothing we can do to make God love us less.[78]

With that kind of love behind us, in us, and before us, we seem to be left with no better option than to walk in His great love shown on the cross and to let Him be King of our lives.

---

78 Richard Halverson, Philip Yancey

CHAPTER 9

—

WHAT DOES IT MEAN TO BELIEVE IN JESUS?

"The word is near you, in your mouth and in your heart" (that is, the word of faith that we preach), because if you confess with your mouth that Jesus is Lord and believe in your heart that God raised him from the dead, you will be saved. For with the heart one believes and thus has righteousness and with the mouth one confesses and thus has salvation.

Romans 10:8–10 (NET)

Belief in Jesus is the second core of the gospel. Our most important beliefs in life concern what brings us meaning on our journey. For anyone contemplating a decision to follow Jesus, it is important to know whether or not it will move one closer to comprehensively answering life's most important questions. Does it help us make sense of the world around us? Will it help us explain our own life experience in all of its dimensions? Does our belief in the deity of Jesus and the truth of His teaching and work on the cross explain concepts such as love, justice, morals, relationships, joy, good, evil, consciousness, the supernatural, and existence itself? For me, the answer was and is yes to these questions. I have come to the conclusion that the greatest meaning-infusing, life-transforming decision anyone can make is to believe that Jesus was God and to follow Him as their Savior.

I do not think we can merely decide to believe in Jesus like we can decide what color of shirt we want to wear. A belief is an intellectual conclusion about a reality that we think to be true on the deepest possible level. We surmise from our reason, knowledge, and observations what is the best explanation of the world around us. In other words, our beliefs come from repeated observations and learning, leading to conclusions that logically cohere to our experience, perceptions, and knowledge. Beliefs serve as categorical assumptions by which we make sense of all the information we perceive.

There are basic beliefs about our reality, like the color of the sky or the grass, which we can agree on. Beliefs like these are based predominantly on physical observations. Then, there are other beliefs that come more from inference. For example, you may believe that your parents or spouse love you based on how they treat you. Both of these types of beliefs easily fit into our scope of reason.

Next, there are the beliefs about the supernatural, as the existence of a god or gods and their identity and character. People have difficulty agreeing on supernatural beliefs because they are usually not based on empirically observed experiences, and they tend to be more subjective. While we may believe with extreme confidence that each time we take a step, our foot will meet solid ground, the Apostle Peter would tell us that having enough belief to walk on water is a little tougher; it might take some faith in the not-so-common, maybe even faith in occurrences beyond the natural.

Belief in the supernatural may be a struggle for some because they may not be willing to go beyond their own natural experience. The potential problem with using an experience-based epistemology is that our perception and reasoning are sometimes flawed, and our experiences are limited. Simply because one does not experience the supernatural does not give facts to its non-existence. If the concept of the supernatural gives you meaning and purpose, that in itself may attest to its necessity for life, in the same regard as food, shelter, and clothing are necessary. While we can live without the knowledge of the supernatural and even deny it, we are left hungry for answers to questions that observation and reason cannot solve, like: "Why are we reasoning creatures who value love so highly?" It is hard to believe that important human attributes like our knowledge, our consciousness, and even our being alive itself came solely by chance from the natural world and not from a supernatural source.

Belief in Jesus' deity and his work on the cross, to the Christian, is ultimately important in order to exist in a right state with God as a human on this earth, and it affects our eternal existence. Belief in Jesus is not only intellectual; it is supernatural because He was supernatural; this is verified by eyewitness testimony found in the gospels. Our dilemma is that we want natural proof, but the more we explain the supernatural Jesus in natural terms, the more natural He appears and sounds. It is impossible to fully prove the supernatural through natural processes, although, through knowing the natural, we know what is supernatural. Looking to science to prove God or to history to prove miracles takes these disciplines beyond their scope of expertise. Yet, it is important to know that science and history do not disprove Jesus and the miracles associated with Him either.

Theology might improve our certainty of Jesus, along with philosophy, meditation, and prayer, but no matter how deep and hard we dig, at some point, we will need to make a decision on what we believe to be truth. We find ourselves embracing our experience, reason, and belief, trusting that the future will bring similar problems and answers. Our combination of understanding and faith can enable us to take the supernatural step towards Jesus, away from a life without Him. Sometimes it is merely our insatiable need for a relationship with our creator that brings us to seek Jesus. When we are drawn to Him, we are faced with a question: Will we accept that Jesus was supernatural, or will we brush Him off as a natural phenomenon puffed up by His disciples? Accepting Jesus as the creator God does not mean we take some kind of irrational leap of faith. Belief in the supernatural is not irrational but is found to be a necessity of life for those who believe. Belief in and trust in Jesus for salvation, it is not irrational to them, for once one sees the truth, it is the only conclusion imaginable.

Christians believe in Jesus with faith based on the direction that love, truth, and logic take us; however, we do not get to God only by reason because then we are simply creating a God that is reasonable to us. Reason, fact, and logic cannot bring us into a relationship with God. To know the supernatural, we must acknowledge that He is beyond our complete understanding and be able to respond to His simple call of love; God loves us and wants to make Himself known to us.

This strong conclusion is rarely based on just one experience or idea. A believer may have several pillars to their belief in the supernatural and Jesus as the incarnate God. They may see that reason allows for the possibility of God. History presents the evidence that Jesus lived and was resurrected. The world around us demonstrates an intelligent and creative maker. The numerous prophecies fulfilled by Jesus point to the existence of the supernatural plan by a powerful God. Jesus' teachings illustrate the wisdom and character of God. Suffering seeks a God who can alleviate the pain and possibly rescue us from it. Loneliness and emptiness require a comforter to fulfill us with friendship. Guilt longs for the forgiveness of the cross. Pride aches to be humbled by the true glory of God. Pain cries out for the compassion and mercy of a savior.

Evil leaves us desperate for His true love. Belief in Jesus is the only complete answer to many of the negative experiences and questions we have in life.

Everyone is faced with the same choice when they encounter Jesus: Will we believe that Jesus was God and follow Him for our salvation? The incarnation of God in the person of Jesus changed the world, and the biggest change would come after He left—in the hearts of His followers. In His reflective presence, a person's true self and motives are on full display. It is like standing in a scanner machine at the airport, but it is not bombs that are detected; it is all that we have ever thought, said, or done that is on display. When someone knows our faults and can reveal them, it invokes a fight or flight response. There is another way. We can face our brokenness. This vulnerability can only be found in the presence of true love and unconditional acceptance, which is what Jesus offers us. He did not come to condemn us but to give us His love and show us the way, the truth, and the life[79]. He wants to save us and reconcile our relationship with Him.

The Jewish leaders, in charge of what they thought was the kingdom of God, were apparently unwilling to be vulnerable, unable to face what was in their own hearts, and fearful of any loss of power. They rejected Jesus of Nazareth as their Messiah because it meant changing their very foundational way of life. They had built a life of law, and Jesus professed grace and forgiveness. He did not jump through the right hoops or follow the right paths to power. Instead of joining their kingdom of God, He appeared to be against them. People began to follow Jesus and not the leaders. At this juncture, they successfully sought to have Him executed.

What will we do when we come face-to-face with the creator God

---

79 John 14:6

when we are forced to see our true self in the light of His perfect goodness and love? Jesus stands before each one of us, seeking to return us to His family as a father searches for a wayward child. Will we hold on to the perceived control of our less-than-adequate lives and then laugh and decide He is a madman claiming to be God? How can we know that He is the God of the universe when we encounter a plethora of claims of deity and outright counterfeits? If we are inclined at all to listen to Jesus, can we suspend our disbelief, forsake all that we perceive as an alternative answer to our deepest needs, and follow Him? When we encounter the powerful, loving, and true incarnate God, we must decide to reject Him or become His disciples and follow Him. People in the Jerusalem area who lived during the three years of Christ's ministry experienced the physical manifestation of this choice as a reality. This decision can seem more distant for us when we lack His bodily presence, but it is ultimately the same question: Will we believe in and choose to have a relationship with the man Jesus, who proved Himself to be God?[80]

If and when we make the decision to believe, we can be assured of our supernatural transition in what Paul wrote to the first-century church in Rome:

> If you declare with your mouth, "Jesus is Lord," and believe in your heart that God raised him from the dead, you will be saved. For it is with your heart that you believe and are justified, and it is with your mouth that you profess your faith and are saved.
>
> Romans 10:9–10 (NIV)

When we actually believe in our heart that Jesus is Lord and God raised

---

80   John 10:24-33

Him from the dead, it becomes a monumental belief that can bring a life-changing transformation. We begin to see the world through the lens that Jesus is God—the creator of all that exists, who lived and walked on this earth and wants to have a relationship with us. He wants to live in us, to fellowship with us, and to give us a new and amazing life in Him[81]. Humans no longer have to depend solely on natural reason to make sense of the mysteries of life. Or, if one adheres to another religion, that person no longer has to make sense of claims that do not always seem to correspond to the world around him or her. With Christ, the truth becomes clearer each day because He teaches His children what is true. He promised that: "If you hold to my teaching, you are really my disciples. Then you will know the truth, and the truth will set you free" (John 8:31–32, NIV).

We can make this discussion of belief in Jesus as complicated as we like, but for some, the complication is not necessary. For them, it is a simple decision to "believe in the Lord Jesus" because they recognize that He is the way to fill the void inside them, to explain and heal their pain, and to answer life's biggest questions—questions they have been asking all their lives. They know that when they "believe in the Lord Jesus," they are given a new abundant eternal life here and now and a future life with Jesus to come.

---

81 John 14:20

CHAPTER 10

—

WHAT DOES IT MEAN TO
BE SAVED?

Jesus answered, "I am the way and the truth and the life. No one comes to the Father except through me."

John 14:6 (NIV)

The third core of the gospel is that when we believe, we are saved. What does it mean to be saved? Does salvation make us cool? Does it make us:…healthy? …wealthy …happy? …kind? …smart? …content? …moral? …perfect? …whole? …found? …sane? …free? What are we gaining from following Jesus? One foundational transformation of salvation in the believer's life is that it results in them displaying Jesus' love, yet being more loving is not the same as salvation.[82]

Salvation in Jesus is not relying on systems like religions, family structures, government solutions, helpful advice, and self-help strategies to transform our lives. Many of those systems are somewhat helpful but also can be a form of slavery to burdensome tasks that attempt to fix our old dead selves. All of these ideas and institutions, although usually well-intentioned, cannot bring freedom from our brokenness that stems from sin and separation from God.

How did we get to the place that we need to be saved? The book

---

82 1 John 4:7; Romans 5:5

of Genesis teaches that God created us, like Himself, as creatures with whom He desired to share eternity with[83]. It goes on to tell the events of Adam and Eve, who ate the fruit of rebellion and chose to go it alone without God's sustenance, knowledge, and companionship. They started a moral fall that facilitated a separation from the God of love, our intimate teacher and Father[84]. At creation, God gave us our own free will and intended for us to openly and purposefully love as He does. Sadly, our free will also allow for the possibility of rebelling against Him, going the way of self-righteousness, and seeking knowledge for ourselves without God.[85] Human rebellion led to evil behavior and needed laws, judgment, and punishment to control that behavior. Humans need to be saved from who they have become by turning away from their creator and building their own kingdoms, with no place for God in them. Salvation is choosing to follow Jesus, which will change the believer's life towards the restoration of God's love and knowledge, and away from serving oneself as the chief end of life.

Salvation is not merely fire insurance for the next life, where possibly we are looking to improve our dying self, but mostly waiting for heaven in the next life. We receive salvation from our dead self, not salvation of our dead self. Salvation in Jesus is a completely different road. We bury our old, false self that desperately controlled our actions to fill the void and despair left by sin and all it entails. We are then raised in the newness of life to become the self who God truly intended us to be. Our true new self is no longer broken and dead but now alive in His Spirit and in His love[86]. When we choose Jesus, we are not doing it to ensure our

---

83 Genesis 3:22-24
84 Genesis 2:7-3:24
85 Genesis 2:16-17
86 Galatians 2:20

salvation from the fires of hell in the future; we are embracing eternal life here and now.

At the point of belief, wonderful things happen in our lives. God restores life in us, the life and relationship that was lost when Adam went his own way.[6][87] God does this by removing sin from us and restoring the presence of His Spirit.[7][88] It is Jesus in us and ourselves in Him that restores our life. One only has this new eternal life if they have Jesus in them and the restoration He brings. John wrote: "And this is the testimony: God has given us eternal life, and this life is in his Son. Whoever has the Son has life; whoever does not have the Son of God does not have life" (1 John 5:11–12, NIV). One cannot have this new life if he or she does not have the means of the new life in them, which is the indwelling of the Son of God within us.

Let us not forget that this new eternal life in us is predicated on Jesus providing us unconditional forgiveness, freeing us from our path of destruction. Our forgiveness is realized when we accept His suffering death on the cross to substitute for the penalty we deserved for our sins and the evil we have committed.[89] To fully understand this forgiveness, one may ask: *Have we all committed sins so terrible that we deserve to be tortured and crucified?* You may not think so, but the destructive results of our own sins, even though they may not warrant such punishment, cannot be overlooked.

When we learn of the torture and death that Christ suffered,[90] it is difficult to conceive that His sacrifice was not sufficient for our worst of sins[10]. Jesus' gruesome death was capable of overcoming the life-

---

87   1 Corinthians 15:22
88   Galatians 3:14
89   1 John 4:10; Acts 10:43; 1 John 1:9; Colossians. 2:13-15
90   Isaiah 53:4-6
91   Romans 6:21-23

destroying results of our personal sins, no matter how destructive they were. Through Christ's death, God was simultaneously saving us from our own self-imposed destruction, and at the same time, He was saving us from the inevitable consequence of death and separation that resulted from Adam rejecting Him[11][92]. We suffer dearly from sin, humanity's failures, other's sins against us, and our own individual transgressions.[93] The cross is where His perfect justice, love, and mercy collided to provide forgiveness of sins to all who believe and to demonstrate the great forgiveness that we are to embody as believers towards others. Because God loves the world, Jesus went to the cross to give us mercy for our wrongs. God wanted to forgive and redeem humanity so humans could enter into a relationship with Him.

All that said, forgiveness and removal of sin based upon our belief is not the whole of salvation. It is because our sins are removed that we can be free from bondage to the law of sin and death[94] and live by the Spirit, which is the crux of our salvation. Jesus bought our freedom through His loving act on the cross. Our salvation is realized when one chooses to receive His forgiveness, understands that Jesus takes away their sins,[95] and walks led by the Holy Spirit.[96] When the Spirit makes His home in us[97], we start to become a beautiful work of art because God takes our broken and tattered lives[98] and begins to perfect us in His love[99].

---

92 Genesis 2:17

93 Romans 1:18-32

94 Romans 8:2

95 Colossians 2:14-35; Acts 26:18

96 John 20:22; Romans 8:9; Acts 8:17, 19:2; 1 Corinthians 3:16; John 14:16; 1 John 3:24

97 John 14:20

98 Romans 7:24; Ephesians 2:1-7

99 1 John 2:5, 4:12, 17-18; 2 Corinthians 5:17

When we make the life-defining decision to "believe in the Lord Jesus,[100]" we become a new creation at the point of our profession of faith. With this step towards Jesus, we begin this new life, living on a completely new path of grace, love, and the knowledge of the truth, away from our previous path of destruction, as we listen to God's Spirit in us. It is amazing as we discover that one's understanding of the truth and impact of salvation cannot be exhausted, yet it is not an endless quest with no clear beginning. The gospel is so simple at a foundational level that a child can understand it. For some, this new life is the precious gift of walking with Jesus daily in His love, and that is enough. Others are moved by the Spirit on an intellectual journey, unraveling the mysteries of the gospel and its implications for their lives. For most of us, it is somewhere in between the two. Understanding the simplicity of salvation is extremely important, but knowing more about the grace and truth that Jesus imparts to us at salvation is extremely helpful to continue growing on this journey and experiencing the promised abundant life.[101]

Our decision to embrace salvation in Jesus is a decision to embrace His love and the truth He wants to teach us. There are multiple sources to discover the truth about salvation and its impact on our lives. Our being filled with the Spirit of truth begins our journey with Jesus as He guides us and teaches us. In addition to the Spirit, we have God's written Word, the Bible.

We would know little of God, His message of love, or the means of salvation through grace if we did not have the Bible. The insights about His love and salvation I am sharing in this book have come from the Spirit teaching me through the study of God's great message He has left for us. It gives us the means to know who the one true and living God

---

100 Acts 16:31 (NASB)
101 John 10:10

is, and His promised path of eternal life is through Jesus.[102] The Bible, combined with the Spirit, guides the Christian on this new journey of truth and love.

No matter how or where we find Jesus, we rejoice in knowing that Jesus came to rescue us from our dark road of following rules as a means to rid ourselves of wrongdoing and the thorny path of following religion to restore our relationship with God. It is by faith in the love that Jesus demonstrated on the cross, and the transforming power of His Spirit, that we are changed and rescued. Jesus takes away the things in our lives that destroy us, especially our sin, but also the law. Paul explains this in his letter to the Colossian church:

> And you, being dead in your trespasses and the uncircumcision of your flesh, He has made alive together with Him, having forgiven you all trespasses, having wiped out the handwriting of requirements that was against us, which was contrary to us. And He has taken it out of the way, having nailed it to the cross.
>
> Colossians 2:13–14 (NKJV)

Jesus came to bring an end to the reign of law, judgment, punishment, and death. He ended the law and its reign of condemnation.[103] He brought the opposite approach when He demonstrated His sacrifice, forgiveness, and mercy through His death on the cross and triumphed over the law of sin and death by His resurrection from the dead. Salvation frees us from condemnation of sin and the law and brings us directly into a relationship with God.

---

102 John 14:6
103 1 Corinthians 3:6-7

The gospel of Jesus is a powerful, life-transforming message. His plan of salvation is perfect in how it relates to the human spirit. It is comprehensive in how it heals us, forgives us, and brings new life through Jesus manifesting His love in us through the indwelling us with the Spirit. It brings freedom from sin, freedom from guilt, freedom from shame, and freedom to be who God wants us to be without these shackles of the past or a fear of the future. "Sin shall no longer be your master" (Romans 6:14, NIV), for there is no sin between God and us.[104] The gospel has power to transform our lives and save us, but as I have described, it may be a different power and salvation than we might expect or want.

---

104 Romans 8:1, 8:33-39

Chapter 11

How Is Our World Changed by Following Jesus?

Continue working out your salvation with awe and reverence, for the one bringing forth in you both the desire and the effort – for the sake of his good pleasure – is God.

Philippians 2:12–13 (NET)

We come to Jesus thinking He is going to solve all our problems. We envision that He is going to set up His kingdom in our lives, and life is going to function as it should. Still, we continue to have the potential to cause destruction in our lives through foolish mistakes, doing evil against God, ourselves, and each other. We are weak and broken, and at times, we even deny Christ. Although God does amazing work in us, our dysfunction and problems still persist.

One might think, as a changed believer, they would be able to overcome sin in their lives. Quickly we experience that this is not the case. Overcoming sin is a complex idea that I will examine in depth later in this book, and our changed life is a puzzle piece to understanding it.

In order to understand the change that takes place in our lives, it might be helpful to define some terms and explain some spiritual concepts commonly used by scripture in reference to the believer's life:

The flesh is one's brain and body, which includes its activities based on chemical and electrical firings. The flesh is the part of us that behaves most like an animal and can cause one's habits, desires, and patterns of thought. An atheist would focus on healing the flesh because, in general, they do not believe a person exists beyond the flesh. For Christians, when our spirits were dead, we were ruled by the flesh; when our spirits were made alive, we put to death the things of the flesh (Romans 8:13).

Our *spirit*, our immaterial self, or possibly called our person, is restored and made whole in a relationship with God when we choose to follow Jesus. The Christian first focuses on living by the Spirit—the part of us that lives forever—before we seek to change our earthly behavior.

The *world* is the system of meeting our fleshly needs and wants without the love of Jesus transforming us. Living for the world can involve seeking success, power, and control at the expense of others: many times, wanting and taking more than we need, and putting ourselves first. It can also be characterized by someone seeking safety and comfort over doing acts of love. We are to be in the world but are not to love the world (1 John 2:15–17).

Satan is a fallen angel who has an agenda to thwart God's plan and is allowed to test our faith. He, along with his fellow workers, are attempting to lead us to live as slaves to our flesh and the world so he can be in control.

Sin is a state where we give in to the flesh, the world, or Satan and commit regrettable acts which are the opposite of love.

God's forgiveness is a gift where, no matter how much we sin, we can let go of our past failures and start over, setting aside our guilt and shame.

God's love is a state of His acceptance and desire to be with us, and His wanting to know us and experience who we are. His love is unconditional, and there is nothing we can do to change His love for us. It has already been chiseled on His body at the cross. He has the markings of love that cannot be removed.

Truth is the knowledge of how the world works, along with how God works with us in the world.

Our faith is our decision to acknowledge and believe in God and what He has done. In faith, we set aside our old self who is a slave to the flesh, the world, Satan, and sin, and choose to walk in God's forgiveness, His love, and His truth, to discover our new self which has been given an abundant life that we did not know was possible in our old self. We begin to discover the new purpose He has for us and the self He intended us to be.

The Holy Spirit is the person of God who guides us in love and truth. It is the Spirit who leads us in the direction of love. The flesh, the world, and Satan have no power to control us as we live to love as Jesus loved, in the power of the Spirit.

We are changed as believers by walking in the Spirit in faith, living to love, and seeing the truth, especially about who we are in God and how loved we are. Although we are not changed overnight, it does not mean we do not change at all. When we choose to believe and follow Christ, we enter a new growth process of life, known as sanctification. It is where the Spirit grows us away from our slavery to sin and fear and grows us toward God's love as His children. God moves in each follower's life according to His purpose. In the midst of our journey, it is often hard to see what He is doing.

Moses was eighty years old when he encountered God at the burning bush[105]. This is a good reminder that it is never too late for any of us to step into God's plan. God called Moses to do a great task after years

---

105   Exodus 3:1-6

of struggle and wondering. He was entering retirement age, where he needed a physical crutch like his staff. God also knew that he needed a spiritual crutch, as well, for the task He was calling him to do. He gave Moses the burning bush experience and a staff with supernatural powers[106]. His world had drastically changed from a misguided shepherd to a prophet who would change the world.

Although we proclaim that we want to encounter God in this manner, I am not sure we can actually handle the impact on our lives. Our actions from that point on would need to reflect the supernatural gift given to us. Even Moses failed at handling God's supernatural gift when he struck the rock at Kadesh instead of speaking to it. The first-century Jews obviously could not handle the incarnation of the supernatural, as shown by the majority of Jewish leaders' responses to Jesus. I fear most humans today would do no better.

God supernaturally interacts with each one of us in a means that He determines is right for us on an individual basis. For some, it is a still small voice, and others see miracles. Blaise Pascal, the great French mathematician and scientist, wrote of his supernatural encounter with God, which was found sewn in his coat pocket after his death:

The year of grace 1654,

Monday, 23 November,

…From about half past ten at night until about half past midnight,

FIRE.

GOD of Abraham, GOD of Isaac, GOD of Jacob

not of the philosophers and of the learned.

Certitude. Certitude. Feeling. Joy. Peace.

---

106 Exodus 4:1-5

GOD of Jesus Christ.

My God and your God.

Your GOD will be my God.

Forgetfulness of the world and of everything, except GOD.

He is only found by the ways taught in the Gospel.

Grandeur of the human soul.

Righteous Father, the world has not known you, but I have known you.

Joy, joy, joy, tears of joy.

I have departed from him:

They have forsaken me, the fount of living water.

My God, will you leave me?

Let me not be separated from him forever.

This is eternal life, that they know you, the one true God, and the one that you sent, Jesus Christ.

Jesus Christ.

Jesus Christ.

I left him; I fled him, renounced, crucified.

Let me never be separated from him.

He is only kept securely by the ways taught in the Gospel:

Renunciation, total and sweet.

Complete submission to Jesus Christ and to my director.

Eternally in joy for a day's exercise on the earth.

May I not forget your words. Amen[107].

---

107 Fusselman, Midge, "What Blaise Pascal Saw In A November Night of Fire That Inaugurated A Year Of Grace," "The Federalist," 2020, https://thefeder alist.com/2017/11/23/blaise-pascal-saw-november-night-fire-inaugurated-year-grace/

This inspiring testimony of a supernatural encounter is an amazing example of a spiritual experience with the supernatural God, Jesus Christ, even for a highly educated, accomplished person. This type of experience is important to one's faith because our mind and reason can trick and fail us. It appears Pascal was aware of this weakness and therefore kept a reminder of God speaking with him at all times.

A concrete experiential marker in one's relationship can be the anchor that holds one in the storm. It is like the feeling of passionate love one initially has for their mate. This love grows into a companion love and then matures into committed love as you both grow, mature, and experience difficulties and successes in your relationship. This matured love does not disregard the present reality, nor does it forget the initial events that began the marriage. A healthy relationship with God is one that remembers and holds on to the past but is not stuck there; it is living and vibrant on a daily basis.

Our beliefs are not sustained by a fleeting moment but the reality of the whole perspective that we bring to the table as we believe. A supernatural experience bolstering our belief can be as important as reason, but it should not stop there. If one is capable, he or she should seek to grow a belief that takes into account the supernatural but looks to reason as well.

The fact is that most believers have a supernatural experience at salvation that they often fail to recognize. It is when Jesus begins to change their life through the indwelling of the Spirit. This is one of the great miracles God does in a believer's life, considering how hard it is to get anyone to change their mind or behavior, let alone both. God does this miracle all the time in people who believe in and follow Jesus, yet we seem to overlook its magnitude and importance. Despite how impressive changing one's life is, the spectacular supernatural seems to be a desire of many to authenticate their belief in God.

I often wondered, as a young man, why Jesus does not sustain us with a plethora of supernatural experiences to bolster our faith? That would be nice, right? It was fortunate that I knew the verse, "You shall not tempt the Lord your God" (Matthew 4:7, NKJV), or I might have done a stupid act to try to force Him to manifest His presence.

Even if God does save us from an accident, do we give Him credit? I rolled my Jeep down an embankment, three complete rollovers at 65 mph, with no seat belt, and survived it with barely a scratch. Did God save me from severe injury or even death in that accident? The answer is "yes," but can I prove it? There are several times I can look back and say God most likely did spare my life, guide me, and open and close doors.

Some do get a miracle to spur on their belief, which is great, but a supernatural experience can also short circuit the process of going through the formation of belief based on a daily walk with God. This is done in the hard grind of study, prayer, and faith lived out in everyday circumstances. Constant supernatural intervention could very well become a crutch that hinders one from growing a deeper faith.

Personally, I feel the supernatural presence of Jesus in my life daily. He is constantly guiding me to love in the smallest of circumstances. Sometimes, while singing praise songs, God has brought me into awareness of His special presence. Meditation, at times, gives me alertness of His Spirit in me. For a period of several months in my late twenties, when I would meditate, I would enter into a special awareness of His presence and long to stay there. As these experiences were happening, I felt so full that I thought I could do amazing feats for God and was willing to go to the toughest and loneliest places for Him, if only I always had His special presence with me.

Another instance when I remember a specific experience of God's presence was in 1984. I was a teenager at a Bill Gothard seminar at McNichols Sports Arena in Denver, Colorado. We were singing hymns a cappella style. The place was packed with more than ten thousand people, and as we sang, the arena began to rumble and shake from our voices. The voices were resonating, causing the whole building to vibrate and hum. It was an amazing experience that felt supernatural. I later went to other concerts in that arena, including the U2 concert, "Rattle and Hum," but there was never again a rattle and hum like the one I felt while singing hymns as a junior in high school.

Earlier in my junior year, my father invited me to attend a Mike Warneke Christian comedy show. Interestingly, while Warneke had some disheartening personal problems, God still used him to preach a powerful message about the love of Jesus. I felt the supernatural love of Jesus fill my heart that night, which changed my life by making me aware of the destructive path I was on. This experience was not limited to me. My friend's older sister, who was not a Christian, accepted an invitation to come with me, and she, too, felt that same supernatural love overwhelm her. For the past couple of months, we had both been living enslaved to our chosen vices, mostly involving sex and drugs. We left that arena crying and praising God for the love He showed us. God had reached out and touched us through this broken man, and it changed my life. He grabbed me at that moment and began to lead me to a new life.

As we look back at the past, sometimes we can clearly see the supernatural in the circumstances God orchestrates. My close friend from high school followed Jesus but was still in and out of trouble his whole adult life. Even though he went forward at a Billy Graham crusade while we were still in high school, his lifestyle did not change. His faith did give him a place to turn to for help, and Jesus was there for him as he continued to struggle with his destructive behavior. Craig lived a troubled and chaotic life and died at the age of thirty-five with his new pastor John by his side. It was strange to me that he had died at that age because I had a strong premonition that I would die at thirty-five and told several people about it. I even had slight anxiety as I turned that fateful age. I now understand that mysterious thought was about my close friend from high school, or perhaps, it would have been me too if I had not allowed the love of Jesus to change my life. It is fairly certain, if not for the grace of God in my life, I would have been lying there with him in the grave.

It is not only my or Craig's journey, but all of our journeys have twists and turns that seem to interact with the supernatural in unique ways. We do not know at the time where our lives are going, and sometimes it takes all our strength to hang on and not fall off. Sadly, some do fall short of a full life, but I am sure God does not want that for anyone.

Although we receive the riches of God's love at salvation,[108] a typical Christian does not experience them. One only surrenders selected parts of their lives that they choose and then wonders why God does not bless their whole life. It seems that God will not give us what we need until we release what we are clutching onto as our worldly means of salvation. Our many distractions block God's gifts[109]. It is only when we let go of our methods outside of God that we use to fill our needs and wants and trust Christ to provide that He gives us what we need in return.

Jesus does not, or at least has not, set up salvation of physical blessings—the one we want; instead, He gives us His salvation of bringing love and truth into our hearts,[110] which is the fulfillment we all

---

108 Romans 12:2
109 James 4:2-3
110 James 2:5, 2:8; Romans 5:8

truly need. We are not called to a kingdom of good works, power, riches, safety, or comfort, but a family of love[111]. At salvation, we become a receiver of every good gift and blessing from God[112] and a member of His family in which nothing can separate us from His love[113]. We are His children merely because we choose to believe in Jesus, accept Him, and love Him in response to His choosing us, accepting us, and loving us. When we embrace God's kingdom of love and truth and disregard the world's vision of success, our whole world is changed.

As we grow in our new relationship with God, we seek to know Him, and He seeks to know us.[114] We can rest in His kindness and love for us because this love never changes, even though He knows our every thought and deed. We share our needs with Him, understanding that He has our best interest in mind[115]. We rejoice in the fact that He has removed our moral debts, and we strive not to hold obligations or harbor grudges towards others.[116] We seek to love and not judge or do evil to others, and we pray that God would protect us from others that would harm us[117]. Lastly, we have peace and contentment knowing that God is in control of all that happens, and He is offering us a new life in a new kingdom.[118]

In this new life, Jesus offers hope of this new relationship with God:

---

111 Matthew 6:24-34; Romans 12:1-2; 1 Corinthians 13; Philippians 2:1-8; John 18:36
112 Ephesians 1:3
113 Romans 8:14-17, 38-39; Galatians 4:6-7
114 John 14:15-21
115 John 14:15-21
116 Matthew 6:12; Romans 13:8
117 Matthew 6:13; Romans 12:21
118 Romans 8:26-39

Therefore, if anyone is in Christ, the new creation has come: The old has gone, the new is here! All this is from God, who reconciled us to himself through Christ and gave us the ministry of reconciliation: that God was reconciling the world to himself in Christ, not counting people's sins against them. And he has committed to us the message of reconciliation.

2 Corinthians 5:17–19 (NIV)

Jesus offers hope for the resolution of our past sins and a new life free from condemnation from sin[119]. Our separation from God has been done away with, and it is replaced by a ministry of forgiveness, love, and restored relationships.

In this new life, our motive for life changes. We live for a new king who commands us to give and to sacrifice and not to live a life of taking whatever we can to meet our needs. "The thief comes only to steal and kill and destroy; I came that they may have life, and have it abundantly" (John 10:10, NASB). We can live life abundantly by the Spirit, in the love and truth He brings, or we can live life as the thief: stealing, killing, and destroying. It can be a great and abundant life when it is lived by His Spirit.[120]

Seeking His kingdom, we are given the hope and the reality of the presence of Christ, now and in the future. Even though we have a purpose and destiny in this life, it is a temporary season in our eternal life with Christ.

---

119   1 John 1:9, 3:20; 2 Corinthians 5:17-19
120   John 1:4, 10:10, 12:25; Romans 8:2

In My Father's house are many mansions; if it were not so, I would have told you. I go to prepare a place for you. And if I go and prepare a place for you, I will come again and receive you to Myself; that where I am, there you may be also.

John 14:2–3 (NKJV)

Christ's Spirit is dwelling with us in this life, but this life is not all there is.[121] Physical death for Christians is changing places from living with the Lord on earth to living with the Lord in heaven[122]. Jesus is always with us, and He has prepared specific places and specific ways for us to be with Him in this life and the next[122]. Wherever Jesus is, we are with Him, and He is with us wherever we are. He desires to live and reign with us, and He hopes we desire to say yes to entering His court.

---

121 John 5:24
122 John 5:24 (NIV)
123 John 14:1-6

CHAPTER 12

THE HOLY SPIRIT'S ROLE IN OUR SALVATION

And if the Spirit of him who raised Jesus from the dead is living in you, he who raised Christ from the dead will also give life to your mortal bodies because of his Spirit who lives in you. ...For those who are led by the Spirit of God are the children of God. The Spirit you received does not make you slaves, so that you live in fear again; rather, the Spirit you received brought about your adoption to sonship. And by him we cry, "Abba, Father." The Spirit himself testifies with our spirit that we are God's children.

Romans 8:11, 14–16 (NIV)

We do not walk alone in our new relationship with Jesus. When John the Baptist announced Jesus, he proclaimed that Jesus would baptize us with the Spirit[124]. Jesus later told His disciples that He would send them a comforter, referring to the Spirit coming to live in us.[125] Once saved, our bodies become the temple of the Holy Spirit[126]. The Spirit is the person of the Godhead who intermingles with our spirit and lives in us, teaching us truth, perfecting us in love, and comforting

---

124 Matthew 3:11
125 John 14:16-17, 15:26
126 1 Corinthians 6:19

us.[127] God is in us, and we are in Him[128].

Consider this list of some of the profound claims about the Spirit that Jesus, the disciple John, and the Apostle Paul made:

The Spirit is our help.

But when the Helper comes, whom I shall send to you from the Father, the Spirit of truth who proceeds from the Father, He will testify of Me.

The Spirit is our teacher.

But the anointing which you have received from Him abides in you, and you do not need that anyone teach you; but as the same anointing teaches you concerning all things, and is true, and is not a lie, and just as it has taught you, you will abide in Him.

The Spirit is a spirit of bold power, love, and sound mind.

Therefore I remind you to stir up the gift of God which is in you through the laying on of my hands. For God has not given us a spirit of fear, but of power and of love and of a sound mind.

We are taught by the Spirit to love one another.

But concerning brotherly love, you have no need that I should write to you, for you yourselves are taught by God to love one another.

1 Thessalonians 4:9

---

127 2 Timothy 1:7
128 1 John 4:16; John 14:20

Living by the Spirit brings amazing transformation.

But the fruit of the Spirit is love, joy, peace, longsuffering, kindness, goodness, faithfulness, gentleness, self-control. Against such there is no law.

Galatians 5:22–23

The Spirit gives us all unique gifts to build up the church body.

But the manifestation of the Spirit is given to each one for the profit of all: for to one is given the word of wisdom through the Spirit, to another the word of knowledge through the same Spirit, to another faith by the same Spirit, to another gifts of healings by the same Spirit, to another the working of miracles, to another prophecy, to another discerning of spirits, to another different kinds of tongues, to another the interpretation of tongues. But one and the same Spirit works all these things, distributing to each one individually as He wills.

The Spirit has an amazing role to play in our lives and in our choices as we grow with fellow believers.

Our lives and our world are not changed through our own effort. On the contrary, we are given His power through the Holy Spirit to act as a healing balm to restore our past, present, and future and to help us with our deepest needs[129]. We begin to be changed by a relationship with our creator God through the power of the Holy Spirit in us. Listening to the Spirit brings truth to our lives to help set us free from our old ways, which controlled and enslaved us[130]. The truth taught to us by

---

129 Romans 8:26
130 Galatians 5:16

the Spirit helps us to make sense of the crazy mixture of wrong and right intentions that are in our hearts.[131] This new relationship with the Spirit comforts us, enabling us to cope with our insatiable loneliness.[132] He calms our fear of the unknown.[133] He gives us reason to live[134]. He confirms that we are as important as we think we are but only because of God's love, not because of our morality or our works[135]. He tells us we are infinitely valuable when we see ourselves as worthless.[136] Our lives are changed by the indwelling of the Holy Spirit and all the gifts He brings when He comes to indwell in us.

These claimed effects of the Spirit in us are amazing and experientially seem almost incomprehensible. We can often struggle with seeing these blessings and transformations take place in us. Paul says to "continue to work out your salvation with awe and reverence" (Philippians 2:12, NET). Now, this might confuse us as to who is doing the work in us, but he goes on to say, "for the one bringing forth in you both the desire and the effort – for the sake of his good pleasure – is God" (Philippians 2:13, NET). Paul is encouraging us to cooperate with the complicated transformation that the Spirit is doing inside of us.

My quest in understanding the Spirit started when I was a senior in high school, and I wanted to experience the supernatural presence of the Holy Spirit. I had grown up in a Baptist church that rarely seemed to mention Him. My mother defected to the charismatic movement because they showed her love and did not discriminate against her for being divorced. I sat through more than one sermon where a preacher

---

131 Romans 7:19
132 2 Corinthians 1:3-5
133 Philippians 4:6-7
134 Romans 12:1-2
135 John 3:16
136 John 8:10-11

professed that his car miraculously did not run out of gas even though the gauge read empty. Sick and broken people would come to the front of the church to be prayed for and profess to be healed. I witnessed people speaking in tongues and slain in the Spirit, although I did not experience either myself.

At times, I wondered if it was real. I found myself even more confused when the pastor's wife died of cancer. Still, I begged God for a supernatural filling of the Spirit. I wanted confirmation that God was real and that I could touch Him, and He would touch me in a unique way. I pleaded with Him for the gift of tongues, but I only received sounds that seemed a product of my own creation. All of it left me wondering more and more about how the Spirit interacts with us.

I was not completely discouraged. Two events happened in my life, at around eighteen years old, that seemed to demonstrate God's presence. The first was when God healed my warts after my mother prayed for them. For years I had unsightly warts on both of my hands. After having a doctor remove them, only to reappear several months later, I turned to my mom for prayer. Within a week, they were gone, never to return. I still have the scars to remind me where they resided. It was an amazing little blessing that God used in my life.

The second event was that of the "Happy Camper" van. I was accepted to be a counselor at Camp Bethel, and they sent out a need to the local churches for a van to transport kids one mile from the camp to the lake. For some reason, I took the task on to provide the van and went to the Lord in prayer. I prayed, "God if it is Your will, You will have my father agree to the use of his old van. Also, I have $20 for the project; may you bless the $20 and provide for the material for seats." My father said yes. I found free seat frames from a converted school bus and bought $10 worth of orange and black seat covering material from a yard sale, I broke out our old sewing machine to sew the covers, cut up an old foam mattress for cushions, purchased one sheet of plywood for backing and a bit of hardware, and for $20, I had fitted the van for twenty kids. The final touch was to paint "Happy Campers" on the side in gold. It was an amazing project that I saw God's hand at each step of the way, which tremendously bolstered my belief in God.

These were not my only experiences, and I think most believers have tales to share about the Spirit's work when we seek Him. As I got older, I continued to wonder about the Holy Spirit, seek Him, and even find Him supernaturally on occasion. I am convinced that He is with me, and I understand more and more why He does not continually make His presence known in an overwhelmingly supernatural way.

If given too many supernatural experiences by the Spirit, I would have unsubstantiated confidence and influence over others. Simon, an old sorcerer and a new Christian, wanted to buy the gift of "the laying on of hands" that Peter and John possessed.[137] He envied the power it would give him and most likely would have abused it. A supernatural encounter with the Spirit is like any gift that God gives us, including love. These gifts can be used for godly purposes, but they can be misused, too. Although a supernatural encounter with the Spirit is what we think we want, it can be difficult to know how to respond when we are experiencing it. Even if we respond appropriately initially, we can still fall into the trap of pride and allow our hearts to be corrupted by power and influence.

Even the best of people are vulnerable to misusing the supernatural power of God. Think of the prophet Elisha who cursed the youth who were mocking him, and two bears mauled forty-two of them.[138] Even though the prophet Elisha was a man of God, it appears he misused his

---

137 Acts 8:18-19
138 2 Kings 2:24

power. Moses made the mistake of striking the rock instead of speaking to it[139], using the power of God, not in obedience, but as a magic trick. Another sad example is the mistake of Peter, where he presided over the death of Ananias and Sapphira, which brought fear over all the church[140]. This action is an anathema to the love and grace Jesus brought. It appears to be more along the lines of Peter thinking he was restoring the kingdom of Israel to the earth through the church. The power of the Spirit may be what we think we want, but sometimes I am not so sure. It may be safer and more edifying to trust the Spirit to participate in our lives in the way He sees fit, according to what we truly need.

Even without the "supernatural" experience, walking by the Spirit is a whole new way of life. It is walking with a comforter, guide, and renewer of our souls who deeply cares about the predicaments and outcomes of our life. He is the person of God within us who helps us when we are weak and do not even know what to pray. He is interceding to God on our behalf, especially when we do not have even a glimpse of the big picture.

In the same way the Spirit also helps our weakness; for we do not know how to pray as we should, but the Spirit Himself intercedes for us with groanings too deep for words; and He who searches the hearts knows what the mind of the Spirit is, because He intercedes for the saints according to the will of God. And we know that God causes all things to work together for good to those who love God, to those who are called according to His purpose. For those whom He foreknew, He also predestined to become conformed to the image of His Son, so that He would

---

139   Numbers 20:1-13
140   Acts 4:32-5:11

be the firstborn among many brethren; and these whom He predestined, He also called; and these whom He called, He also justified; and these whom He justified, He also glorified.

Romans 8:26–30 (NASB)

Walking in the Spirit is walking with a destiny to display the image of God again as we were created to do in the beginning. He is calling us, He justifies our sins, and He gives us glory, as He did for the saints in the past. The Spirit in us is the key to us working out God's destiny for us.

The Spirit is our power to love as Christ loved when we step out in faith. The Spirit interacts with us through a new law written on our hearts. He has a universal goal of truth and love and a specific purpose that God tailors to each individual[141]. Together, we are all working to be perfected in His love but at our own paces, in our own ways, and at different stages.[142] We have a picture of what it looks like in the New Testament, but since it is a relationship between God and a unique individual, it can look different for each person.[143]

This mysterious transforming power of the all-powerful Holy Spirit transforms us on the inside, yet He seems to do His work in a non-overwhelming way. He gives us power to love and understand the world around us. He manifests loving character in our lives. He anoints us and teaches us truths, especially truths about His salvation and love. He comforts us, and He manifests His gifts in our lives to edify the body of Christ. The Christian life is not a self-help system; it is a supernatural journey with God, where the Spirit of God enters us and performs

---

141 John 14:17, 26
142 1 John 2:5, 4:12, 18
143 John 15:15

miracles on whatever scale He sees fit.

Part 2: The New Covenant of the Cross

CHAPTER 13

———

HOW MY PERSONAL TRAGEDY AS A CHILD SHAPES MY VIEW OF THE CROSS

And hope does not disappoint, because the love of God has been poured out in our hearts through the Holy Spirit who was given to us.

Romans 5:5 (NET)

I was the victim of violence for the first nineteen years of my life. I have vague memories as a young child of six, alone, crying, huddled in a corner while my father violently beat my mother. From that point on, I went from a happy kid to a somewhat depressed child. I entered a life of survival, and luckily, as I grew older, I envisioned that someday I would escape this prison.

My father used violence on my mother in an attempt to change her behavior or to punish her for her actions he did not approve of. Obviously, his motivation and mental reasoning are more complicated than can be explained here, but this is a fair summary of the situation. His violence, although horrendous, is not atypical of humans. We are all capable of doing awful actions and hurtful speech to appease ourselves or to change and force others to comply with our wishes to meet our needs and wants.

My father's heinous physical abuse and destructive words were completely unacceptable and extremely hurtful and damaging. Most of us show restraint and self-control in our public world, but then we may self-righteously turn our guns on those we disagree with privately, or even worse, hurt and destroy the ones we love.

Receiving Jesus and acknowledging His sacrifice on the cross should have freed my father from a life of violence, but sometimes, our brokenness in our brain and flesh cannot be fixed. In the case of my father, there were plenty of times he was beyond repair.

The following incident happened in 1982 when I was in the eighth grade. I wrote it down in 1986, my freshman year in college. Please be warned that this story contains domestic violence. Fill free to skip this story if you think it will be a problem for you.

Mom, Margaret, had finished hooking up the utilities to another trailer house. She had unusual talents for a woman in those days.

The trailer was parked in one of the worst trailer courts in Billings, Montana. A real dumpy place with gravel roads, no fences, and not far from the sugar beet factory. Because of the close proximity, one could smell the stink of boiling beets all winter, which smelled a bit like a sour kitchen sink. My mother had moved this trailer 120 miles from Cody, Wyoming—where we previously lived—and parked it a few spaces away from the trailer she was living in she called the Corinthian after its manufacture.

Mom bought the Corinthian for $500 after it had a fire in it. The entire trailer had a lingering smell of a toxic fire. One could see some charred paneling in places. Mom had managed to get it partially fixed, but failed to finish it, so we were left with rough wood floors and unpainted drywall. It was not only the fire that made the place a mess; the house was filled from floor to ceiling with boxes and other wall-to-wall clutter. I was excited to move out into this cleaner trailer.

The trailer was the newest and my favorite. We called it the "Red and White" trailer for obvious reasons. My mother also owned other trailer houses and houses; the "Yellow" trailer, the "Star" trailer, the "Green" house, and the "Klucas" house. These were the valued possessions that she had somehow accumulated over the years from working as a teacher, cook, waitress, laundry worker, landlord, and other odd jobs. Although she liked owning property, they were also a symbolic place of escape and shelter for her from the violence. We had moved to Billings over a year before. We moved about once a year when I was a child, fleeing to a better life but staying within a one-hundred-and-fifty-mile radius of Northern Wyoming and Southern Montana. It never seemed far enough to get away from the dysfunction.

In the past, my home had been too disgusting to bring a friend over. The homes were either halfway remodeled or piled full of boxes of clothes that my mother had found in the garbage at a secondhand store called "The Bargain Box." To this day, that name haunts me. I did not have many friends, but I would never dream of inviting one to my house if I did.

I was fourteen now, and for some strange reason, I was hoping that maybe my dream would be fulfilled with this trailer. What dream? The dream was that I would have a house, or home, a place that was clean and free from the clutter of boxes and junk because of my mother's hoarding. This would be a place where I could bring a friend over and not be ashamed.

I had been moved into the trailer for about a week. It was wonderful to be able to walk all over the house without walking through a maze of boxes and stepping over trash on the floor.

My father, Wayne, had come up for a visit from Greybull, Wyoming, a little town of 1500 people, 135 miles away. I detested the town of Greybull where he lived. I had many bad memories and because of the cruelty of the kids I grew up with. I never wanted to live there, so I chose to live in Billings in the mess. Mom and Dad were recently divorced at that time, and mom's boyfriend was around occasionally. Even with another man in the picture, Dad still came up trying to get back together with Mom. Eventually, they did remarry when I was in tenth grade, but they rarely lived together till Mom was unable to live away from him because of her health.

When he heard that Mom was moving up the Red and White trailer to Billings, he expected that she was going to rent it because it would cost money to have it there. I think he was paying the bills for the new trailer and wanted her to have an income from it. When he found out I wanted to live there, he informed me that my mother agreed she would rent it. She denied it to me later, but things were confusing with Mom; she would say what she needed to say to make people happy or to get out of trouble. My heart dropped, I wanted to cry, but I kept a stiff upper lip. I knew all of this was too good to be true when I moved in. Now it was back to the half remodeled, burnt, box-cluttered trailer. Mom tried to make it up to me by offering me the bigger back bedroom, which I knew I would have to settle for because it would make living in that mess a little easier.

The day was not over. That night my father was going to leave early since they were not married, but he kept hanging around and would not leave. Finally, he and my mother started arguing, probably about my mother's boyfriend, Tom, but I do not remember. She was still sleeping with Tom on occasion, and he might have been up there at the time, hiding at the neighbor's house. Either way, I am sure my mother was putting my dad's sexual advances off. First came the arguing and then the cursing. They began yelling about why she was going to the neighbors. Dad guessed that Tom was there and accused Mom of having sex with him even though Mom denied it. This was all done with violent yelling and foul language.

Part of it was that Mom liked to sit down and visit. Dad was also mad that she was not helping and spending time with him after he drove two hours to be with her. The mistrust was deep as well as a controlling spirit, jealousy, and hurt. That yelling match settled down, and Dad and I were able to finish our work.

When it was time for him to go home, the battle started up again. There were more accusations of adultery, horrible names slung, and profanity-laced accusations aired. Mom denied and twisted her answers to attempt to calm down the situation, but there was no end to his temper.

By now, he was grabbing her hair and jerking her around as he yelled about how he would extract his retribution for her adultery.

"Stop, Wayne. You're hurting me! Please stop!" she said, crying loudly!

I was lying in my bed, gritting my teeth. That was my mother he was hurting. My father had done this countless times. I was not a little kid anymore who hid, lonely, in some corner all alone and powerless to do anything about this, like all of the times before. I had been thinking earlier that day, "I will not let them physically fight again." I knew that if I let this go on anymore, I would be torn apart inside. I thought about the club that I had made and had it hidden in the bottom of my closet. Finally, when the fighting started, scared and cowardly, I jumped out of bed, grabbed my club, ran down the hall, and yelled, "Let go of her, or I'll kill you!"

My father, astonished, let go of my mother, and they both stopped and stared at me. At age sixty-four, he was much stronger than me, but with the club, I was more of a threat to him.

"I could have you put in jail for this," he threatened.

"Go ahead, but you're not going to touch her!" Fear started to grip me, "Get out of here, just get out of here!" I yelled.

He stood his ground with a bewildering stare. I was waiting for him to jump me.

Then my mother stepped in calmly, "Wayne, you better leave."

He left the trailer, went out, and got in his van.

"Ernie, put down the club," she said to me as tears silently rolled down my cheeks.

"No, Mother, he is not going to hurt you anymore. I won't let him."

"Okay, calm down. I'm going to talk to him."

"Why?" I felt like she was undermining what I had accomplished. (Maybe it did help because they only physically fought once more after this, about a year later.)

"What did he say?" I asked when she returned half an hour later.

"He didn't know what had gotten into you."

"Is he going home?" I asked.

"Yes," she uttered.

I share this poignant story from my life to make a point about how all of our walks with God have strange twists and bumps. Both my mom and dad were Christians that read their Bible regularly and attended church. With all the fighting, adultery, and poverty, I think I can say firsthand that Jesus does not take away all suffering. Anyone who thinks that He does may be confused.

Our past shapes and molds us in interesting and unique ways. On one occasion, my father beat my mother so severely he put her in the hospital. That was the only time he was ever put in jail for his actions. The rest of the time, the police, neighbors, our friends, and even our pastor rarely intervened. I am sure my father confessed his sins, but he lived by the law. The problem with living by the law is that it leads to violence because if you have a law, you must have consequences for sinning and breaking that law. Although his consequences were horrifically unbalanced, are not all consequences condemning and painful?

I see living out the law as a big part of the destruction in this world. This cannot be what Jesus wanted. It cannot be that He died on the cross so we could live by the law better. Once a standard of what is right is determined, now others must be coerced into following this standard. Guilt, confession, rebuke, repentance, judging, withholding love, violence, imprisonment, and death are all ways in which people are negatively persuaded into following the standard if positive ways do not work. In the case of my father, he could not stop enforcing what he believed was right and could not stop trying to force and change my mother to that standard.

We all can easily fall into the coercion trap of the law. This is why it is important to understand how Jesus took away the law. He went to the cross for all of our sin and destruction. He changed the entire mechanism of how we become sanctified. People are changed through emulating His forgiveness and sacrificial love with God's Spirit of love poured out into their hearts. They no longer live by the law of sin and death, which depends on judgment and consequences. This new love in our hearts is the description of how the Spirit brings us new life in Christ Jesus. Jesus' work on the cross turned an upside-down world of judgment and condemnation, found through living by the law, into a *love-side-up* world of sacrificial and unconditional love found through living by the way of the cross.

I heard it said that "Satan takes what is beautiful and ruins it, God takes what is ruined and makes it beautiful[144]." God can make everyone beautiful if their standard of beauty is love flowing from a person and not some standard of moral behavior, power, physical looks, and influence.

Practicing the love of Jesus instills in us the ability to be truly good to one another, even if they do not deserve it. This unconditional love does not come through obeying moral laws. I like to say; religion can make able people reasonable sinners, but only Jesus can make every one of us good. I say "able people" because religion only works for those who have the ability to keep its standards. We must understand that to be good is to be a loving person made good by what Christ did on the cross. When my Christian, Bible reading, church-attending father beat my mother, he might have thought of himself as a reasonable sinner, but he was not good. Neither his confession in Christ, his going to church, his reading the Bible, his acts of service, nor his following certain moral standards made him good. He needed the love of Jesus to flow in him and through him. I will take a loving sinner over a mean moral person any day. Jesus in us leads us to be loving moral people, but love comes first. My father did not need to be a more legally righteous person by following a law; he needed to be a more lovingly righteous person, worthy of being called righteous by his love.

---

144 Unknown, quoted on KLOVE by announcer, June 2020.

I must say that life has been relatively kind to me after my childhood. I have enjoyed the wonders of getting an education, marriage, building a family, owning property, and having various fulfilling jobs. It seems Jesus has tremendously blessed me. All of my needs are met, and I praise Him for that. This is not to say that it has all come without struggle, but in the struggle, God has held me up in His love.

Money, power, the right people, or material possessions will not fully bring what we desire. All these things can leave us empty and sometimes turn us into not-so-loving people. Peace and contentment in our lives are ultimately achieved by knowing and trusting the love of Jesus, found at the cross, not in the things that the world promotes to bring the good life. Most paths we choose purport to give us a sense of purpose and meaning, some lasting and some not. To have true and lasting meaning in life, we need a relationship with Jesus to guide us as we travel this road of life how it was meant to be traveled. We walk by the Spirit, God's heavenly guide of truth and love in our lives, and with a blessed earthly purpose that we choose to do within the boundaries of that love.

When we choose to walk with God, He has an individual destiny for each one of us. We all are given our own unique call and story. I have shared a little bit of the darker side of mine, but it is not necessarily worse than anyone else's. God has done a tremendous number of positive things in my life, and we all have tragedy and triumph in our stories. God is going to take our stories and make them beautiful works of art. I do not want to be pitied, and I do not want to be admired for my story. I want to be seen as someone whose life story was transformed into something beautiful because I participated in the work of Jesus Christ in me. I began to seek His kingdom over my own. God has offered to make something special out of each one of our stories. He has called us to join His family and walk with Him, and He will help us succeed in ways we hardly thought possible.

CHAPTER 14

THROUGH THE CROSS, ONE IS DECLARED RIGHTEOUS

He made Him who knew no sin to be sin on our behalf, so that we might become the righteousness of God in Him.

2 Corinthians 5:21 (NASB)

The cross was the defining moment in Jesus' ministry. The act of love that Jesus committed on the cross is what makes it possible to reconcile our relationship with God. Much of the Bible is a love story of God wanting a relationship with us. He loved us so much that He sent Jesus to facilitate the possibility of restoring a right relationship with Him. Upon faith in Christ, our sins are taken away, and our nature is changed from sinner to sinless, which enables us to enter into an intimate relationship with God. This interaction with God is what was intended for humans from the beginning of creation. Our worthiness to enter into this relationship with God is called the righteousness of God. We are made worthy of being in the presence of the King.

Most of my life, I have thought that being righteous was a state of doing what is right in a moral sense. The G. W. Bromiley Bible dictionary explains righteousness as a state of a relationship, not an accomplishment of ethical behavior:

In the OT, righteousness involves the fulfillment of the demands of a relationship …the OT usually has the covenant with Yahweh in view (e.g., Isa. 51:7; Ezk. 18:19, 21) …When a person fulfills the obligations of a relationship, that person is said to be righteous[145].

[At the time of Christ, before the cross, righteousness had changed to a degree:]

The qualities associated with righteousness include mercy, generosity, honesty, moderation, and active concern for the poor and oppressed; qualities of unrighteousness include, greed, violence, and oppression …Righteous persons generally are those whose merits outweigh their transgressions.[146]

[They had the concept of the righteous being "rewarded and the wicked punished.[147]" What Christ demonstrated on the cross changed the definition of righteousness:]

In the NT, one finds again the primacy of the relational aspect of righteousness. The righteous are those who participate in and preserve a covenant relationship with God or other persons. God's righteousness is shown in that He has saved humanity in Christ[148].

---

145 Bromiley, Geoffrey W., The International Standard Bible Encyclopedia, Vol. 4, Q-Z, Pg,193, Eerdmans, 1988.
146 Bromiley Bible Encyclopedia, Pg,193.
147 Bromiley Bible Encyclopedia, Pg,193.
148 Bromiley Bible Encyclopedia, Pg,193.

[Paul further develops the meaning of righteousness. From Paul's writings, Bromley concludes that:]

Only the righteousness of God revealed in the cross and granted to the believer through faith in Christ can defeat death and reconcile a person to God. ...Thus, the righteousness of God cannot be a mere property, ethical attribute, or quality. The righteousness of God in the cross is the saving link between God and sinful humanity; no ethical attribute can ever endure the stress of being such a connection[149].

The righteousness of God is not achieved by a personal effort to sanctify ourselves, perfecting our moral goodness as prescribed by law. Our righteousness is solely found in the righteous act of Jesus on the cross that is given to us as a result of our faith in Him. By faith, we receive forgiveness and the removal of sin and are able to renew our relationship with God that He intended from the beginning. We are declared righteous at the moment we put our faith in Jesus.

The act of Jesus taking the penalty for our sins on the cross, which instantly and forever makes us clean through His death, is what theologians describe as justification. Imputed righteousness is more than justification. God did not merely take away the penalty of sin but sin as well. It does not make sense to say we are made righteous because we will no longer receive punishment for our actions; our sins must be taken away for us to be righteous. As former sinners separated from God, we are now justified to enter into His presence because Jesus paid the price for our sin, and He took away our sins. We become the righteousness of

---

149   Bromiley Bible Encyclopedia, Pg,193.

God when we receive this gift by faith.[150]

It also stands to reason that if a righteous person is now worthy of being in God's presence, they are worthy to have God's Spirit dwell in them. In order for God to enter into us, there must be no sin in us because there is no sin in God.[151] Being in God's presence begins the moment you believe in and choose to follow Jesus, and His Spirit abides with your spirit.

Our *righteousness*, our worthiness to have God in us and not be condemned, comes solely from what Jesus did on the cross and not through the law. Paul states: "I do not set aside God's grace, because if righteousness could come through the law, then Christ died for nothing!" (Galatians 2:21, NET). The burden of having to follow the law to be in covenant with God ended when Jesus completed the Mosaic covenant through His sinless life and the shedding of His blood. We now are able to receive righteousness as a gift, not bound by our obedience to the Mosaic law. It is given to us solely by our faith in God and His provision of righteousness[152].

It is unclear if righteousness was ever intended to be achieved by following the Mosaic law. The Apostle Paul pointed out that Abraham's righteousness was not achieved by following the law; it was given to him through his faith in God. He also surmised that King David's idea of righteousness came from forgiveness and not works. Paul wrote:

For if Abraham was declared righteous by the works of the law, he has something to boast about – but not before God. For what does the scripture say? "Abraham believed God, and it was

---

150 2 Corinthians 5:21
151 1 John 3:5
152 2 Corinthians 3:7-11

credited to him as righteousness." Now to the one who works, his pay is not credited due to grace but due to obligation. But to the one who does not work, but believes in the one who declares the ungodly righteous, his faith is credited as righteousness. So even David himself speaks regarding the blessedness of the man to whom God credits righteousness apart from works: "Blessed are those whose lawless deeds are forgiven, and whose sins are covered; blessed is the one against whom the Lord will never count sin."

Romans 4:2–8 (NET)

There are unfortunate events in Abraham's and David's lives that were not virtuous. We could include other prominent Old Testament figures in the list of the unrighteous because of their deeds, like Isaac, Jacob, and all Jacob's sons. This "cloud of witnesses" all pleased God by their faith in Him and not by their ability to follow the law with their works.[153] They were destined to receive the righteousness of God someday, a perfect relationship with Him, and they did, "together with us."[154]

As I look back at myself as a young Christian seeking to be good, I remember thinking that I could only know if I was good and worthy to be in God's presence if I had rules to live by. I was seeking a righteousness of my own doing. This is a process of becoming a good person who does not break any laws and does good instead of evil. It may be hard to understand, but that way of thinking is the product of religious works; it is part of our fleshly effort to make ourselves righteous. When living under the law to be righteous, one is either a law abider or a lawbreaker, but either way, we are slaves to the law to become morally righteous or

---

153 Hebrews 12:1 (NET)
154 Hebrews 11:40 (NET)

to rebel against the moral law.

God wants us to correctly understand that what God sees as our source of righteousness is not living according to the law but having faith in what Christ accomplished on the cross. He displayed righteousness through forgiveness and love, which was demonstrated through His humility and self-sacrifice. Any effort away from righteousness by faith and towards works according to a law only produces personal righteousness of our own.[155] This type of achieved righteousness system is usually more measured by what we have done for Him and not by what He did for us on the cross. The true source of God's righteousness is faith in God and reliance on the gift given at the cross.

---

155 Romans 10:3-4

CHAPTER 15

THE CROSS WAS THE END OF THE OLD COVENANT LAW

For Christ is the end of the law, with the result that there is righteousness for everyone who believes.

Romans 10:4 (NET)

Humans continually find themselves circling back to the same question: *What is the right way to fix humanity?* The simplest and quickest answer is to reconcile them to their creator, but it is too big of a question to begin to answer fully in this chapter. I will narrow it down: *Is following the Mosaic law the right way to fix the Christian?* And a follow-up question might be: *Should the Christian follow the law at all?* My experience tells me that the Messianic Jews and many other sects of Christianity would give a resounding, "Yes!" while recent antinomians of the likes of Andy Stanley, Andrew Farley, and Aaron Budjen are against the idea of using the law to bring sanctification.

The three writers mentioned have attempted to bring an end to using the Mosaic covenant as a tool for believers to achieve righteousness and sanctification. Andy Stanley, writer, pastor, and founder of enormously impacting North Point Ministries based out of Atlanta, states in his book, *Irresistible*: "Participants in the new covenant are not required to obey most of the commandments found in the first half of their

Bibles."[156] Andrew Farley, writer and pastor of Church Without Religion, wrote a book on the end of the law entitled *God Without Religion*. In it, he clearly explains and defends the end of the Mosaic covenant and that we cannot mix law with the grace found in the new covenant.[157] Aaron Budjen, former rabbi, turned Christian pastor and radio host of Living God Ministries radio program, vehemently opposes using the law to establish any righteousness. He believes that obeying the law is nullifying the death of Christ.[158] These three men, and many others, have used an avalanche of scripture to point out that we are not to use the Mosaic law to reach a level of desired righteousness.

I am going to come right out and say it; I fully agree with these three men that Christians should not functionally use all or even part of the Mosaic law as a guide to their personal sanctification. It is a very easy temptation considering how the first chapter of Joshua reads:

Carefully obey all the law my servant Moses charged you to

keep! Do not swerve from it to the right or to the left, so that you may be successful in all you do. This law scroll must not leave your lips! You must memorize it day and night so you can carefully obey all that is written in it. Then you will prosper and be successful.

Joshua 1:7–8 (NET)

---

156 Stanley, Andy, Irresistible: Reclaiming the New that Jesus Unleashed for the World, pg. 196, Zondervan, Grand Rapids, 2018.

157 Farley, Andrew, God Without Religion, book summary, Baker Books, Grand Rapids, 2011.

158 Budjen, Aaron, "Hebrews 6:1 Dead Works," Hebrews Message, Living God Ministries web site, https://www.livinggodministries.net/living_god_minis tries/radio_archive/audio_files/hebrews_20_ch6_1_dead_works.mp3

The promise of earthly blessings is a temptation that we all want. Joshua implies that if you obey the law, then blessings you will have. But blessings only came to those who could obey the law. Virtually everyone in this society would find themselves cursed and unable to obey the law. In fact, the physically defective could never fully obey the priestly laws. God told Moses to write this law concerning the priests:

Say to Aaron: 'For the generations to come none of your

descendants who has a defect may come near to offer the food of his God. …no man who is blind or lame, disfigured or deformed; no man with a crippled foot or hand, or who is a hunchback or a dwarf, or who has any eye defect, or who has festering or running sores. …No descendant of Aaron the priest who has any defect is to come near to present the food offerings to the Lord. …he must not go near the curtain or approach the altar, and so desecrate my sanctuary.'

Leviticus 21:17–21, 23 (NIV)

Only the pure, unblemished priests could approach the presence of God. The blemished descendant of Aaron could never achieve full righteousness.

While the law brought glory for those who were willing and able to follow it, it also brought condemnation for those who failed to follow or could not follow it. One would imagine that all failed at some point, and their glory faded, and they were condemned.

For if there was glory in the ministry that produced condemnation, how much more does the ministry that produces righteousness excel in glory! For indeed, what had been glorious now has no glory because of the tremendously greater glory of what replaced it.

2 Corinthians 3:9–10 (NET)

Through Christ's death, since Christ died for all, we are all able to enter into glory and stay in God's glory[159]. This permanent glory comes through Jesus and not the fading glory of following the law.

One might still want to cling to the law and Joshua's promise, but maybe not all of it, possibly just the ten commandments. I think a lot of believers would like to see the ten commandments promoted and upheld. I would agree in principle to using them for the health of a society, but the old covenant is no longer a source of contention between ourselves and God, not even the ones written on stone. Consider what Paul wrote: "For the letter kills, but the Spirit gives life. But if the ministry that produced death – carved in letters on stone tablets" (2 Corinthians 3:6–7, NET). Not even the ten commandments were spared by Paul from the removal of the law for the believer.

For many believers in the God of the Bible, a universal law like the ten commandments brings a sense of safety and comfort. We think if we hang it in a courthouse or codify it with ecclesiastical or government power, we have established a solution to our problems. This is not usually the case. At best, we have forced compliance to a solution but not fixed a problem. The problem usually lies much deeper than a law could ever fix. The law is not wrong in deterring evil with the threat of death, but it merely can only provide a temporary hiatus from a condition that will

---

159 2 Corinthians 5:14

not be fixed by behavior correction. For a time, people on a personal level and societies as a whole experience transformation from ethical ideas and moral directions. The effectiveness of a system of laws is usually short-lived because humans are in a state of decay. Just read the biblical books from Judges through Chronicles.

I was in a youth group meeting one night, and a leader spoke up and confessed he had broken all of the ten commandments while trying to make the point that Christians do not follow the law. The room was silent, and I was in a state of shock and intentionally holding back my reaction at the awkwardness of the situation. It appeared we were in a room full of believers who trusted the law to make people good, or at least not kill one another. This leader openly admitted that not even the ten commandments were working for him. Then in a small voice, a young woman, who truly desired not to overreact to his comment, said this: "I guess I am okay with you maybe breaking nine of the commandments, but the 'Thou shall not murder' one makes me a little uncomfortable." The leader explained that he had once given a young lady a ride to an abortion clinic. His response seemed to ease the tension concerning violence, but I am not sure it brought grace to his confession. There were quite a few more broken commandments that I was uncomfortable with, like adultery, of which this man lost his marriage over a few years later. It clearly seems to be detrimental to merely shed the law and replace it with people doing what is right in their own eyes. When the youth leader suggested the irrelevance of the law in the way he did, it brought fear because he did not explain the new life of love found in Christ Jesus.

Not only is the law insufficient to make us righteous, but it is also powerless to bring people into a loving relationship with God, ourselves, and our neighbors. On the other hand, it is not powerless in its ability to convict. The law's ability to condemn is exponentially more powerful than our ability to overcome sin. It will convict us until we are lowered to the status of a worm. In the face of its conviction, if we can stand at all, we will stand condemned. How can one use this instrument of condemnation to help themselves to be sanctified and live the new life that Jesus gives? The point of Paul in Romans chapters six, seven, and eight is that the law will not bring sanctification, only condemnation.

In Romans, Paul concludes that the law is completed when he wrote that "the law of the life-giving Spirit in Christ Jesus has set you free from the law of sin and death" (Romans 8:2, NET). The law brought exactly that, "sin and death." The Mosaic law seemed to only make people more aware of their sin and showed them the impossibility of achieving perfection by their effort.[160] The law demonstrates the reality that a person cannot be righteous and loving through their own striving, even if they have a perfect law. When one does get close to following the law, do they perform their deeds in love? It is foolish to think that somehow, we are going to discover a better law to facilitate our works righteousness now that we have grace. Instead, we should be living free from the law of sin and death, by the Spirit, in the grace He provided. God's goal for humans, even when we were under the law, has always been that we love Him, our neighbors, and ourselves. The law of Moses, given to help achieve that goal, could not bring it to completion and often brings the opposite[161].

When Paul refers to the law as the "law of sin and death," he is clearly describing its outcome[162]. With the law, death had been instituted by God as a deterrent to restrain humans from rebellion and sin. Death for behavior did not start with the law. Death began its reign with

---

160 Romans 7
161 Romans 8:3
162 Romans 8:2 (NET)

Adam and Eve in the garden when they rebelled. Humanity became so irredeemable at the time of Noah; God's only choice was to wipe them out in a great sweeping death. In the law, there is plenty of death to go around for animals and people; it is truly the "ministry that produced death."[163] It seems to me that secular society appears to want to shed its attachment to death, which is good but problematic in terms of controlling people's behavior. It cannot merely shed the deterrence of death to restrain people's behavior, something has to replace it, or people will again become as it was in the days of Noah. Paul, too, promoted the shedding of condemnation, but only because he knew the love of the cross, the blessings of the new life in Christ, and the power of the Spirit in us.

Even the Israelites obeying the law out of obligation and not out of love would not make them worthy of being in His presence. This is shown in Paul's explanation of why the Israelites' understanding of establishing their own righteousness was misled:

> For I can testify that they are zealous for God, but their zeal is not in line with the truth. For ignoring the righteousness that comes from God, and seeking instead to establish their own righteousness, they did not submit to God's righteousness. For Christ is the end of the law, with the result that there is righteousness for everyone who believes. For Moses writes about the righteousness that is by the law: "The one who does these things will live by them." But the righteousness that is by faith says: "Do not say in your heart, 'Who will ascend into heaven?'" (that is, to bring Christ down) or "Who will descend into the abyss?" (that is, to bring Christ up from the dead). But what does

---

163 2 Corinthians 3:7 (NET)

it say? "The word is near you, in your mouth and in your heart" (that is, the word of faith that we preach).

Romans 10:2–8 (NET)

The first-century Jew's idea of self-made righteousness from following the Mosaic law was "not in line with the truth.[9]" They sought to make themselves worthy of being in the presence of God by following the law. It appears God always intended to accept people into His presence by their faith alone, and it was a man-inspired movement to be righteous by obligation to the law. "Christ is the end of [using] the law with the result that there is righteousness to everyone who believes" (Romans 10:4, NASB). He is the end of using the law to have a relationship with God, and from this flows that the cross was the end of using the law for our sanctification. Following the law does not bring Christ closer to us, and our sin against the law does not make Christ more significant. Our faith brings Christ into our mouths and hearts.

In our new life with Jesus, without the law, sins according to the law should no longer be the issue because we are not in the old covenant with God, given by Moses. In fact, Gentiles were never actually under that covenant. In Acts 15, we have a record of a historic meeting of the leaders of the church in Jerusalem. They were deciding on whether Gentiles were obligated to follow the law as believers in Jesus. The answer was no, and they were recommended to follow some general moral obligations unrelated to the law of Moses. The case should have been closed after this council, but it was not. In Galatians, Paul ran into men who wanted Gentile converts to be circumcised. Paul demanded a stop to it and declared that following the law to become right would alienate them from Christ. Instead of following the law, he said, "The only thing that matters is faith working through love" (Galatians 5:6,

---

164 Romans 10:2 (NET)

NET).

What then should the believer do with the Mosaic law since it is not used as a source of guilt and condemnation in the process of sanctification? The law is very important in knowing wisdom and good and evil. In it, we can find tremendous knowledge about human behavior and even wisdom on how to love God, our neighbor, and ourselves in a community structure. Unfortunately, it has been mostly used[165] by the believer to find an exceedingly long list of dos and don'ts. Even though no one can come close to following the list, it is a fairly effective system by which we can clobber our neighbors and ourselves.[166] That was not God's intention. He was hoping that humans would love His law and see its true purpose and goal. Instead, it seemed to bring pride and control for the ones who kept it and complete wretchedness for the ones who turned from it.

It is good news that we no longer need to live under the law to be morally righteous. If the law could not make the Israelites behave right, it certainly is not going to succeed with the Gentiles. Fortunately, our sanctification will not be realized because of works according to the law because Christ already gave us righteousness. Even though we know we are declared righteous; often, we do not feel or act that way in the flesh. In fact, we feel and know we need some improvement.

So how is a Christian fixed, if not by the law? The answer comes in two parts. First, by knowing we are now a people who have an unchanging, loving relationship with God. The next step of sanctification comes in light of this loving relationship. It comes through allowing the Spirit to grow us to resemble what God has done in us.

Paul wrote that our sanctification in the flesh is done by the Spirit

165
166 Matthew 23:13-39

of Christ who lives in us through our faith in Jesus and His work on the cross. We have been declared righteous by our faith, and we are sanctified by the Spirit in us, apart from the law, or Christ died in vain.

> I am crucified with Christ: nevertheless I live; yet not I, but Christ liveth in me: and the life which I now live in the flesh I live by the faith of the Son of God, who loved me, and gave himself for me. I do not frustrate the grace of God: for if righteousness [comes] by the law, then Christ is dead in vain.
>
> Galatians 2:20–21 (KJV)

If one could be sanctified by following the law, it would dilute the need and purpose of the death of Jesus[167]. But we know that His death was not in vain. Ultimately, before Christ, the only way for humans to complete the covenant of the law was through their own earthly death and a future of deserved punishment. On the cross, Christ's death fulfilled the requirement of death, ending the reign of death and beginning the reign of life here in this life on earth and the afterlife. The old covenant found in the Mosaic law was a part of that reign of death, and that reign was completed and ended with Jesus dying on the cross. The crucifixion of Jesus was not just the end of the old covenant, but it also established the new covenant, which I will discuss in the next chapter.

(For more discussion, see Appendix C on "1 John 3, Law Versus Love" and Appendix D for a verse list on the removal of the law.)

---

167 Hebrews 10:26-31

CHAPTER 16

THE CROSS ESTABLISHES A NEW COVENANT

How much more will the blood of Christ, who through the eternal Spirit offered himself without blemish to God, purify our consciences from dead works to worship the living God. And so he is the mediator of a new covenant, so that those who are called may receive the eternal inheritance he has promised, since he died to set them free from the violations committed under the first covenant.

Hebrews 9:14–15 (NET)

When I speak of freedom from the old covenant, represented by the law, I am not speaking of freedom for unbelievers. They still live under the law and the deterrent of death. At salvation, we are purified from the works of death and brought into a relationship with the living God, a living relationship not based on death for failure but eternal life when we believe. We receive a new covenant of eternal life, adoption as His children, and indwelling of the Spirit. We are set free from the sins of the old covenant, which were enforced through violence and death.

The new covenant is somewhat a prescription in how a believer is sanctified. It removes the law from a person's life as the means of sanctification and replaces it with "faith working through love."[168] The process of sanctification is not a one-time event but is a daily, moment-by-moment adventure with the Spirit.

Sanctification via the new covenant is not the same as salvation. When one is saved, they are justified and declared righteous. When one thinks of being justified, one might think of someone making an excuse or a defense for their actions. Our behavior as sinners is unjustifiable according to the Mosaic law and often even our own rules. We are guilty of transgressions deserving of punishment, even death. Jesus ransomed us from the inevitable destruction we deserved and took the penalty upon Himself. God the Father accepted His loving sacrifice as a substitutionary payment to free us from the law of sin and its consequences. Now we can stand before God as forgiven and miraculously regarded as a different person because we are in Christ, not in danger of being cast out. To cast us out would be to cast Jesus out because He is in us and covers us. This state of justification and righteousness is solely because of what Jesus did for us, and we are now justified to be at God's table.

When I speak sanctification, I am not speaking of something that makes us right with God in terms of salvation. Sanctification is the process of a Christian transforming into a person who loves as Jesus loves, which happens after salvation. New covenant sanctification, which is sanctification in terms of love and not law, is not promoted by all Christians. There is a divide in what believers see as sanctification after our justification is established. Many think of sanctification as a moral behavioral improvement according to external standards. To believe that is to completely miss the work of Christ. He wants to transform us into the image of God by growing us to be a believer who loves as He

---

168 Galatians 5:6 (NET)

loved.[169] This is quite different from improvement according to the law. Sanctification is ultimately demonstrated when we begin to display on the outside the new creation that God made us on the inside. We are being taught by the Spirit to love with the sacrificial love of the cross, becoming loving in our hearts, words, and deeds. We are being changed into the loving person God has already made us to be in Christ.[170] Having an increasing love enabled by the Spirit view of sanctification versus the Spirit enabling us to follow the law view is a foundational difference in how sanctification is approached.

Another troublesome divider in how one looks at sanctification in the new covenant is what a believer sees as the purpose of grace in the process. Does grace free us from the law and take away our sins, or does grace give us strength to follow the law, and then grace offers forgiveness and restoration when we fail? If one believes we are sanctified by following the law and that grace is to help us accomplish that task, they run into a few hard questions to answer. The first one that comes to mind for me is: *If we are not saved by works according to the Mosaic law, how can we be sanctified by works according to that same law or any new law?* It seems entirely arbitrary to determine exactly which laws we are to abide by. After we are justified and declared righteous by faith, must we still do more to be more right with God? Struggling to be right according to the law is an impossible task that even grace cannot accomplish in a person.

Having a hope that we will increase in our goodness is demonstrated by us living out His example of love in faith. That is the essence of our sanctification. Jesus said as much when He proclaimed His new commandment as life couched in love: "Love one another; as I have loved you" (John 13:34, NKJV). Sanctification is a transformation done

---

169   2 Corinthians 3:18
170   Galatians 2:20

by His Spirit in us with his love being poured out into our hearts.[171] Practical sanctification is not the believer living more and more by the law of Moses or any other law, but by the believer loving more and more like Jesus. Sanctification can be thought of like diving into a loving relationship with God, and then out of that, flows love for our neighbors and ourselves.

Paul juxtaposes the positions of sanctification so clearly to the Galatians:

> You who are trying to be declared righteous by the law have been alienated from Christ; you have fallen away from grace! For through the Spirit, by faith, we wait expectantly for the hope of righteousness. For in Christ Jesus neither circumcision nor uncircumcision carries any weight – the only thing that matters is faith working through love.
>
> Galatians 5:4–6 (NET)

Sometimes it is hard to see that the only thing that matters is our faith working through love when it seems rulers, leaders, and pastors promote obedience to the law as the measuring point of sanctification. Sanctification for the believer is almost the opposite. Jesus created a way to have a relationship with us that did not involve enslavement to rules and constant condemnation. He took on our deserved violence for us, so we no longer have to live under the threat of the violence of the law.

Living by the law is living by the flesh to attempt to overcome sin. We are trying to use our strength and ability to follow the law to overcome the needs and desires within us that predestine our sin. The new law of

---

171 Romans 5:1-5

the life-giving Spirit is much different.[172] God's Spirit in us overcomes the flesh. The Spirit fills us with His love, and that love moves us to love like Jesus. When we are filled with His love, we are able to achieve selfless love for God and our neighbor. This selfless, unconditional love fulfills the whole law. The law cannot make us more loving and thus more sanctified; that is not what the law does. The only resemblance of law for the believer under the new covenant is the commandment to love as Jesus loved. It would be more of a sin to go back to following the Mosaic law in order to be sanctified than any transgression of the law one commits.

Those who still live under the law for their sanctification do not understand the new covenant we are in and are blocked from seeing the freedom and truth we have in Jesus: "But until this very day whenever Moses is read, a veil lies over their minds" (2 Corinthians 3:15, NET). When one finally takes hold of an understanding of the end of the law, it is like a veil is removed from their eyes. They no longer have the fading glory that comes and goes with their ability to follow the law. "And we all, with unveiled faces reflecting the glory of the Lord, are being transformed into the same image from one degree of glory to another, which is from the Lord, who is the Spirit" (2 Corinthians 3:18, NET). This glory is so amazing that we can continually walk in God's presence, never separated from Him by any action or thought.

Jesus established a new covenant in which He takes sin away by taking away the law, reconciling our relationship with God, and giving us newfound freedom and power to make loving decisions. Freed from all condemnation and lavished with love, we live in an entirely different mindset. Our new life in Christ is based on walking with the Spirit, learning how to love God, our neighbors, and ourselves well, not on

---

172 Romans 8:2

161

learning rules to keep us from sinning. It is not a life of seeing how much we can get if we follow the right rules, but a life of how much we can give without regard for the old rules, except the rule of love.

We follow a Savior who gave His all for us in His love. Jesus is growing this love in us as we become more and more like Him, living a life worthy of His presence in us and worthy of the new life He has given us. His ultimate goal is to move us from living in a state of slavery to sin and separation from Him under the law, whether the core cause is foolish living or religious living, and to bring us into a state of relationship with Him; being freely perfected in His love, through the power and guidance of the Holy Spirit. This is truly the process of sanctification under the new covenant established by the cross.

CHAPTER 17

THE CROSS TAKES AWAY SIN

Jesus was revealed to take away sins.

1 John 3:5 (NET)

Whether one believes they are under the law, under grace, apart from the law, or some other variation, every Christian must come to grips with the reality of their own mistakes, as in their own evil behavior, and what to do about it. The answer to this core question of how to resolve one's failures profoundly affects their success in overcoming sin. The traditional Christian solutions to this problem are admission or confession, repentance, and then for some, penance. The issue is that this system of overcoming sin has not made a noticeable difference in the problem for so many. For some, they find themselves falling deeper and deeper into sin. Even the leaders promoting the system often have a few skeletons in their closets. Maybe we have been thinking about overcoming sin in the wrong way. As long as sin is the issue, sin will remain the central focus of the Christian life, and this makes it more difficult to overcome.

The problem we face is that none of us can fully avoid sinning by knowing all of society's rules, religion's morals, government's laws, and others' expectations. It is easy to commit minor sins in our day-today interactions. These sins often require apologies, while repentance or even penance may be demanded in some cases. Our transgression against another person may be so severe that we cannot recover from the repercussions, and our physical presence is no longer welcome. Breaking the government's laws requires the police and the courts to remedy the problem. Sin is a daily, moment-by-moment part of living, and we are not without a plethora of opportunities to fail at living according to the rules.

More than often, it seems that we receive the "just desserts" of our bad behavior in this life, with or without Jesus. On the other hand, there are those who seem to get a free pass on everything. If one does not receive their due justice and punishment, will it come in the next life? The Bible contends that God has eternal consequences, where He enforces justice in the afterlife for the unloving or evil behavior we perpetrate[173]. For the nonbeliever, there is promised suffering that justice would demand, and for the believer, there is promised removal of the evil that cannot be in the presence of God[174].

But before we try to understand what to do about sin, let's attempt to define it. The literal definition of the main word translated "sin" from Greek is "missing the mark,[175]" as in not achieving a standard or failing to follow the law. Think of speeding. Once people go over the speed limit, they are breaking the law. Even if it is only one mile over, a sin has been committed. For believers, sin can mean failing to live up to God's law found in the Old Testament, failure to follow the admonitions and prohibitions of the New Testament, or both. It can also encompass other rules they are obligated to.

173 Romans 9:27
174 2 Corinthians 5:10
175 BibleHub.com, "Strong's Concordance," https://www.Biblehub.com/greek/266. htm

Another common sentiment among Christians is that sin is any thought or action that can separate us from God. This could be the breaking of a biblical rule, but it could also consist of denying God, walking in darkness, making foolish decisions, or even failing to believe in and love Him. For many, they associate a connection to the church as a connection to God, so any act that transgresses an institutional list of rules denoting "bad" behavior and "good" behavior is considered sin.

Whether devoutly religious or not, sin can be the transgression of a personal ethic, like disobeying family rules or assaulting your marriage vows. One's list of bad behavior would usually include humanity's commonly held morals, like do not murder and do not hate. One may also think of sin as breaking government laws, breaching laws of political correctness, doing what is generally considered evil by society, or doing something as little as acting in a way that others do not like. Behaving unfairly, unjustly, unwelcomingly, or unlovingly toward one's neighbor would be considered sin for most. One can even sin against themselves in similar ways.

It is not unusual for people to have a list of sins to know the difference between right and wrong. Often, they are carried in one's memory, almost on a subconscious level, and not written down. Although there may be some agreement on the big taboos, agreeing on a specific list of sins remains an impossible task because of the multiple opinions concerning what defines an offense. With all the possibilities of transgression, sin can become a complicated, condemning problem for those who seek to be sanctified by not sinning.

Christians sometimes simplify the definition of sin, defining it as going against the will of God, which is found in scripture. That sounds simple enough, but the statement does not narrow down the specific sins for the believer.

How do most Christians know which specific actions are sins? I have already demonstrated that it cannot be following the Mosaic law. This is especially true since no one can keep all the Old Testament laws without a temple and live animal sacrifices. Still, there is a desire to skip most of it and simply start with a framework like the ten commandments to give us a list of sins. Or one might begin their list with the earliest form of laws given to Noah recorded in Genesis 9. One tenant of this law is the deterrent of life for a life. Another possible place to derive a list of sins is Acts chapter fifteen, where Paul inspired a decision concerning how the Gentiles are to conduct themselves as Christians. The church leaders concluded that they did not need to become Jews but that Gentile converts should "abstain from things offered to idols, from blood, from things strangled, and from sexual immorality" (Acts 15:29, NKJV). There are several possible starting points for Christians if they want to build and follow a new and reasonable law defining sin.

Selectively pulling from multiple biblical sources to compile a list of what sin is, does appear to be the process evoked by most believers. We take a smattering of Old Testament laws and add lists of sins and admonitions found in the New Testament to create a system of moral guidance. Between Christians, there is generally a consensus on what the appropriate core combination is, but the peripheral sins vary from church to church. The different stances on what is and is not sin can partially explain the differences in the denominations.

Often, in churches, the list goes unspoken, and we are simply expected to know it as a participant. Do we have to follow a distinct set of rules, forgive, love, say the Lord's prayer, and do other positive acts to prevent sin? We may even be motivated to switch churches because we are not comfortable with the current list of sins held by the one that we attend. Sometimes the new list of sins becomes more burdensome and overbearing than the original Mosaic law. The new moral obligations may come with new rules of enforcement. Confusion can result as one tries to differentiate between their right standing with the church and their right standing with God.

Living by a list of sins more than often does not seem to consistently work at sanctifying one from sinning. I have seen people, who most would refer to as mature Christians, say and do some awful things in secret that most would categorize as evil. When a mature Christian fails according to a law, it feeds into the religious practice of prompting more confession and repentance when the sins are exposed or prompting denial when sins are hidden. All of this guilt and repentance is entirely dependent on what list of rules one is following and may not even come close to pleasing God or the Holy Spirit in us.

With a list of sins, there is always the question of how close can I get to the sin without it actually counting as sinning? Often there is a desire to live in the gray areas. In my life, this was definitely bolstered by living according to a law. When I sought to sanctify myself via a list of rules and religious duties to achieve some level of purity, I needed to find a way to let my sin out. I found myself devising ways to skirt the rules, especially if it was a special circumstance, like a date with a dream girl or a night of revelry with the guys. Because I had behaved so well according to my list, I now deserved a little pleasure in the gray areas.

It seems that at all levels of devotion to God under a list of rules, there is room to vicariously live out one's struggle with sin in seemingly benign activities. We may participate in watching violent scenes and raunchy humor on TV or in movies. We may join with evil while playing video games, magical dice, and fantasy card games. Maybe one's weakness is dicey romance novels or coarse talk at work. One common struggle among most people is a form of coveting; possibly by watching endless home fix-it shows, leading us to desire a different house; cooking shows, giving us a longing for foods much better than what we already have; or fashion shows to improve our clothing. While these types of shows are innocent and fun, too much dwelling on what is better than our current situation can lead to discontentment and coveting. There are many seemingly benign activities that possibly let Christians, who are living by law, enjoy sin without sinning in the actual sense. This passive means of engaging in sin seems to be an attempt to vicariously experience the ways of the world while we are able to continue our self-achieved level of sanctification according to our lists of rules. One's outside behavior may be perfected, but their inner life is still in conflict.[176]

A deeper effect of living by a list of rules defining sin is that it profoundly affects how we treat ourselves and each other in terms of judgment. One of the immediate consequences we face when we transgress our morals is guilt and shame. While we know that beneficial guilt and shame can lead one to change their ways, judging ourselves with destructive guilt and shame can psychologically destroy our mental stability. Also, when we discover and conquer a sin, do we keep it to ourselves, or do we judge others by comparing their failure to our success?

Despite the certainty of most Christian's eventual failure at keeping rules, seeing oneself as virtuous because of achievements and standards may be what props up one's worldview. A system of virtue makes one feel better because they see themselves as right and those who disagree to be in the wrong. Even though some Christians do not follow their own rules, they tell themselves that they are still better than those on the wrong side: "They are truly the evil in the world, not me." They often condemn those who disagree with them on what they determine are the

---

176 Matthew 23:28

important and moral issues, giving themselves a form of sanctity and thus becoming self-righteous.

Sanctifying ourselves through works of virtue gives us a status that puts us above our brother or sister, who has not achieved the level we have. This type of thinking tends to elevate believers to different levels of sanctification. What level are you on? Not as high as your pastor but not as low as the church alcoholic, the person who went bankrupt, or the couple who failed at marriage? Self-righteousness can only lead to eventual disillusionment and an empty pride because we cannot live up to our own standards.

As a Christian becomes more self-righteous, they are now increasingly dissatisfied with those around them and then fail to bathe others, who disappoint or oppose them, in the same grace as Christ did them! Maybe a self-righteous person is unwilling to sacrifice for those who they characterize as having allegedly wasted their life by living it wrongly. They might contemplate that if the suffering individual had lived according to the right rules and systems of success, they would not be in a bad way, and therefore, they do not deserve the help that they seek. Or, they may have compassionate virtue, not attributing the person's plight to behavior that person has done but attributing it to evil perpetrated by others. The self-righteous Christian may virtuously dedicate their lives to preventing others from doing evil. They may even become perpetrators of violence to save others from suffering. Their virtue may become as important or more important than their faith. When one's virtue is elevated, it becomes difficult to publicly admit their failures because of the level of rightness they have assigned themselves amongst the perceived bad behavior of others around them.

When we go to church, we obviously do not generally get away from rules-based righteousness. On Sundays, we are often reminded of our failure to live according to a new list of sins touted from the pulpit and how to fix our deviation. It seems to me that the churches I have experienced continue to preach that righteousness comes more from following rules rather than from our new relationship established by Christ's work on the cross. Churches seem to have become a place to exchange or enforce the curse of man's attempts at ethical righteousness by pointing out the church goer's sin, with its consequences, and insisting on repentance as our means of reconciliation to God.

In making and promoting a new law, the church is not doing something new at all. The Jewish leaders of Jesus' time burdened the people with not only their interpretation of the Mosaic law but also additional rules, insisting that righteousness came from keeping them. They saw those who obeyed the rules as blessed and those who broke them as cursed. The converse was also believed; if one was poor or unhealthy, they were a sinner, and if one was rich and in reasonably good health, they were a righteous person[177]. This prejudice was not any more true in Jesus' time than it is today. The ones with all the money and influence are not any more righteous than the poor. The Jewish leaders were mixed up in influence and power and were attempting to create the kingdom of God by their wisdom and strength. They wanted a kingdom of laws and order that would keep them in control. They could not let go of their false kingdom for the real king of love who was right in front of them. Jesus would do away with their stronghold of rules by His message of grace, mercy, and love towards sinners. He does the same for us today, and the church should not be attempting to rebuild a religious structure of rules to bring sanctification in the face of true sanctification and reconciliation brought by faith, truth, and love.

Please don't get me wrong; I believe that a loving church is extremely

---

177 John 9:2

important in the Christian life. Jesus prayed concerning it:

> I pray not only for these, but also for those who believe in Me through their message. May they all be one, as You, Father, are in Me and I am in You. May they also be one in Us, so the world may believe You sent Me. I have given them the glory You have given Me. May they be one as We are one. I am in them and You are in Me. May they be made completely one, so the world may know You have sent Me and have loved them as You have loved Me.
>
> John 17:20–23 (HCSB)

In practice, the church should be a surrogate family with righteous relationships that are characterized by love, support, and forgiveness. God wants us to live in a church family where we genuinely love and care for one another. He does not want us to be in the kind of relationships where we hold back because we are hurt whenever we open up. God desires the church to be a place where we can be free to be transparent and express ourselves because all our failures are forgiven and forgotten and all our successes are rejoiced. The church family should be a place where we are wanted, accepted, and celebrated; a place where people are unselfishly supporting our destiny for our betterment; and a place of truth and love. The church could be an unstoppable force if it was a community of loving relationships, free from destructive judgment and condemnation.

My hope in mentioning the common practice of the church is that they will see the hopelessness of using sin, rules, and obedience for sanctification and turn to sanctification by following the Spirit and being perfected in the love of the cross. Guilt-laden preaching tends to teach that practicing religious works is the process to be sanctified. This leaves the believer discouraged because of inconsistent success. When one fails, guilt is readily provided, prodding them to repentance and confession, or causing rebellion. Opinions of what is right are not what brings us together in a church; it is usually what tears us apart.

We should no longer be trying to live the Christian life by avoiding sin according to lists taken from the Mosaic law because we are no longer under the old covenant. Sanctification by the new covenant also is not going to New Testament passages or other sources to find lists of sins. Lists of sins will overwhelm and enslave us. This should no longer be the case because God is not using a law to define sins between ourselves and Himself. Lists of sins should not exist for this purpose, especially not as a tool to control and condemn ourselves and others. We have been declared righteous, and there is no law or sin between ourselves and God. For the believer, while we still have earthly obligations, the concept of sin and condemnation has been replaced with the new concept of living by the Spirit in truth and love.

The Apostle Paul said, under the law, we are slaves to what we obey.[178] When we hold on to rules to define sin, we eventually will be forced to choose a means of coping with the struggle between the law and our sin. This choice takes two forms. One, we attempt to obey the law and become a slave to fighting sin. When struggling to do right, we will find ourselves continually attempting to find ways to live according to our knowledge of good and evil. Or two, we rebel against the law and allow sin to rule in our lives, fully indulging in destructive behavior. Many Christians believe that struggling with sin is a main part of the Christian life. In holding and practicing this belief, they are not free from sin and the law; they are still living under its curse.

When someone is a slave to sin and in a state of rebellion, they

---

178 Romans 6:16

172

disregard the requirements of the law and sometimes intentionally do the opposite. Their hearts become wicked and evil, seeking whom they can devour. A person can become bent on destruction looking to steal, kill, or destroy to get their needs met. If they do not develop shame and remorse, they may develop a passion for destroying those who condemn them. Their sin and passion can become insatiable and without restraint, beyond their own preservation. They become slaves to sin and bear its destruction.

It is easy to see how irresponsible living keeps us in a state of indulging sin, but it can be a little harder to understand that a significant amount of Christian teaching is keeping us in a state of fighting sin. As I demonstrated earlier, the Christian church, in general, prompts its followers to be loving in action and deed, yet they also seem to emphasize one's state of sin. Keeping the focus on sin keeps one in bondage to sin and unable to freely and fully experience the change that God's love brings. Any focus on sin according to a list of laws makes sin the issue and our master.

If one chooses, as a Christian, to follow the law to define their sin, that slavery looks different than rebellion. Romans 7 is commonly thought of as Paul's personal experience of the Christian's new struggle with sin as a believer. While Paul does indeed describe the sin conflict and the role of law, it is for a higher purpose. He was explaining how it is impossible to live a pure life by following the law, even as a Christian. He contends that the law actually stirs up and points out our sin, making us powerless to overcome it: "For while we were in the flesh, the sinful passions, which were aroused by the Law, were at work in the members of our body to bear fruit for death" (Romans 7:5, NASB). Our struggle with sin and the law is only overcome when we turn to Jesus to rescue us from the slavery to sin, which is partially caused by the law: "But now we have been released from the Law, having died to that by which we were bound, so that we serve in newness of the Spirit and not in oldness of the letter" (Romans 7:6, NASB). Paul wrote this passage in his correspondence to the Romans to explain how we have died to the law, and we serve in the newness of the Spirit. The life of struggle with the law, which has a stranglehold on our lives, has been eliminated. Sin has no power over us when we walk in the Spirit and follow Jesus' love as our guide to being sanctified. But if we walk according to the law, or any moral or religious rules for that matter, we are under its power and a slave to sin.

When Paul wrote that we "are not under Law but under grace" (Romans 6:14, NASB), he was clearly explaining the magnitude of Jesus taking away our sins. Since we are no longer under the Mosaic law, sin cannot be disobeying a law we are no longer obligated to.[179] Logically speaking, how can Christians sin if Jesus has taken away the law delineating their sins? The only way to have sinned, in its legal sense, is to transgress a law, but the law no longer applies to the believer. Paul wrote directly about the end of the law in his letter to the Colossians:

> Having wiped out the handwriting of requirements that was against us, which was contrary to us. And He has taken it out of the way, having nailed it to the cross. Having disarmed principalities and powers, He made a public spectacle of them, triumphing over them in it.
>
> Colossians 2:14–15 (NKJV)

Jesus' plan was to wipe out the written requirements by which we judge.

---

179 Romans 6:14-15

In doing this, He not only removed the law but the power of those in charge to institute a new law. If we entrust the "principalities and powers" to give us a new list of sins, we are making a new law and starting the sin condemnation cycle all over again. We are working to recreate a substitution of the law Jesus nailed to the cross.

When Christians define sin as failing to follow a law or "missing the mark," they are not living in the new covenant, which embraces the new freedom we have in Christ. When living by moral rules defining sin, we are slaves because we, as imperfect humans, in our greatest effort, cannot hit the mark consistently. At some point in our lives, we may achieve a level of accuracy, but these times are quickly fading. When we miss it, no one cares how often we hit it. Even when we are spiritual, acting holy, or following a set of morals, we are most likely doing it by our own effort, which misses the mark.

What hits the mark is the work that Christ accomplished on the cross as the perfect, spotless Lamb that worked to repair the destruction of sin in our lives and restore our relationship with God. The sacrificial lamb of the Old Testament law only covered sins temporarily for a temporary communion with God. The perfect Lamb of God took away our sins permanently[180] to restore forever the relationship with God that was lost. What we cannot and could not fix, Christ can and already did on the cross. God has restored us to walk with Him in a sinless, loving relationship.

Christians are not subject to all the normal definitions of sin imposed by those around us as we live in this earthly realm because we live in newfound freedom in Christ. Jesus took our sins away and nailed them to the cross[181]. The old commandment that separated believers from

180   1 John 3:5; John 1:29
181   Colossians 2:14

God was done away with. It was replaced by the new commandment of Jesus:

> A new commandment I give to you, that you love one another, even as I have loved you, that you also love one another. By this all men will know that you are My disciples, if you have love for one another.
>
> John 13:34–35 (NASB)

This new commandment should change the definition of sin for all believers. The only sin left between a believer and God is failure to show the love Jesus showed us, especially on the cross. This sin is actually between the ones we harm. The old sins of the flesh, as defined by religion and the Mosaic law, are part of the old life and old covenant of the law of sin and death, and they no longer have a place in condemning the Christian for their behavior.

Rules, laws, and religious systems do not decide what sin is for the believer. Our sin now is to not listen to the Spirit as He leads us to live out this new covenant to love one another as Jesus loves us. The problem with rules and systems is that they bring condemnation upon failure, whereas when we live by the Spirit, we do not start with the threat of condemnation. This is not a license to do whatever we want, good or bad, because He lets us know when we fail to love with the love of the cross. It is crucial in our quest to define sin that we distinguish between "rules" and a failure to love as Jesus loved.

We have entered into the new covenant where God makes us righteous by our faith, and we are not judged according to sins. In fact, we cannot sin according to law because Jesus took away the law, and by doing so, accomplished the removal of sins reckoned by any law. God adopts us into His family and loves us with a Father's unconditional, sacrificial love that does not change based upon how much we sin according to a law or do good deeds. We can no longer be separated from God by sin or any other action or power that exists. We are held in God's love, and as a Father, He stops all attempts to take us away from His love. Once we believe in Him, all our transgressions are no longer a threat to our relationship with God. Sin no longer separates us from Him.

The final truth is that God is not even going to judge Christians by how much they loved. All law, sin, and judgment are removed based upon one's belief in Jesus, and that happens at the very moment in time we choose to believe and follow Jesus.

All this being said, even if we live by the Spirit in Christ's love, we will never be perfect in this life. We can and do commit unloving acts towards God, others, and ourselves. Believers can walk in darkness and show hate for others. Believers can live with a love for the things of the world. We can cause all sorts of problems and destruction to the point of ruining our witnesses and sometimes ending our lives. These acts are not done solely by some entity called our flesh, for we are whole beings. These acts are not done by an outside force called sin; if a force exists, it is given power by our own evil fleshly desires. But, be forewarned; you cannot bring your darkness and evil with you to be with Jesus in the next life. Living in darkness is the opposite of the sanctification spurred on by the Spirit in us, who wants to perfect us in God's love and transform us on earth into the person we will be in heaven.

By the power of the Spirit in us, we can choose to walk in the light, or by our flesh, we can choose to walk in darkness. We can choose to love or choose to hate. We can choose to love the things of the world or choose to despise the things of the world and seek the things of God. We can choose to take advantage of others, using them for our sexual pleasure, financial success, or to improve our position in life, or we can choose to live the cross and to sacrificially love others. In the new covenant, sin is anytime we choose not to love as Jesus loved. This is the New Testament definition of sin; it is referred to as "not following his commandment."[182] Christians do not sin according to any written law, but they do sin quite often according to Jesus' new law of love. Our ability to love will grow as we allow ourselves to be sanctified by God's Spirit, who teaches His children how to love well.

Please do not stop reading or throw this book away because I said we are not to live by moral laws. I understand that there is a real struggle between our complete freedom in Christ from sin according to rules and a world which functions entirely by rules. Rightly so, one might still protest that we need laws to constrain our behavior, especially for those who are not made new by the Spirit. It seems that government laws, religion, family rules, and cultural pressure are often effective in changing designated outside behavior. But what about changing a person's desires on the inside? It is a noble goal to fix a person's behavior, but seeing a person change from the inside, with a desire to do good, and acting out of love as a result of salvation, is a change that is on a higher level.

Living a life by the Spirit, one in which we are completely set free from rules to guide and condemn us, is hard to realize and participate in if we still cannot let go of using the Bible for a list of sins and admonitions as the path to being sanctified. It is a reasonable position because the Bible is necessary for knowing the truth concerning salvation, good and evil, darkness and light, truth and falsehood, and love and hate. Still, it must be used from the right perspective.[183] The right understanding of the Bible as a whole is that it functions as a vehicle to know God and to know what is true about matters it addresses. Being righteous based on the knowledge of good and evil has never been what God wanted for us. He wants the same thing He has always wanted, to be our God, walking in a relationship with us, teaching us to love.

---

182 1 John 2:4
183 2 Timothy 3:16

CHAPTER 18

THE CROSS SETS US FREE FROM CONDEMNATION

For God did not send his Son into the world to condemn the world, but that the world should be saved through him.

John 3:17 (NET)

The most life-changing implication of the cross taking away sin is the removal of all condemnation from God towards the believer. In Paul's gospel presentation in Romans, he comes to a climax in chapter eight after his lengthy opine in chapter seven about how it is impossible to overcome sin through living by the law. He begins chapter eight by exclaiming the truth about how we relate to sin when we are in Jesus:

There is therefore now no condemnation for those who are in Christ Jesus. For the law of the life-giving Spirit in Christ Jesus has set you free from the law of sin and death.

Romans 8:1–2 (NET)

During my senior year in college, I had the privilege of rooming with a student from Tanzania, Charles Deogratias. He was tall, sophisticated, and had a great sense of pride in his heritage, along with his zeal for Jesus. Charles had come halfway around the world to get a degree at a Christian university in ministry. It has been a while, but I still vividly remember him constantly quoting Romans 8:1 (CSB) out loud in his thick Tanzanian accent: "Therefore, there is now no condemnation for those who are in Christ Jesus." He must have said it at least once, if not repeatedly, every time he saw me, almost reciting it out of habit. Maybe he perceived that I did not live by grace but instead focused on the law and condemnation of myself. I failed to understand my African brother's obsession with this verse until years later.

Romans 8:1 is one of the most important verses that the Apostle Paul wrote. It is the pivotal center point in his complex and thorough explanation of the gospel. He explodes with his conclusion that we have no condemnation because we have been set free from a life of sin and death according to the law. We are set free to make any choice we want without any threat of condemnation. He knew that, in Christ, we could be completely free because the same power that sets us free also leads us to make good and loving decisions concerning those around us. Our freedom from condemnation came from the one who demonstrated the greatest example of sacrificial love and then gave us His Spirit to empower us to do the same.

The paradigm shift from a life of bondage under the law to a life of freedom in the Spirit is so mind-wrecking that most of us fail to understand it, even after Paul spends eight chapters explaining it in his letter to the Romans. Jesus' act on the cross has forgiven us, healed us,[184] and taken all of our sins away[185]. He has given us His Spirit of life in Christ[186], His love has overwhelmed us,[187]   nd our adoption has given us a whole new life and destiny and our adoption has given us a whole

184   Colossians 1:14; 1 John 1:9; Acts 26:18
185   1 John 3:5; Romans 8:2
186   Romans 8:2
187   Romans 8:39

180

new life and destiny[188]; We live a blessed life as children of God the Father.[189] Understanding this amazing, transforming new birth, which happens at salvation, precipitates our understanding of abundant life with no condemnation.

At the climax in chapter eight, Paul begins the chapter with his bold statement of no condemnation and ends the chapter with his life-changing, religion-destroying proclamation that nothing can separate us from God's love. Prescribed sins of religion certainly cannot separate us from God. God is love, and in Him, there is no sin.[190] If we are in God and He is in us, and His love is in us, there is no possibility for sin to be in us.[191] We have the possibility of no sin because we are not under an old covenant of laws, rewards, and punishments; we are under a new covenant of living by the Spirit, and there is no law left to condemn us with or separate us from God.

The amazing fact is that when we accept Christ, all condemnation is removed, and we are freed "from the law of sin and death." The law of sin and death follows the pattern of law, sin, and judgment. This judgment either results in repentance, obedience, and then reward, or results in rebellion, which results in more condemnation, enforcement, and punishment.[192] If one is still living by rules, will they not judge and dole out condemnation according to transgressions of those rules? There is no condemnation without a law. Without condemnation, the law has no power over believers. We are free from all law and all condemnation, especially that which would separate us from God.

---

188 Romans 8:29-30
189 1 John 3:1; Romans 8:15-17
190 1 John 3:9
191 1 John 3:9, 4:7-8
192 1 John 4:18

In contrast to realizing that they have no condemnation, some Christians are still teaching that we must obey God according to rules or morals and that we will be punished when we do wrong and rewarded when we do right. This is the "carrot and the stick[193]" argument, as Aaron Budjen likes to label it. Conditional blessing is also how it appears the Jews in Jesus' day perceived God's interactions with humans. This is apparent when the disciples saw a blind man and asked Jesus, "Who sinned, this man or his parents, that he was born blind?" (John 9:2, NKJV). It is often insinuated that bad things happen to us because we are out of the will of God, which seems to be a form of Christian karma. This is not how a loving Father treats His children.

I have found that even when one believes in total grace, with only the commandment to love, they still have hidden taboo sins. It seems some hold the thought in the back of their minds: What is the one thing that I could do that would destroy my relationship with God and maybe end my forgiveness? I know that practitioners of grace say that they do not believe that such a taboo trespass exists, but deep down, fear of judgment for committing a forbidden sin can still haunt us! For the believer, this belief in a drastic sin should not exist. In fact, no sin except the sin of unbelief before we know Jesus separates us from God's love[195] or summons God's condemnation. Complete forgiveness, spiritual blessings, and unending love are not compatible with believing in some sort of condemnation for a sin like suicide or murder. Jesus took sin away and the law, as I explained in the last few chapters. Therefore, since there is no sin and no law, there is no legitimate source for thinking one is condemned by God and that He has removed His love or fellowship.

---

193   Budjen, Aaron, "Cloth and Wine," Living God Ministries, https://www.liv inggodministries.net/living_god_ministries/radio_archive/audio_files/cloth_ and_wine.mp3

194   Romans 8:39

This is not to say that we do not feel and receive condemnation from others. It can come from all sides, especially when we commit an act against a believed moral found in the Bible or a transgression of our church community rules. It is apparent that we experience judgment from the world if we commit any action that they deem immoral. We face an increased condemnation as believers from unbelievers because of their preconceived beliefs about what Christians should and should not do. Even our families, Christian or not, will scorn us if we offend the established family traditions. And sadly, we condemn ourselves. We can be extremely judgmental of our own person in regard to our actions, based on our perception of rights and wrongs, which may or may not be accurate. Satan is the worst source of condemnation in our lives. He works to condemn us using all of the above sources and more if given a chance. God speaks concerning Satan: "For the accuser of our brothers and sisters, who accuses them before our God day and night" (Revelation 12:10, NIV), will be cast down. Someday, we will even be completely free from the condemnation from others, ourselves, and even Satan.

In the new covenant, with our only commandment being to love as Jesus loved, one might possibly find a reason for self-condemnation when they fail to show this love. Even that failure cannot separate us from God. We are more likely estranged from one another or ourselves, but not from God. Any wrong we have done has already been paid for, and we are completely forgiven by Him and are continually in fellowship with God.[195] He is not going to discipline us each time we get it wrong, nor is God going to leave us alone until we get it right.[196] His Spirit will guide us and convict us of behavior He does not want us to do, and

---

195   1 John 1:7; 1 John 1:9; Romans 8:39
196   Hebrews 13:5-6

He will lead us to the behavior He desires for us[197]. A Christian can sin against God and others, but not by transgressing any list of rules. A Christian sins by failing to love God, others, and themselves[198]. This does not, by any means, change God's love toward us or our forgiven status. It may change our heart, blinding us to the Spirit's work in us and through us, but that is not the same as God condemning us or breaking fellowship.[199]

Knowing that condemnation is not practiced by God against believers, I am compelled to not practice condemnation against others or myself. Can I love someone and condemn them at the same time? Maybe as an appointed parent, boss, or public office holder, but not as a brother, sister, or friend. The same grace should be afforded to one another as God affords to us[200].

We are wise to remember Paul's claim that nothing "will be able to separate us from the love of God that is in Christ Jesus our Lord" (Romans 8:39, NIV); and the observation that "the righteous will live by faith" (Romans 1:17, NIV). The Old Testament patriarchs were certainly not righteous by following the law, but because of their faith, God loved them and chose not to condemn them. Neither are we condemned based upon our actions.

It is not uncommon for Christians to see themselves as becoming sanctified through keeping a code of ethics. When they fail, they often feel separated from God. Some even think they have lost their salvation. The usual process is to feel condemnation and then confess, repent, and believe that they receive forgiveness and restoration. This process

---

197   Romans 8:26; 2 Timothy 1:7; Galatians 5:16, 25
198   1 John 2:5
199   Hebrews 6:4-6
200   Philippians 2:1-6

is living by the law of sin and death and riding on a rollercoaster of uncertainty. Instead, by faith, we should be free to live by the Spirit in truth and love with no threat of condemnation. We have the promise of the inseparable love of the Father as we ride the unpredictable winds of the Spirit, always in His love and fellowship, without condemnation. True and permanent forgiveness will set you free from sin and most certainly set you free from condemnation to live a new, amazing, uninhibited life in Jesus and by the Spirit.

CHAPTER 19

THE PURPOSE OF CONFESSION FOR BELIEVERS IS TRANSFORMED BY THE CROSS

So confess your sins to one another.

James 5:16 (NET)

In reality, Christians continue to fail to do what is right, no matter what they believe about condemnation. No one has discovered a magic cure to make us only love and not make mistakes. I remember all of the insane fights between my mother and father. So much of the time, my father was trying to get my mother to admit her wrongs, most likely to justify his hurt and anger. Even if we could somehow achieve perfection alone, maybe living in a cave, what would happen in our hearts when someone wronged us? Would we cite the rule they have broken against us and then demand their confession?

There is an immense divide in the way Christians respond when they fail. This dilemma hinges on how we believe God responds to the wrongs one commits and how we respond to God when we do, say, or think something we believe to be a sin. Does He break fellowship with us and need us to repent to receive forgiveness, or is there nothing we can do that will separate us from God's love? Do we need to repent and confess our sins to make our relationship right with God, or are our sins already forgiven and to ask for forgiveness would be a failure to acknowledge what Christ already completed at the cross?

A majority of Christians I know would say that we sin in terms of rule-breaking and failure to do righteous acts, and as a result, we have to repent and confess our sins to restore our relationship with God. The belief that God is separating Himself from ourselves and that we must repent to alleviate a problem is a form of judgment and condemnation from which we are freed. In some Christian denominations, there are entire systems of condemnation in relation to confessing. Those from a protestant church tradition may interpret the Catholic practice of confessing to a priest as going beyond the biblical description of confession[201], but one commonly held protestant belief about confession is that it restores a believer's relationship with God, an idea that is not found in the Bible.

This is where the problem and source of sin for the believer is crucial. It is usually claimed that once we realize our sin as defined by laws, we must repent, confess, and receive forgiveness and a restored relationship with God. Those who practice this procedure usually throw up a blanket confession for all the sins they were unaware of. Some might differentiate between accidental sins and willful sins. I agree a believer's sin gets in the way of having fellowship with God; that is why God took them away. The core of the sin problem for the believer is believing that we sin according to a law and then practice repentance and confession of that sin.[202] This thinking and practice condemns us and separates us from His love.[203] Instead, we should live without the law of sin and death, in the complete forgiveness of the cross, led by the Spirit, who

---

201 James 5:16

202 Hebrews 10:29

203 Hebrews 6:4-6

guides us in God's love.

What should happen when we do wrong to another person? We might be confronted by someone, be convicted by our own conscience, or be made aware by the Holy Spirit of wrongdoing. One's normal practice may be to repent and confess to God for forgiveness according to the broken rule and the guilt and shame they feel, and hope to receive forgiveness and restored fellowship. Sometimes we apologize and confess to one another, but not always. I contend that while it is necessary to openly confess our failures to each other to restore relationships[204], it is important to know that God's love has not changed for us, and our relationship with Him is never broken[205]. Our love, acceptance, and relationship with the Father are not in question, and there is no action that would rescind our ability to meet with God in the fullness of His love. In fact, as God is perfecting us in His love, a willingness to openly admit our failures to one another is a big part of the process. The awareness of the complete love and forgiveness we have already received empowers us to confess because we have nothing to fear. Confession is openly admitting to one another when one has failed to show the love of Jesus. It is healthy and needed to confess our sins to one another on most occasions when it is beneficial to the offended party.

If we have to confess our sins to God, how and what do we confess? Is it by repenting prostrate on the floor, crying out for the forgiveness of our sins before God? Or is it a simple, "What's up, God; I'm sorry"? For some, it seems there is a spiritual exchange of the old practice of animal sacrifice for a new practice of personal confession and repentance.[206] How can we know what to confess if we are not using a system of

---

204   James 5:16
205   Romans 8:39
206   Hebrews 10:1

rules to guide us? How are we free from condemnation if our actions are counted against us, and we need repentance and forgiveness to fix ourselves? After salvation, having to confess our sins to God to receive forgiveness is living by the law of sin, judgment, condemnation, and death[207].

We need to be careful that we are not trying to duplicate what Jesus has already accomplished on the cross when we confess[208]. If we are confessing anything but our failure to love as Jesus did, are we not forced to look for a commandment or rule we transgressed? Are we using rules to condemn ourselves and others into confession? Heaping laws on people is what the Pharisees did in Jesus' day, and He had a few not-so-choice words for them[209]. In a system of sanctification by works through the use of confession and repentance, there seems to be no end to discovering sins to repent and confess of.

The idea of a believer's confession for the forgiveness of sins is mainly derived from what the Apostle John wrote in 1 John 1:9 (NKJV): "If we confess our sins, He is faithful and righteous to forgive us our sins and to cleanse us from all unrighteousness." In most of Christianity, this verse is thought of as a basic instruction to confess, which allows one to receive forgiveness and right standing with God. This use of the verse does not seem to fit with the finality of the forgiveness for sin that Jesus completed on the cross and the promise that nothing can separate us from God's love. This practice also seems to not cohere with Paul and John's other statements about our sins being completely forgiven and taken away, especially when juxtaposed with Paul's statement that "there is no condemnation for those who are in Christ Jesus" (Romans 8:1, NIV). If freedom from condemnation, forgiveness, and our relationship

207 Hebrews 6:4-6
208 Hebrews 10:29
209 Matthew 23:1-36

with God is conditional on anything, including confessing our sins, can we ever truly be completely forgiven or have a relationship with Him? This belief and practice can cast doubt in our hearts about the security and the permanence of our status with God.

To attempt to answer this dilemma, please take a closer look at 1 John 1:

> If we say that we have fellowship with Him and yet walk in the darkness, we lie and do not practice the truth; but if we walk in the Light as He Himself is in the Light, we have fellowship with one another, and the blood of Jesus His Son cleanses us from all sin. If we say that we have no sin, we are deceiving ourselves and the truth is not in us. If we confess our sins, He is faithful and righteous to forgive us our sins and to cleanse us from all unrighteousness. If we say that we have not sinned, we make Him a liar and His word is not in us.
>
> 1 John 1:6–10 (NASB)

In verses six and seven, there is a situation that occurs when one claims, as I do, that a believer does not sin by transgressing the Mosaic law or failing to do a prescribed good. We are left with a question: How do I know what the right behavior is? I know the answer: Walk in the Spirit.[210] But what does that look like? John and Paul both seem to describe this new journey as walking in the light and not walking in darkness.[211] John goes on in the later chapters of this letter to juxtapose love versus hate in a similar fashion as darkness and light.[212] Walking in the light is

---

210   Galatians 5:16 (NKJV)

211   1 John 1:6-7, Colossians 1:12-13

212   1 John 2:9-11, Colossians 1:13-14

walking by the Spirit in His freedom, truth, and love, knowing we are fully cleansed from all unrighteousness.[213] We are freed from sin and law, which enslaves us to the temptations of this world that distract us from love and lead to darkness. We are freed so that we may walk in the light of his truth and love.

Verses eight and nine touch on how we all will struggle to stay in His light and miss the goal to love as Jesus loved. When we fail to love, we sin. A forgiven person should have no hindrances in openly admitting their failure to love when the Spirit or someone else points it out. Do not worry about this happening; people will definitely point out our problems. When we fail, we usually do not need others to convict us. We often see our own failures, most likely with the Spirit's prompting. Our willingness to openly accept our failures should not lead to overwhelming guilt and shame. Confession for the believer is to participate with the Spirit in sending away[214] (forgiving) our failures (sins), pruning[215] (cleansing) us of any hindrances[216] to loving (unrighteousness), and teaching us to demonstrate God's love. We are spurred on to love well the next time, to love according to the grace that we have received.

In verse ten, we see that no law can lift one to the perfect eternal height of Jesus' love; only His Spirit in us can lead us towards that point. Achieving sanctification by our works only leads us to the darkness of hiding or denying our unloving behavior ("if we say that we have not sinned").

Reaching a level of practical sanctification that we have achieved

---

213 1 John 1:9

214 Liddel-Scott-Jones Definitions, Entry for Strongs #863, Studylight.org, 2020, https://www.studylight.org/lexicons/greek/863.html

215 Liddel, Strongs #2511, https://www.studylight.org/lexicons/greek/2511.html

216 Liddel, Strongs #93, https://www.studylight.org/lexicons/greek/93.html

on our own only puts us in a place where we are not open to the love of God molding us. How many of us have been hurt by someone who was considered a highly spiritual, moral person in the church? Failure to love by Christian leadership has caused deep wounding. No one is past walking in the darkness; not even the Apostle John was. When we think we are, we "make Him a liar and His word is not in us."

I am not taking John's admonition lightly to confess, but when we believe our right standing with God is broken by sin, based on rules, and our fellowship with God is restored based on confession, that puts us in the driver's seat of the relationship. This self-control can produce an attitude that can actually break fellowship with God and others, achieving the opposite of what we think confession achieves. If I am guilty of a failure to love, I should openly confess to others and God and be openly willing to let God cleanse me of my unloving ways.[217] This is not done out of fear, guilt, shame, and a need to restore a relationship; it is done out of a desire to be perfected in God's love. Denial is the opposite of confession and love. We should not deny or hide our weaknesses or our lack of love, nor should we have any reason to because we are unconditionally loved and not condemned by God.

John states in both verses six and ten that if we deny our failings, we make God out to be a liar. Fear and condemnation foster denial of one's failings. My mother, for understandable reasons, almost always denied any activity that my father angrily accused her of. It had become just a reflex for her to deny any wrongdoing in the face of his judgment and condemnation. An open willingness to confess and not deny when we fail to love is vastly different from the general procedure of confession taught for when we sin according to a rule. One is done out of love, and the other is done out of fear and not love. Confession out of love and

---

217   1 John 1:9

193

not fear is the way of Jesus because we know: "There is no fear in love" (1 John 4:18, NASB).

To answer those who insist that Christians must confess their sins to receive forgiveness, those in the modern grace movement contend that this verse is clearly for non-Christians. It cannot apply to Christians because it says forgiveness of sins and our sins were forgiven at the cross. While the modern grace movement does make an important point about forgiveness, I am not ready to only apply this verse only to non-Christians.

The more traditional answer is that it is not forgiveness you are getting through confession because one receives that the first time they confess and become a Christian. But through repentance and confession, a Christian is thought to restore their relationship with God. One might legitimately ask, "When are we law-abiding and all of our sins confessed?" If one honestly answers, it's "never." Then when is it that we can actually have fellowship with God?

In the end, I think the perspective of both the modern grace movement and traditional Christian thought agree that we are not actually receiving forgiveness again when we confess. Naturally, there is still disagreement over whether or not one has to confess their sins at all since we are already forgiven.

There is a fundamental problem with the idea of restored fellowship. 1 John 1:9 does not say confession and then restored relationship, but confession and forgiveness. I find it interesting that most evangelicals who stand on this verse to demand confession squirm away from the forgiveness part and add the idea of a restored relationship. One passage used to support the idea of loss of fellowship is found in Ephesians: "Do not grieve the Holy Spirit of God, by whom you were sealed for the day of redemption" (Ephesians 4:30, NKJV). Does grieving the

Holy Spirit cause us to lose fellowship in the sense of separation? If I do something to my daughter to make her mad, we may have words, but she is still my daughter. I do not stop loving her, and she does not stop loving me. It would grieve me if my daughter stopped loving me and communicated it to me, but it would not change my love for her. It would also grieve me if she abandoned Jesus and lived a destructive life, yet I would still love her. My grief would not be against her but for her huge loss. God grieves for the loss and destruction that we bring into our lives through our bad choices. He is not separating Himself from us with His grief; He is crying for us and with us. We are not condemned, we do not lose our forgiveness, and we still have our relationship with God no matter what we do[218].

The threat of loss of fellowship should not exist for the believer. Loss of fellowship may actually come from one convincing themselves that they can confess all their sins as the key to having fellowship with God. John later wrote that "if our heart condemns us, God is greater than our heart" (1 John 3:20, NKJV). We may feel out of fellowship, but God's open arms have not changed. He is not standing there looking at us with crossed arms and a scowl on His face waiting for us to come back with our tail between our legs, confessing and repenting of our sins. Nor does He hand out treats with a happy face to those who do not mess up or to those who are truly repentant and confess with sincerity. God is always standing there as the good Father with open arms to love us despite what we have done or whether we confess or repent correctly.

The story of the prodigal son and the loving father that Jesus spoke about is such a profound illustration of the love of God in a Christian's life and how it will not go away no matter what we do[219]. Just as the

---

218 Romans 8:38-39
219 Luke 13:11-32

brother in the story was angry when his father threw a party for his wayward son, so also some Christians choose to speak of condemnation for those who have strayed from the Lord and returned rather than celebrate their return. They do not understand that the Father, even though wronged deeply, never stopped loving His son.

How can we turn Christ's free and complete gift of salvation, which is not based on works, into a legalistic, law-pounding religion to get people to somehow become sanctified through confession and no longer commit sins as we define them? How long will we beat up one another and ourselves? The rest of our lives, possibly, because we cannot achieve sanctification by confessing sins as defined by a written law that we are no longer under. Sanctification comes through forgiveness, truth, and love, not penance and confession according to the law.

In our walk with Jesus, we will all fail to love with His love. One would ultimately hope that as we grow closer to being perfected in His love, the possibility of hateful and evil acts would grow further away from us. When we commit bad or unfortunate behavior and talk to God and others about it, it should not be done in fear of separation from God[220]. In a perfect world, others would not condemn us either. When we come to God in confession, it is in a spirit of thankfulness for His unending love and sorrow for not listening to Him or practicing love as we know we should.

A righteousness based on faith in what God did and does for us means that our forgiveness and relationship with God the Father is based solely on our decision to have a relationship with Jesus, not whether or not we have confessed all or most of our sins. There are no levels of sanctification achieved for confession and good behavior; that sounds

---

220 1 John 4:18

more like a prison term than a loving relationship with God. Confession openly allows others and the Spirit to help us and teach us to love better. In Christ, we are free from the type of confession that condemns us and are free to grow in God's love through an open confession of our failure to love. We are not motivated to deny our wrongdoing but rest in the Spirit to guide us in His love. We can freely confess all that we are accused of for the sake of love. It is entirely different from looking at a list of rules and obligations, spoken or unspoken, condemning ourselves according to that list, and then needing to repent of and confess our transgressions. At that point, one does not have the righteousness and freedom that the cross brings, but instead, they are a slave to their list of sins.

Since we are bathed in God's great love and forgiveness and motivated by our desire to love as He loved us, we can openly acknowledge, to God and to one another, when we sin, as defined by a failure to love. This freedom is key to allowing God's Spirit to work in us and transform us. This interaction with God and others is extremely helpful for maturity and growth in one's life, bringing one closer to God and other people. This open, humble, and trusting conversation allows the Spirit to change us as we are shown our shortcomings in our attempts to love. Hopefully, as we mature in our faith, our conversations will not be about what we have done wrong but what we are doing right.

Part 3: Transformed by the Love of the Cross

CHAPTER 20

SANCTIFICATION IS ACCOMPLISHED THROUGH LIVING THE LOVE OF THE CROSS AND THE TRUTHS OF OUR SALVATION

I have been crucified with Christ, and it is no longer I who live, but Christ lives in me. So the life I now live in the body, I live because of the faithfulness of the Son of God, who loved me and gave himself for me.

Galatians 2:20 (NET)

I have thrown a lot at you in these last few chapters. Chapter 14 emphasized that we are made completely righteous at the moment we trust in Jesus. Chapter 15 contends that the old covenant law does not apply to believers. Chapter 16 demonstrates how the cross of Jesus establishes a new covenant and defines sin according to Jesus' new commandment to love as He loves us. Chapter 17 takes freedom from the law a step further to explain that Jesus takes away all sin, and we are free from all rules to live and judge others and ourselves by. Chapters 18 and 19 establish that we are free from God's condemnation and relieved of the need for confession to God. In this next section, I want to focus on the new covenant and how sanctification is demonstrated through us living out the love of the cross.

Jesus came to bring love into the world by dying in our place so we could restore our relationship with God. On the cross, Jesus demonstrated sacrificial love as a new way to live in contrast to a violent, self-serving humanity. He did not come to fix the world according to human definitions of right and wrong; Jesus came to make our relationship right with Him, right with others, and right with ourselves. He came to teach us to love and to give us the power to love.

Coming for a relationship couched in love looks different from what some contend Jesus came for. If He came to change the world through improved government or social programs, He failed. If He came to feed the hungry or heal all the sick, then He failed. If He came to end all war, He failed. If He came to alleviate suffering, He failed. What Jesus came to do was take away the sin of the world in order to provide a means to renew a loving relationship with Him and subsequently our relationship with others and ourselves[221]. In that endeavor, His success was far beyond measure, for through the cross, He taught us that love was more important than life itself.

God loved us so much that He sacrificed His Son, Jesus, "that we should be called the children of God" (1 John 3:1, NASB). Once adopted as His children, God lavishes us with His great love. His love will never be taken away because of our failures, and His love for us does not increase when we follow the rules. Receiving Jesus' salvific act of love on the cross brings us into a right relationship with God. Our transformation comes from us being restored through forgiveness and being filled with His life-giving Spirit[222]. The filling of the Spirit and our adoption as His children could only happen because Jesus took away our sins on the cross.

---

221 John 1:29
222 Romans 5:5

It took an act of God to begin to change the hearts of those who would believe. Even with Christ's great loving sacrifice on the cross as our example of love, Christians for centuries have gotten it wrong about how to overcome their struggles through promoting a process of religious works. They have gotten it wrong about the means of sanctification with practices such as following laws, repentance, confession, penance, self-flagellation, and practicing good deeds. Believers have gotten the church's role in sanctification wrong, thinking that the church was the arbitrator of blessings for good behavior and the corrector of bad. Believers have gotten their personal piety and its relation to sanctification wrong. Christians have promoted several ways of sanctification other than love, and those ways have sometimes led to unloving actions through enforcing their legalistic ways of righteousness over God's love.

Human knowledge of good and evil has been the bane of mankind, and it is what we use to judge others, ourselves, and even God. The unfortunate truth is that humans need someone or some source greater than themselves to define morality, or else our own definitions will become self-serving. Religious or secular, the definitions of right and wrong in human hands quickly become a tool by which we are judged and condemned. Even Moses' law, which sought to teach us to love properly, devolved into a religion of judgment. Under a religion of rules, love becomes conditional, and reciprocity is required.

Some rely on rules to prevent them from living by the flesh. When we think of the flesh, we immediately think in terms of indulging the flesh in pleasure, comfort, and safety. The other way to live by the flesh is by restraining it with religion, personal effort, and altruisms. When we cross the line of indulging the flesh, we face condemnation and punishment. When we live the pious life of restraining the flesh, we are outwardly praised, but living by the law still produces the fruits of the flesh. It degrades our ability to love those who do not measure up and causes pride in our ability to follow rules.

Practicing a form of Christianity where we become sanctified according to following a list of rules was not Christ's plan. His new plan is to sanctify us by our faith in His truth and our practice of the sacrificial love of the cross.[223] Our sanctification begins when Jesus takes away our sins. He then sets aside the system of rules, laws, obligations, and altruisms, replacing them with one command: to love as He loves. Our practical sanctification is realized in our love for God, our treatment of our neighbors, and our respect for ourselves as we emulate the love of Jesus. This loving behavior can only be accomplished by God's strength and with the truth and knowledge that is provided by the Holy Spirit. We are no longer following rules to judge ourselves and others; instead, we seek and listen to the Spirit guiding us to love and to do good, and not to hate and do evil.

Even those that agree that Christians live by grace and the work of the Spirit for their sanctification often find themselves thinking that they still need both rules and the work of the cross to restrain the flesh. Living under both grace and the law is a distorted view of grace. When Christians fail, they often feel or believe that they are estranged from God. This reaction is affirmed when others point out one's sin according to the law and provide remedies such as confession and repentance. The pattern of failure, guilt, confession, and perceived forgiveness is all too familiar, only to start it all over again the next day or hour or moment. Those who participate in this formula are failing to take off the old law and put on the new garment of forgiveness and love that Jesus has given us. Having grace and using it as a means to follow the law is the

---

223 Philippians 3:9, Galatians 5:6

act of sewing a new patch on an old garment[224]. This tear-and-repair lifestyle and ministry will trap a Christian into living by the flesh and not experiencing the fruits of the Spirit. Jesus gives us a new garment, a whole new way of life. When we are filled with God's Spirit, we should not be using grace to help us live by the ministry of death, trying to repair our old garment of religion.[225] This only makes more holes. We need the new covenant of a life of love that Christ brings through His Spirit because we are no longer under the law of sin and death.

Jesus puts the Spirit's new wine of truth and love into new wineskins—our redeemed selves—that will not burst. This is an amazing transformation. Despite this truth, it seems legalistic Christians are still attempting to put God's new wine into their old religious wineskin and then wondering why Jesus has not made a difference in their life. In that scenario, our lives crash and burn in the same swiftness and severity as the non-believer because we are still living by the world's rules. For those who try to point out that the work of the cross ended religious traditions and the world's rules in the church, they are not welcome either. One cannot forcibly insert Jesus' new covenant into religion, and if they try, they may end up crucified like Christ. Sanctification by truth and love has no quarters with sanctification by rules. It is destined for an explosion. Jesus' new wine must be put into new wineskins that will not burst[6]. This new wine in new wineskins is our source of sanctification from the inside out.

Consider what the Apostle Paul says to the Thessalonians about being sanctified:

---

224 Matthew 2:21
225 2 Corinthians 3:7
226 Matthew 2:22

As for other matters, brothers and sisters, we instructed you how to live in order to please God, as in fact you are living. Now we ask you and urge you in the Lord Jesus to do this more and more. For you know what instructions we gave you by the authority of the Lord Jesus. It is God's will that you should be sanctified: that you should avoid sexual immorality; that each of you should learn to control your own body in a way that is holy and honorable, not in passionate lust like the pagans, who do not know God; and that in this matter no one should wrong or take advantage of a brother or sister. The Lord will punish all those who commit such sins, as we told you and warned you before. For God did not call us to be impure, but to live a holy life. Therefore, anyone who rejects this instruction does not reject a human being but God, the very God who gives you his Holy Spirit.

1 Thessalonians 4:1–8 (NIV)

As Paul addresses sexual actions here, he does not refer to the Mosaic law. He is pointing out the obvious; if you love your brothers and sisters, you will not do evil to them by taking advantage of them. Grotesquely using others to meet our needs is the opposite of the way of Jesus. We are to sacrifice ourselves for the sake of loving others, not sacrifice them for our pleasure.

Paul then goes from negative to positive, addressing what we should be doing:

Now about your love for one another we do not need to write to you, for you yourselves have been taught by God to love each other. And in fact, you do love all of God's family throughout Macedonia. Yet we urge you, brothers and sisters, to do so more and more.

1 Thessalonians 4:9–11 (NIV)

This is Paul's description of what it means to be sanctified through love. Again, Paul is not quoting the Mosaic law to condemn them for their hurtful actions. In fact, he reminds them that they were "taught by God to love each other." It is a great struggle for some to learn to love by the Spirit and not judge by the law. God's Spirit is right there to guide us on the right path. The Spirit continues to work on us, and we need to be open to His training in love.

It is recorded in Mark 7:15 (NIV) where Jesus said: "Nothing outside a person can defile them by going into them. Rather, it is what comes out of a person that defiles them." This statement was inside out to the Jews. How could Jesus say that eating the wrong foods or touching an item that was unclean would not defile a person? His claim was against the law of Moses. Jesus had reversed their interpretation of the rules by saying it was not what goes in but what comes out. When living by the law, it was most definitely what someone did or touched on the outside that made them unclean. When living by the Spirit, if hate comes out, one is unclean; when love comes out, one is clean.

Jesus said He came to take away sin, making sin according to the law a non-issue for the believer, but in what sense?[227] Believers can definitely do evil, hateful actions, and sin by failing to love, but that is a completely different definition of sin than living according to rules or the Mosaic law. Jesus ended the curse of the law by becoming the curse for us.[228] The ministry of death that was carved on stone as the ten commandments

---

227   John 1:29
228   Galatians 3:13

no longer apply to us[229]. We have entered the ministry of life in Christ Jesus.[10] The law of the Spirit is the new law written on our hearts, teaching us to love[11]. Every day, I fail to love in some capacity, and the Spirit continues to grow me in His love. The new law of the Spirit is a beautiful relationship. It is not slavery to a written law that defines transgression and punishment. There is no focus on sin according to a rule broken or a failed duty. There is no condemnation; we simply learn from mistakes leading to greater love. We are in a new covenant, following a new command; to love one another as he loved us as we are led by the Spirit.

---

229 2 Corinthians 3:7
230 Romans 8:2
231 Romans 8:2

CHAPTER 21

THE LOVE OF THE CROSS IS LIVED BY THE SPIRIT

For the law of the life-giving Spirit in Christ Jesus has set you free from the law of sin and death.

Romans 8:2 (NET)

A few people who have heard the story of my father's abuse of my mother have had a disturbing response. They assume that I am abusive because they think that the son will repeat his father's behavior unless something extraordinary happens. Some are even brave enough, or perhaps thoughtless enough, to openly ask how I overcame this handicap, or they express amazement that I am not abusive like my father. To set the record straight, I am not abusive in any way like my father was. That is not to say that I could not easily have slipped into a life of abuse, but I chose not to succumb to any form of it. My entire life, I have had God with me, which I am convinced, was a big part of my saving grace. While I think it is a careless application of behavioral theory to assume that the child of an abuser will be abusive, I understand that it might be easy to mimic a learned behavior.

My story is different than my father's, and I was determined not to be like him. I succeeded in many ways, except my temper. Many today may not relate to having anger responses to an offense, but I see it quite often in society. I have seen grown men get into a fight over a parking space. People can get into a simple argument over someone taking a bite out of their grilled cheese sandwich, and it can escalate to the point of violence.[232] Anger is a debilitating disease that puts one in an almost uncontrollable state. Although I had trouble controlling my anger at times, I luckily could control my behavior when I was angry. This is what got me out of a lot of trouble. Still, I hated my anger and was, at times, very depressed over it. No matter what I tried, it would always rear its ugly head. It was not until I realized the complete forgiveness and love in Jesus, and the removal of all law, that I began to have control over my anger. As God taught me about his freedom and the love He offered, I could sense the Spirit instilling in me the freedom not to be angry. There was no rule by which I was condemned by God. If that was true, then by what rule am I condemning and punishing the object of my anger. Was this not someone Jesus died for? How could I now curse them?

When I allowed the Spirit to change me, a renewing miracle of love took place in my life. I became "a new creation; old things …passed away; behold all things have become new" (2 Corinthians 5:17, NKJV). We all experience this newness of life when we live by the Spirit and not by the law. Living by the law shuts out the Spirit's ministry in our hearts because it focuses us on how to behave by rules, which prevents us from being taught how to love by His Spirit[233]. His Spirit speaks to us, guiding us in our daily situations. The Spirit displays Himself as we discern between the right and wrong courses of action, based on the love and truth He has taught us. Our ability to love grows in us each day

---

232 Musumeci, Natalie, Man Shoots at wife and daughter over grilled cheese sandwich: cops, January 9, 2017, New York Post, nypost.com, https://nypost.com/2017/01/09/man-shoots-at-wife-and-daughter-over-grilled-cheese-sandwich-cops/

233

as we are led by the Spirit to love more. As the love of God continues to grow in us, our propensity to do evil is greatly diminished.[234]

Before we become Christians, the difference between a good person and a bad person depends on whether or not someone has learned to perform morally and socially acceptable ways of getting their needs fulfilled. For many Christians, the difference between a good and bad Christian is also based on how they behave according to biblical and social norms, or they may also point to a Christian's displayed relationship with God. For a follower of the new covenant, neither one is fully correct. Our definition of a good Christian should be based on whether one lives a life of love guided by the Spirit. Will we allow the Spirit to meet our needs, or will we use old practices and habits to meet them ourselves? Will we use others or perpetrate evil to meet our needs, or will we depend on God to provide? We are on the path of sanctification towards the light when we know that the source of love and life comes from the Spirit, and we no longer have to take from others to meet our needs. Instead, we can choose to live a life of love, giving to others and not taking. We live to love, not live for love.

This transformation is not a process of following rules or practicing confession for restoration. As we have discussed, that process leads to legal sanctification, a process that must be repeated the next day, hour, or moment. The transformation by the Spirit is a process of Him teaching us truth and sanctifying us in the love of the cross. When we follow Jesus, we are not merely exchanging the law of Moses for a better law found in the New Testament.[235] This is especially important to understand when we are explaining the blessings of Jesus to a Muslim or a Mormon, for example. We should not be trying to convince them that we have a better

---

234 1 John 4:15-21
235 Galatians 2:21

law. Instead, we should be trying to show them that sin and the law are destroying them and ourselves. We need to point them to Jesus, who takes away sin and the law and gives us His Spirit to live and love by.

This relationship I am explaining is one in which the goal of sanctification is to become a more loving person by demonstrating the love of the cross in their life. Religion's concept of good and Jesus' concept of good diverge at the crossroads of how one becomes sanctified. Does goodness come by following a list of rules, leading to a practical level of sanctification if you succeed and condemnation if you fail? Or does our goodness only come through embracing Jesus' sacrifice on the cross by which we are subsequently sanctified by emulating His love? I would contend that one is good only if they have faith in God by which they are declared good. Then, in response to God's gifts of unconditional forgiveness and love, a person loves with God's love in the power of the Spirit. The Spirit guides us in truth concerning salvation and pours out His love in our hearts. It is through this truth and love He puts in us that we are sanctified and become more and more loving.[236] This growth in us happens because we are given the want and the power to love as He loved us. Being taught by the Spirit to love as Jesus loves is our way of sanctification as believers.

With no possibility of condemnation and being bathed in God's unconditional and immense love, we are free to make whatever decision we need to. It is interesting that in these circumstances of freedom, we make much better decisions than when chained to past failures and future fears. Jesus said to Nicodemus, "The wind blows wherever it will, and you hear the sound it makes, but do not know where it comes from and where it is going. So it is with everyone who is born of the Spirit" (John 3:8, NET). Complete freedom in Christ is an amazing state to strive for.

---

236 1 Thessalonians 4:1-12

We experience freedom differently than ever before because "if the son sets you free, you will be really free" (John 8:36, NET).

This freedom from the law of sin and death is hard for some to agree with. There may be a few points of contention from a large swath of believers when I say we live by love and not the law, especially when I say that Jesus came to take away our sins.[237] One may not believe, as I contend, that in order to take away sins, the law must be taken away. If we live by a law, transgressions will always exist. Fear of taking away the law and other lists of sin should be alleviated by the fact that we are indwelt by the Holy Spirit perfecting us in His love.

The Bible is very clear that a new law is written on our hearts because of the Spirit in us[238]. We live a life by the Spirit; therefore, we are free to love as the Spirit leads us. Jeremiah declared a future where the law would be inside of believers:

> "Behold, days are coming," declares the Lord, "when I will make a new covenant. …I will put My law within them and on their heart I will write it; and I will be their God, and they shall be My people. They will not teach again, each man his neighbor and each man his brother, saying, 'Know the Lord,' for they will all know Me, from the least of them to the greatest of them," declares the Lord, "for I will forgive their iniquity, and their sin I will remember no more."
>
> Jeremiah 31:31, 33–34 (NASB)

Jeremiah states that the law will be written on the hearts of God's people,

---

237 Romans 6:6, 8:1-2, 11:27; Hebrews 10:17-18; 1 John 3:5; John 1:29
238 Hebrews 10:16

and their sin will be remembered no more. They will not have to be taught to fix their sins every Sunday. This prophecy is specifically applied to Christians by the writer of Hebrews in chapter ten, verses sixteen and seventeen, where the author quotes this passage from the book of Jeremiah. If we have the law written on our hearts, then why do we seek a new written law to point out our sins?

It took me until my forties to learn that this new goodness and righteousness comes from loving as Jesus did, living by His Spirit, and not following a list of rules to condemn or to judge others and myself. This is what freed me from my anger and an instinct to punish others and myself for wrongs done. Living a Spirit-filled life is living with the continual awareness of God's love, His forgiveness, and His freedom to love. It is truly bringing the kingdom of God to earth—a kingdom of truth and love in our hearts, minds, and lives—not a utopian kingdom that humans may conceive. The Spirit in us is required for us to be good and loving because it is in the trepidation of walking in the Spirit, not clearly knowing the way, that we are taught God's humility, truth, and love.

Ever hear the expression that "Rome wasn't built in a day"? The Jews of Jesus' day expressed a similar thought: the temple was not built in three days. It is an interesting comparison of the work of the Spirit in our lives versus religion. It took religion forty-six years to build the temple, which was a way of building a relationship with God. Jesus made this relationship possible for everyone in only three days. Such a great transformation as Jesus does in our lives cannot be done with religion and rules even if one had forty-six years to rebuild their life as I tried in mine. Jesus can make us new creations as fast as we are able to go along with His work in us. Believers do not always cooperate with God's plan, and sometimes Jesus has to lovingly drag us along kicking and screaming.

Even though we have such a great source of freedom, forgiveness, and love, we will still struggle. We often will feel torn in this world. It may feel like we have one foot in the temporal world of religion, where achievement and following rules are what matters most, and one foot in the eternal world of the Spirit, where sanctification is achieved by His love in us. It is hard to walk in the light, and we often fail to demonstrate His love. The darkness of following the law or rebelling against the law can start to control us, and then we give in to our desires of the flesh. At those times, all that seems to count is our failure, and we forget all of our success and progress in putting on God's love. But God's love and forgiveness never fail us, and we should not be tempted to abandon the message of freedom and turn back to sin or turn back to rules and religion.

Today, as in the past, Christians often want to know what the terms of righteousness are so we can fulfill them by our own strength. The Spirit's power is an afterthought. We are metaphorically pushing our Christian car down the road without even using the gas that is the Spirit's power in us. The law gives us insight into knowing what is not love. The law tells us what the ancient Jewish culture, under God's direction, determined was good, evil, foolishness, and wisdom; yet the law is not the fuel source that makes us good on the inside. Only God's Spirit can do that.

So then, if we are not approaching the Bible looking for rules, how should we approach the Bible? One common mistake is taking New Testament passages as prescriptive passages for new ways to live when they are actually descriptions of what the new life in Christ looks like. This is best illustrated by the fruits of the Spirit in Galatians. It is a list of results of the Spirit's work in us, not a list of characteristics for Christians to work on. These passages are tools to let you know when we are getting it right—looking at the dashboard to see what your speed does not change your speed or make the car go faster or slower. Adjusting the fuel source through the pedal is what changes the car's speed. The Christian's fuel is the Holy Spirit, not the dashboard of potential rules we find in the New Testament.

Going down a highway in a car with the Spirit as our fuel is a great illustration of how to live this life of sanctification by the Spirit—living in Christ while guided by the Spirit powers our car and keeps us in the middle of the road. The Spirit does this by teaching us His truth and moving us to love without the law. On one side of the road is rebellion and hate, where one may indulge in evil, selfish, and hurtful acts. If we drive off this side of the road, we agree that the law is an effective tool to inform us of our distance from truth and love. Only God's Spirit and love can bring us back to the center of the road without throwing us off to the other side.

The other side of the road is religion, where one lives by the law to become sanctified. In religion, there is law, judgment, guilt, shame, and punishment. Religion is slavery to the law of sin and death, where good works become our righteousness and actually estrange us from the love of God. Again, only God's Spirit and love can bring us back to the middle of the road without sending us off the other side.

The means to control the vehicle and keep it centered on truth and love is the Spirit powering us to live Jesus' example of love. If we look at sin or religion, just as when we are driving a car, we will go the direction we look and fail to live by the Spirit in the center. Paul expresses this sentiment in his letter to the Romans, where he talks about being a slave to sin in chapter six, living by the law in chapter seven, and living by the Spirit in chapter eight. God wants us right in the middle of the highway living by His Spirit, learning the knowledge of salvation, and practicing the love of Jesus.

Some might say: *If I understand truth and love, why do I need a relationship with God?* Imagine that, as a toddler, we take a few steps without our parents, and then we run from them and fall. The love of our true father through the power of the Spirit is the amazing ingredient that keeps us from falling flat on our faces. We walk in God's love by the power of the Spirit and go on the journey of abundant life that God longs for us to take.

Our strength to live the abundant life in us is given by the Holy Spirit doing a work of love in our hearts out of His love for us. When we live by the Spirit, we do not avoid the rules of the world that we must obey, but the rules do not own and control us. As God's children, we are free. We do not use our freedom to indulge whatever behavior we want, but we use our freedom to put the truth of God and His love first, above all else.

This new life that we live is one where the Spirit indwells our hearts and plays multiple roles in our lives, most notably showing us the truth concerning salvation and sanctification. The knowledge that the Spirit is giving us has the power to set us free. Changing one's beliefs and perspectives can change one's whole life. Knowing about how much God loves us and does not condemn us can open up amazing doors to a new freedom. Knowing the harm of our behavior can give us the resolve and power to overcome bad behavior. When we know for certain the consequences of abusive behavior, we may find the power to commit to not abusing someone despite what they do to us. The power of the Spirit guiding us is in truth and love is life-changing. Even in our darkest times, the Spirit is there for us, praying for us when we are unable[239].

As we set the law aside and contemplate loving as Jesus loved, it

239 Romans 8:26-27

can be overwhelming and feel unattainable. When we are called to love with the love of Jesus, the Spirit does most of the restoring, and we do very little. We are sanctified by the power of the Spirit as we walk with Jesus. We do have a small part that we are given to do on our end. First, we must believe in and follow Jesus. Then, at the very least, we must choose to listen to the Spirit. There is still more we can do on our end to be involved in our sanctification. We choose to meet with God. We choose to seek love over law. And, we choose not to judge by the law but to emulate Christ's grace and love. The reality is that truth and love are poured into our hearts by the Spirit and are available for us if we choose to participate in His way of sanctification.[240]

Walking in love by the Spirit defines true success in this life. This is not even close to what the world deems as success. A truly fulfilled life comes from us growing in love, sharing God's love, and knowing the truth as best we can. Success grows with hope, endures with faith, and is demonstrated by love. Success is when a person truly knows that what matters most is their relationship with God, others, and themselves. The highest success is when a person is so overwhelmed by the love of God that they realize that no sacrifice is too great in order to have God's love and to share it with others.

With all the gifts of love and grace He has lavished us with, it seems it should be easy to love ourselves and others with His love and not indulge our old self, but this is still a struggle. In our resolve through God's love and through the power of the Holy Spirit, we are able to participate in eternal life, living life by His love in an environment that is filled with both suffering and delightful temptations for the old self. We will struggle, but God will grow us through our struggles: "For our struggle is not against flesh and blood, but against the rulers, against the

---

240 Romans 5:5; John 14:16-17

powers, against the world rulers of this darkness, against the spiritual forces of evil in the heavens" (Ephesians 6:12, NET). Our struggle is a struggle for the honest and kind version of ourselves that already exists with God. It is not a struggle in which we lose our place with God, but a struggle for what we will be like when we go to be with Him. Do not fear what can kill the body, but fear what can kill the soul, the part that will continue with you into eternity.[241]

As Christians, God's Spirit is helping us to experience this love and truth, bringing "love, joy, peace, patience, kindness, goodness, faithfulness, gentleness, and self-control" into our lives.[242] Although one may argue that people from all religions share these attributes, Christians are unique because God has poured out His love in their hearts through His Spirit. This power in us makes our experience different from the world's experience of truth, love, and other positive behaviors because it is empowered and directed by the Spirit and entirely based on sacrifice for the sake of loving others as Jesus did on the cross. His Spirit desires to give believers the gifts that make them kind, truthful, free, and abundantly alive. This lifelong journey to be perfected in God's love is the ultimate quest of the Christian's struggle, and "we are more than conquerors through Him who loved us" (Romans 8:37, NKJV). As we live out our daily lives, the Spirit guides us in His love, even in our trials. We are to "count it all joy" as we grow from suffering.[243] Living by the Spirit in His love and truth gives us hope for the future. Even in suffering, our faith in Christ increases, and our love for God, others, and ourselves grows.

God's Spirit in us wants to perfect us in the sacrificial love that He demonstrated on the cross. Demonstrating this cross-type of love in

---

241   Matthew 10:28
242   Galantians 5:22 (NET)
243   James 1:2 (NKJV)

our earthly state is leading us to emulate our heavenly state, which at salvation was made worthy of being in His loving presence. Sanctification is truly becoming the loving person God has already declared us to be. This loving state of sanctification is infinitely better than sanctification achieved by following a rule. It is a transformation that comes by faith and is manifested in our lives by His Spirit, teaching us to love as Jesus loved us.

CHAPTER 22

WHAT IS THE LOVE OF THE CROSS?

We have come to know love by this: that Jesus laid down his life for us; thus we ought to lay down our lives for our fellow Christians.

1 John 3:16 (NET)

Paul described this gift of love as a gift that is "way beyond comparison."[244] Jesus was the greatest example of love ever known when He, the creator of the universe, volunteered to die on the cross to save us from our sins and reconcile us to Him. With the shedding of His blood, Jesus established a new covenant relationship that only has one duty: "Love one another. Just as I have loved you" (John 13:34, NET). Emulating the love of Jesus is not done solely in our own strength. The willingness to lay "down our lives for our fellow Christians" does not come by following our knowledge of what we think is good and evil; it comes by the Spirit, and it flows out of our relationship with Jesus where we are taught to love as He has demonstrated for us.[245]

The commandment to love does not lead us back to the law, as some might argue. Paul says in his letter to the Romans that "[l]ove does no harm to a neighbor. Therefore, love is the fulfillment of the law" (Romans 13:10, NIV). One might simply ask, *Is not the law teaching us how*

1
2

to love our neighbor, and therefore one should follow the law and the prophets? It does not circle back around that way. While love may fulfill the requirements of the law, following the law does not fulfill the requirements of love. The new commandment is not that we should go back to living by a law to know how to love. Not at all. Instead, it is instructing us to love as Jesus loved, in which we will inevitably fulfill the requirements of the law and much more. The new covenant, with its only stipulation to love, replaced the covenant of the Mosaic law that Jesus completed and left hanging nailed the cross.

Having love as our new commandment and completely letting go of the old law, our modern rules, and altruisms to be good, frees us to live and love by the Spirit; it turns our world love-side-up. Our sanctification is based on loving as Jesus loved. It is in sharp contrast to moral laws or human virtues. The sacrificial love of the cross proclaims that being good does not make us loving; living in His love makes us good. Reducing suffering does not make us loving; loving with God's love reduces suffering. Working on the "fruits of the Spirit" in our lives does not make us more virtuous; living by the Spirit grows the "fruits of the Spirit" in us.[246] The transformation that the Spirit accomplishes in us is not done by our own striving to improve ourselves and the world around us. Exulting virtues without submitting to the supremacy of the sacrificial love of the cross and the Spirit's work can produce a proud person who appears to be morally righteous on the outside but on the inside does not have the love of God. Participating in the love of God through faith in Jesus and relying on the power of His Spirit—not on rules and good deeds—is when we truly exhibit His gift of love, even in the most trying of times.

Helping us to love is the main voice with which the Spirit speaks to

---

246 Galatians 5:18, 22-23

us on a daily, moment-by-moment basis. Since we are no longer under any law and we live by the Spirit, we are dependent on His voice to guide us in a love that sanctifies us more than any law ever could. While the law was to give us guidelines of what was not love, it was powerless to direct us in love on a relational basis where love is most needed. We need to know the right words to say and the right actions to take at the moment. For example, when a family member is angry at us, or should we give someone in need our last twenty dollars. We need to know how to share our time with our spouse and kids to communicate to them how valuable they are. Being guided by the Spirit to live by love is the process of sanctification that no law can come close to motivating us to do. Sin is no longer our focus or the problem; being perfected in God's love that was demonstrated on the cross by the power of His Spirit is now the path that we follow.

The Christian life is no longer about rules and obligations mandated for the believer in the form of a law because we are propelled by the Spirit pouring out love in our hearts. God's Spirit gives every believer the gift of love and steers us in the ways of God's love. God has done away with sin and condemnation according to rules, and we have entered a new path of life by the Spirit. When we allow God's Spirit to guide us in His love, we fulfill the pertinent aspects of the law without even trying. God is in us, and we are moving in His power as we love. At salvation, we are forgiven, made righteous, and loved; we do not need to do works of piety to sanctify ourselves except to love as Jesus loves in the movement of the Spirit.

Seeking to allow God to change us in His love is how we become more like what we will fully be in eternity. Eternal life is not just in the future but is the gift God has bestowed on us right here in the present. The more we realize and share His love, the more we experience eternity right now on this earth. We are living out eternity in this life in how we treat God and one another and in how we respond in love to life, in all its rewards and struggles.

Having established that our new commandment is to love one another, one might ask: What is love? To answer this question, we need to look no further than the cross, where Jesus laid down His life for us. I know that to be true, but how is that sacrificial love applied practically on a day-to-day basis? I do not have the opportunity to do such a heroic act as dying each day, but maybe giving hugs, doing dishes, saying kind words, and working hard to make ends meet are the acts of love Jesus is leading me to do in my life. God's love looks a little different for each one of us as the Spirit leads us.

The Oxford English Dictionary gives a profound definition of religious love:

[Love is] the benevolence and affection of God towards an

individual or towards creation; (also) the affectionate devotion due to God from an individual; regard and consideration of one human being towards another prompted by a sense of a common relationship to God[247].

I like the words "benevolence," "affection," and "devotion," and I love the phrase "regard and consideration of one human being towards another prompted by a sense of a common relationship to God." This is a beautiful description of the love a believer should have for God and others.

---

247 Oxford English Dictionary, 2020, https://www.oed.com/viewdictionaryentry/ Entry/110566

Here are some interesting and pertinent musings on love by some admired people of the past:

What is hell? I maintain that it is the suffering of being unable to love (Fyodor Dostoyevsky, *The Brothers Karamazov*).[248]

A purpose of human life, no matter who is controlling it, is to love whoever is around to be loved (Kurt Vonnegut, *The Sirens of Titan*).[249]

What is love but acceptance of the other, whatever he is (Anaïs Nin, *A Literate Passion: Letters of Anaïs Nin & Henry Miller*, 1932-1953).[250]

When people talk of love, they speak in terms of its application, its presence, and its absence. It is a quality of one's behavior that we know is either there or missing, but we find it difficult to quantify. Yet, love is not simply an uncontrollable force; it includes a decision to act that is voluntary.

I will give my best shot to define it, which will most likely fall short of the definition love deserves: Human love is truly wanting to know and value a person as they are. It is a deep desire to do what is best for someone and a sincere willingness to sacrifice to give someone what they need, even at one's own great loss. Human love is made possible by unconditional acceptance, based on one's willingness to embrace others

---

248 Popova, Maria, "What Is Love? Famous Definitions from 400 Years of Literary History," May 28th, 2020, https://www.brainpickings.org/2013/01/01/what-is-love/

249 Popova, "What Is Love?"

250 Popova, "What Is Love?"

as they are and set aside our urge to make them what we want them to be. It is a decision not to hold others' wrongs against them. Love is facilitated by genuinely considering others better than ourselves, and it is demonstrated in an attitude of what I can give, not what I can get.

I want to let Greg Boyd, PhD., pastor of Woodland Hills Church in Saint Paul, Minnesota, and professor at Bethel University, sum up the modern human effort to define love. This is found in his 2013 sermon entitled "Sociopath Religion":

> Enemy embracing, other oriented, self-sacrificial, non-violent love …ascribe[s] unsurpassable and unconditional worth to every other human being on the planet …instead of sacrificing them, we sacrifice ourselves for them. …The world is not capable of [this type of love]. To get this kind of love …surrendering your life to Abba Father and letting him download his character into your life—it's called the Holy Spirit. …We can't crank this one out on our own; our self-preservationist instincts …are too strong to will our way into this[251].

He describes love in an intense, powerful way that is challenging and inspiring. I also agree with his point that this love will only come to fruition by the power of the Holy Spirit.

The quintessential, authoritative, and informative treatise on love was written by the Apostle Paul almost two thousand years ago in his first letter to the Corinthians. It is an other-worldly description of love:

If I speak in the tongues of men or of angels, but do not have

---

251 Boyd, Greg, "Sociopath Religion," The Narrow Gate, July 3, 2013, https://you tu.be/-3sZr8IWbKs

love, I am only a resounding gong or a clanging cymbal. If I have the gift of prophecy and can fathom all mysteries and all knowledge, and if I have a faith that can move mountains but do not have love, I am nothing. If I give all I possess to the poor and give over my body to hardship that I may boast, but do not have love, I gain nothing. Love is patient, love is kind. It does not envy, it does not boast, it is not proud. It does not dishonor others, it is not self-seeking, it is not easily angered, it keeps no record of wrongs. Love does not delight in evil but rejoices with the truth. It always protects, always trusts, always hopes, always perseveres. Love never fails. But where there are prophecies, they will cease; where there are tongues, they will be stilled; where there is knowledge, it will pass away. For we know in part and we prophesy in part, but when completeness comes, what is in part disappears. When I was a child, I talked like a child, I thought like a child, I reasoned like a child. When I became a man, I put the ways of childhood behind me. For now we see only a reflection as in a mirror; then we shall see face to face. Now I know in part; then I shall know fully, even as I am fully known. And now these three remain: faith, hope and love. But the greatest of these is love.

1 Corinthians 13:1–13 (NIV)

In this great statement, Paul explains the necessity of love, what love is and is not, the primacy of love, the clarity of love, the maturity of love, and the eternality of love. When one sits and tries to define or explain love, he or she quickly finds out how extraordinary this passage is in portraying righteous and genuine love.

Love is a powerful, moving decision that is empowered by the Spirit, reasoned by our minds, and driven by our emotions—sometimes all at the same time. We watch movies about the loss of loved ones, and our hearts are pulled to emote for the story told. When we experience the reality of the loss of someone we love, we are more than devastated. Our hearts are moved when we hear of heroic acts of love—a person donating a kidney to save a life or a soldier diving on a grenade to protect their comrades. We smile when we see someone speak to a child in an uplifting way that changes the child's whole demeanor or even his or her life. At times, we are at a loss as to how to respond when a person does loving acts of kindness to us. They may give us a hand when we are down, buy us a meal for no apparent reason, or kindly overlook our inappropriate behavior and love us anyway. The Spirit inspires us to love beyond our human abilities. His inspiration to love is so powerful that one can look past all the roadblocks that others put up and choose to act in a way that brings benefit to the other, even if the cost is high to oneself.

While contemplating love, we may think of our mothers. They are one of the first experiences many of us have with love. It is a wonderful gift of love when a mother gives their child kind service and attention. Those who have worked with broken children that have no relationship with their mothers find themselves bewildered about the child's desire for their mothers' love. This is the case even when the mother is a fallen person who cannot or chooses not to love them.

A father's love is also desirable and impactful. It often comes in the form of gentle but firm teaching, correction, encouraging words, and an example of strength when we need it.

Parental love is not easy when parents are balancing their wills and desires with their obligations. They are dealing with careers, personal brokenness, failure, success, disillusionment, pride, and at times, physical ailments, including mental struggles. There are some big hurdles they must step over to be able to love. Perhaps, because love is so difficult to demonstrate at times, it is what makes their loving acts so meaningful. We desire someone to make a great sacrifice for us. It communicates deep into our souls how valuable we are. For many, that sacrificial person may have been our mom and dad, yet for all, that person is Jesus and His death on the cross.

Just in general, love can be exceedingly difficult to demonstrate in our day-to-day lives. All of us can be controlled by a desire for possessions, power, and physical attention. We want to be heard, to be important, to be safe, and sometimes to feel better than our neighbors. We can be driven to have correct politics, a respectable spiritual direction, and an admirable morality. It is sad how we seem to be constantly overwhelmed by our judgment of ourselves and others. We all have people that we feel we are better than, and we all have people that we feel are under us on the social ladder. In our own strength, we can fail to love, especially if we are using reasoned arguments and religious morals to prop ourselves up. We may defend our unloving actions by appealing to experts, emotions, and name-calling. We also may blame circumstances and other people for our lack of love instead of our own foolish, selfish behavior. Our pride and unwillingness to be humble can block the possibility of change in our lives. To become a loving person is no easy task: "There is no one righteous, not even one" (Romans 3:10, NIV).

It is sometimes easier to love those whom we do not know because we have no emotional strings attached to them. It may be hard to love our family, our spouse, or our siblings because of some relational distress from the past. It may be especially hard to love those who would criticize us or take advantage of our vulnerabilities. There is a certain extent when we are with strangers, where we can deny ourselves, which makes it easier to set our inhibitions aside and love with abandonment. Yet, staying fully engaged in our immediate lives and fully loving those around us with whom we have deep emotional attachments is the supernatural milieu the Spirit's love is made of.

To what extent are we called to love? Are we all eventually to be like Mother Teresa, who gave her whole life to serve and love the dying in Calcutta? Mother Teresa was able to focus on love and not sin. If she had let the idea of another's sin get in the way of her love, how could she love those who were clearly sinners? She was also able to set aside the enticements of the world, which enabled her to love without consideration for herself. Although each person's call to respond to the love of the cross may look different, it is the same call. How are you, as a unique individual, called to demonstrate the love of Jesus?

Just like Mother Tereasa, we must respond to God's call to love. First and foremost, we must learn to forgive and love on an individual level. In doing so, we learn how deep and complicated each individual is and how hard it is to love. Unfortunately, the more we love, the more people expect us to love. When someone who shows great love fails, they usually receive intense disappointment. The process of learning to love is developing the stability and the fortitude to exhibit and share love wisely and consistently. Little progress is made if we love immensely for a short time and are intolerable for the majority of our lives.

Love in some ways may seem like money, which can be used for beneficial or destructive causes. If it is used to control, manipulate, or gain for oneself, love can be destructive. I say this to help contemplate why God does not instantly make all Christians miraculously loving. Until we are ready, we cannot sustain the cost and responsibility of love. Love is the most precious commodity of life, yet it is one of the hardest gifts to manifest with authenticity and consistency. If we are not healed by the forgiveness and the love of Jesus, it may prove extremely difficult to handle such a great gift well.

The late president of Fuller Theological Seminary, Edward John Carnell, in his book *The Kingdom of Love and the Pride of Life*, looks at life from a child's perspective: "That a person is good when he is kind and truthful[252]." Carnell points out that, as a child, we are to be quick to forgive, especially if the person had the right intentions[253]. He wrote that there is a principle of "double fulfillment" involved in love[254]. There are two ways to love: open and direct (being kind and truthful) and indirect (failing at love but attempting to love with the best intentions). When we fail, our struggle to learn to love is more important than legal perfection. Love can be difficult, but through the power of God's Spirit in us, we grow more and more loving. In order to be good and be sanctified, we must make God's love our first priority. We must become humble and see the world as a child, making truth and love our highest priorities, and be quick to forgive. These simple practices are the key to enveloping our lives in God's love. It starts by us being a humble, moldable block of clay that God can shape into a beautiful and loving soul.

When we follow Jesus, the greatest gift the Spirit imparts to us is the gift of love.[255] The Spirit is actively teaching us to have love for the Father, one another, and ourselves.[256] Whatever we do with our lives is of no value if it is not done with an understanding of the supremacy of God's love. As His child, the most important and transforming truth <u>you can know </u>is what manner of the love the Father has lavished on

252 Carnell, Edward John Carnell, *The Kingdom of Love and the Pride of Life* (Grand Rapids, MI: Wm. B. Eerdmans, 1960), p. 17
253 Carnell, *The Kingdom of Love*, p. 130
254 Carnell, *The Kingdom of Love*, p. 130
255 1 Corinthians 13
256 1 John 2:15-17

us.[257] *There is nothing you can do to make God love you more, and there is nothing you can do to make God love you less.* You have all of His love, and it is not conditional on anything[258]. Life for the believer is a process of learning to live in light of the love poured out in us.[259] For "[i]f we love one another, God resides in us, and his love is perfected in us" (1 John 4:12, NET)

257 1 John 3:1
258 Romans 8:38-39
259 Romans 5:5

CHAPTER 23

THE LOVE OF THE CROSS IS FORGIVENESS

Then Peter came to him and said, "Lord, how many times must
I forgive my brother who sins against me? As many as seven
times?" Jesus said to him, "Not seven times, I tell you, but
seventy times seven!"

Matthew 18:21–22 (NET)

I stood with my mother, who had recently suffered from a stroke,
gazing over my father's casket, holding back the tears enough to ask
her if she forgave him. Even though he deeply loved her, he was verbally
and physically abusive to her most of their marriage. She nodded her
head and spoke a faint noise resembling a "yes," indicating she forgave
him, or at least I thought she did. Some aspects of my life were hard to
face because I had held onto my unforgiveness for my abusive father.
My moment with mom at the casket was a step in the right direction
of forgiveness. It seems that when we have been hurt and are impacted
deeply by sin, we have a hard time forgetting and forgiving. Walking in
God's love requires us to engage in constant and great forgiveness.[260]

There are generally plenty of people in our daily interactions that
we need to forgive, and that fact is fairly easy to be aware of. It is a
little more difficult to recognize and admit when we need forgiveness

---

260 Luke 17:4

from others. My father hurt me, my mother, and my family with his violence and anger. My mother let me down countless times. They were merely the first. I have been talked about, lied about, taken advantage of, used for my skills, and even rejected at times by my family, friends, and church. I find myself holding on to the trespasses and not forgiving and forgetting. I keep a record of wrongs. *Maybe I will forgive them if they ask me just right*, I often think. It is hard to see that sometimes I may be the one who has committed the wrong and needs to be forgiven.

Transgressions affect us and change us. Unforgiveness amplifies the effect and change by feeding our resentment, judgment, and anger. It is like an old ripped-up, threadbare, dirty coat we carry around for protection. Even though it has no benefit, we feel like we have to keep it for when life gets too uncomfortable. We cannot throw away the worthless coat because it makes us feel safe. Lack of forgiveness, unfortunately, can play a significant role in who we are and can become part of our identity. If we feel someone is trying to hurt us, we can reach into a pocket of that old, ragged coat and find past grievances to either block them or injure them first. Letting go is extremely hard. Keeping that old coat of unforgiveness can lead to our destruction, and if we are not careful, it could kill us. That coat represents the loneliness, self-protection, fear, and vengeance that is in our hearts.

I would define forgiveness as the act of agreeing to let go of our hostility towards someone who has wronged us and a willingness to accept the destruction that the wrong behavior has caused. That is an extremely difficult task to do and not humanly possible in all cases.

Jesus wanted us to have a loving and full relationship with those we are close to, our neighbors, and even our enemies. Without grace and forgiveness from all parties involved, loving and forgiving relationships are extremely rare. When someone offends me, I have to make a choice to forgive them or disassociate myself from them. If I do neither, I enter into an unfair relationship which can quickly evolve into an abusive situation. In order to stay in unfair relationships, we must find ways to cope with the unbalances. Through unforgiveness, we may attempt to punish others for what they did, and obviously, we want to protect ourselves. Forgiveness is especially not easy when it is tied to an intimate person in our lives— someone with whom we are vulnerable and who can hurt us over and over again. A wise, self-protecting person would not foolishly let themselves be vulnerable again and continue to be abused. So, we are sometimes caught between abuse and the ability to forgive. Unfortunately, without forgiveness, it is hard to overcome the destruction of bitterness, condemnation, and alienation one experiences. This does not mean we should play Jesus and surrender ourselves to be abused and killed, but maybe there is somewhere in between total self-protection and total sacrifice where we can facilitate forgiveness and healthy relationships. To have a relationship, we must take the risk and forgive.

One of the hardest examples of forgiving and remaining in a relationship, even for a believer, is in the case of adultery. In our own strength, the reality is that some forgiveness and reconciliation may not seem possible. It is important to know that forgiveness is different from reconciliation, and while a restored relationship may not be on the table, there still should be forgiveness and letting go of hostilities. Holding on to unforgiveness at times hurts the victim more than the perpetrator. In the case of adultery and abuse, the consequences are great. There are emotional, trust, betrayal, and imagination issues that can explode like a nuclear bomb and sometimes even cause physical consequences. Yet, some are able to forgive and even be reconciled.

Restoring a healthy relationship is no less than a miracle after a deep betrayal of trust, such as an act of adultery. When the offender has sorrow for having wronged the one that they love, what great torture, pain, and fear of loss they experience, and what great destruction they feel. When the offended forgives them and chooses not to hold their offense against them,[261] oh, what a relief and joy they are overwhelmed with. At best, the forgiver will even forget about it, or at the very least, they are not going to hate the offender for the offense. Then comes the personal depression and feelings of inadequacy because the forgiveness was undeserved. They may struggle to live with themselves because of what they have done.

In the process of forgiveness, does the hurt party decide on a price to be extracted for the transgression? Does the offender extract payment from themselves? Will there ever be the same trust, the same love that existed before, or the same paradise of abandonment? No, and that is a sad fact of life. Things settle down, but each party will have trouble forgetting the betrayal. Things are not the same, and they never will be. A trust has been broken, and nothing will change that. Life with that person begins a new chapter where they grow together and continue to learn to love and survive the scars.

What I have tried to convey is that relationships and forgiveness are messy. All of our actions have consequences, and forgiveness is not a way to rid ourselves of all or even some consequences. Instead, forgiveness is a way to love in the midst of the consequences. It is a way in, not a way out.

Forgiveness with the intent of restoration is a willingness to accept the effects of the trespass and a willingness to be vulnerable again. It is a decision to continue to love despite the risk and loss to ourselves and

---

261 Luke 11:4

others[262]. When one forgives, they accept the destruction that another's trespass has caused, try to move past it, and attempt to restore the relationship; it is a decision to go against all instinctive reactions that demand self-protection. We naturally want to flee or fight when we are personally hurt, not forgive and love. Even with total forgiveness, the consequences of one's offenses do not go away. But God can make us more loving even in our sin by salvaging the unintended positive part of our wrongfully acquired characteristics and weaving them into the tapestry of who we are.

In the worst of circumstances, only love could be powerful enough to motivate one to be willing to take on the magnitude of the destruction caused by the offending person in order to have a relationship with them. This is the type of love that is found at the cross; it is not trivial and does not lend itself to abuse. It is not only complete love and total forgiveness but also restoration into a right relationship with God through the Spirit. We are held tight in the arms of a Father who loves us, never harms us, and wants what is best for His children. Sometimes it is hard having this great relationship and knowing all of our earthly relationships will fall short.

What does this selfless forgiveness look like for us? It is demonstrating unconditional, sacrificial love as our motive and a willingness to be vulnerable for the sake of loving others.[263] This is a delicate balance where we must intently seek the guidance of the Spirit because we still need boundaries to survive. They are extremely healthy and effective at protecting ourselves and others, yet the Spirit can lead us to open up at times, even though it may be dangerous. Our ability to forgive is something that God grows in us as we know more of His forgiveness,

---

262 Ephesians 4:31-32

263 Matthew 10:38-39

love, and truth. To reach the level of turning the other cheek, we would have to be steeped in God's love so deeply that we realize physical pain is no justification to not love. Forgiveness is what Jesus demonstrated on the cross and what He asks us to emulate. Paul describes love as keeping "no record of wrongs."[264] This one act of love and forgiveness would easily solve most marriage problems! This seemingly simple yet immensely difficult act cannot be done without receiving our own complete forgiveness from Jesus first. When we embrace God's love, it moves us to forgive, forget, and restore relationships; and it moves us to forgive ourselves. We learn to forgive our brothers and sisters, despite the fact that they have hurt us badly and will do it again. The Holy Spirit can work this miracle in our hearts and minds if we let Him.

Jesus modeled this great forgiveness when He took on the magnitude of all of our destruction upon Himself on the cross in order to forgive us. He provided the example and the means for us to restore our relationship with Him and others: "But God demonstrates his own love for us in this: While we were still sinners, Christ died for us" (Romans 5:8–10, NIV). Jesus suffered on the cross while we were still actively causing destruction. The love that Jesus showed us on the cross can never be repaid nor taken for granted. He died to take away all of our individual sins by taking on our deserved consequences upon Himself.[267] He paid the price that we would extract from ourselves, others would demand from us, and the law required. This sacrificial love, demonstrating the means of forgiveness, brought a new reality of a relationship with God. It is to be remembered each time we take communion.[266] This forgiveness we receive from God is the greatest source of our ability to forgive ourselves and others. The

---

264 1 Corinthians 13:5

265 1 John 3:5

266 1 Corinthians 11:24

more we understand and receive God's complete forgiveness as the Spirit transforms us, the more we are empowered to share God's gift of forgiveness. There is great power to love and freedom from our past burdens in forgiveness.

Christ's forgiveness transformed the world by demonstrating that real change, which leads to the right relationships, comes through sacrificial love and forgiveness. This change does not come through the typical method of demonstrating that we are in the right, enacting self-preservation and self-protection through the use of power and violence. That is the opposite of forgiveness and love[267]. When we cling to our rightness, it accentuates the consequences of people's trespasses against us. We often depend on rules (naming sins with power to enforce compliance), self-preservation (a priority to protect one's safety and comfort), and enforcement (violence for non-compliance) to justify our unforgiveness and to achieve justice for the wrong that has been done. Jesus revealed this common practice of people to be an insufficient and sometimes dreadful solution[268]. This way of treating one another was supplanted by the way of forgiveness and love at the cross. Christ demonstrated the superior and victorious change that came through Him suffering on the cross. Showing unconditional love, He was willing to pay the price for something that He did not do. Jesus took away our sins, giving us complete forgiveness and a restored relationship with Him[269].

Christians forgive out of gratitude for what has been done for them; it is not out of fear of punishment as it was for those under the law. Matthew, in his gospel, writes about a king who forgives a great debt. The receiver of that debt turns around and then refuses to forgive someone

---

267 Romans 8:3-14
268 Colossians 2:13-15
269 John 3:14-15

who owes him money. Jesus describes the consequences for the man who would not forgive:

> And his lord, moved with anger, handed him over to the torturers until he should repay all that was owed him. My heavenly Father will also do the same to you, if each of you does not forgive his brother from your heart.
>
> Matthew 18:34–35 (NASB)

This parable resonates with all of us. We can look at it in regard to forgiveness in three ways.

First, we are comforted when the great debt is forgiven and then immediately incensed at the thought that the person forgiven would not forgive another for a lesser debt.

Second, while those without Jesus go to a place of waiting when they die where they will be handed over to the torturers to suffer for their cruelty and unforgiveness in this world, we as believers will not, so this parable applies to us in a different way. It asks the question: If we have been forgiven so much, why would we still not forgive others freely?

There is also a third and deeper point. Jesus is demonstrating how being forgiven does not make everyone a better person. Forgiveness did not work in the wicked man's life in the parable because it is not a magic wand; it only fully works for those who believe and choose to follow Jesus.

God's Spirit and the Son's forgiveness work hand and hand to transform us. We know that the goal of God's love and grace on the cross was to make us loving on the inside; it was not just a coupon to remove our debts. I hope as we humbly live in the unconditional love and forgiveness of God and, filled with His Spirit, we are compelled to extend that love and forgiveness to others. The more we receive, the more we are willing and able to love and forgive beyond our natural ability.

Permanent forgiveness from God is an amazing promise for us as believers[270], and knowing we will not be judged for our failures is extremely important in the realm of forgiving ourselves and others[271]. Still, on a practical note, it may be impossible to fully feel forgiven by God or others if our past failures can be brought up against us. With God, knowing He has completely erased all our sins, gives us freedom from our past. With an individual, it takes a miracle for the offended person to forget and to forgive others for the damage that has been done to them. It takes no less than a miracle for us to forget and to forgive ourselves for the damage we have done to our own person[272]. That miracle comes in the form of Christ's complete forgiveness; the suffering and the cost He went through on the cross to provide that miracle for all of us says it all[273].

As we meditate and are humbled by what Jesus did, it seems foolish to hold on to the sins that others have committed against us, and it seems ungrateful to hold against ourselves the bad decisions we have made because He has done so much more to forgive us by comparison. When we allow His Spirit to enter us and fill us, we are able to wash away the judgment and condemnation in our minds and hearts; past, present, and future. Through forgiveness, we are able to renew our hearts with His unending love.

---

270 Psalm 103:12
271 John 5:24
272 John 13:34
273 John 19:1-30

CHAPTER 24

THE PRACTICAL APPLICATION OF SALVATION GIVEN BY THE CROSS

And these three remain: faith, hope, and love. But the greatest of these is love.

1 Corinthians 13:13 (NET)

It would be nice if, at this point in the book, I broke out that easy button again and explained how all is fixed with a three-step process. I do want to try to put an understanding of salvation and sanctification together for you, but it must come with a caveat. This world is broken, and we are far from perfect. Even if we had the perfect plan and detailed instructions on exactly how to follow them and what to do with every variable, there would be no guarantees. The truth is that we are all on different journeys with varying degrees of understanding the truth of our salvation. Sadly, tragedy seems to strike as often as a triumph, and for many, life can feel like a mundane, non-eventful existence. Even worse, for a significant number, they never even get a chance to even take a breath. Consequently, any idea I give you about the process must come with the understanding that it will help as much as it is true and applies to your life. A large portion of any growth you may experience is between you and God.

Still, I will attempt to explain how we live the abundant life Jesus

241

promised. It comes in such a different way than we think. It is not riches and glory on this earth but an existence much better. It is not found by cherishing worldly ways of pleasure and comfort but by cherishing sacrificial love amongst each other and an intimate relationship with God.

To have abundant life, it is of first importance to understand the immediate eternal life given at salvation, how much God loves us and how He came to take away our sins, which removes all condemnation. These three truths bring freedom which can lead to abundant life in Christ. They bring about the possibility to live without sin ruling our lives. This new freedom is different from what many believers have been taught about how Christianity is lived out. While they follow salvation by grace, they are instructed to embark on a religion that advocates for sanctification based on following rules; rather than understanding that sanctification is to live worthy in His love.[274] The abundant life of Jesus does not come through our own effort to follow the rules, but it comes by following the Spirit in complete grace, forever forgiven of our sins, and without written law to condemn us.

Sanctification is the process of learning to love, which leads to this abundant life. It is a personal journey that the Lord takes His followers on. Jesus moves us closer to His truth and His love by the power of the Holy Spirit. Some start far away and only move a little, while others seem to touch heaven. Life is not the same for everyone, it is not equal, and we definitely would not call it fair. If we see this journey as arriving somewhere, we have missed the point. It is a personal journey about becoming who God wants us to be, specifically, attempting to know a portion of His truth, exhibiting as much heavenly love as possible, and seeking His purpose for our lives on earth.

274 Galatians. 1:6-7

I have written about how life can be dark at different times in all our lives. In that darkness is where hope springs to life. We should not live in the possibilities of despair; we need to reside in the hope of a great ending. Even in the darkest times, seeing hope in a situation makes it brighter. It is amazing and inspirational to look into the eyes of a beautiful soul who has their hope in Jesus, even when they know their days are numbered with cancer. Most of us are not facing such immediate tragedy, but we still have our own battles of negativity. We cultivate hope by trusting in the best possible outcome with the Spirit comforting us and not dwelling on the worst scenario we can conjure up in our minds. We have a choice, to live with hope for the best or to live with the fear of the unknown. Life has bad days, but we have hope which lets us know that bad days do not have to win.

Another gift God has given us, in addition to hope, is faith. I often contemplate the darkness of thinking that this short life is all there is. What would we have if we had no God, no afterlife, no self beyond the chemicals and electrical signals in a structure of flesh and bones? I have believed in God my whole life, except for flirting with the idea of abandoning Him when I was fourteen, so it is difficult for me to conceive of a world where He does not exist. If this short existence is all there is, I think I would be left with little reason for a motivated life that includes kindness and productivity.

Faith in Jesus goes beyond the reality of a God and proposes a God who loves us and wants to dwell in us and be in a relationship with us. He is calling us to be His friend and promises to walk with us in our struggles and successes. He loves us as a parent who would never compromise in their love for their child. He is a God that would sacrifice Himself to have a relationship with us. The power of knowing that great love and understanding that a great and loving God is in control lets us know that it is all going to be alright because He is in charge.

And last, the most important gift is the love that the Spirit pours out into our hearts. Without love, a meaningful life is difficult to come by. What is the purpose of experiencing life if we have no one to share it with? Love tells us that others are as important as ourselves and are worthy of our sacrifice. Love tells us to give and not take. Love tells us to listen and tell the truth. Love is the deep moving force that powers our life, and without it, our lights go out. How do we find it, how do we show it, and how do we keep it? These are very difficult questions for everyone, but for the Christian, we have a solace: the Spirit is guiding us to exhibit unconditional and sacrificial love as Jesus did, with an eternal goal to have His love shown on the cross perfected in us.

To end this chapter, I want to tell you about a man named Kurt, whom I was fortunate to know. The following is a portion of the sermon I wrote for his funeral (revised this format):

I enjoyed knowing Kurt in his last couple of years. He came to "Bible Lounge" at the Sit-N-Bull Saloon, a Bible study at a local bar in the neighborhood. Kurt would show up on occasion, and I also had chatted with him at church.

At the time I knew him, he had an abundance of health problems, lingering trouble with the legal system, and still dabbled with drugs. He would attend Bible study consistently for a while and then suddenly stop coming; that is how he was. He cycled between pulling himself up out of a hole and then falling right back in the same hole.

During one of his downturns, we were able to visit him in the hospital and prayed for his future. At that time, I got to see a glimpse of Kurt's relationship with God. Kurt spoke of his love for his son and how he wished he could have done more for him. He told me about his daughters and how he cared for them and tried to be a part of their lives as much as he could. Kurt loved his mom and dad and appreciated all they had done for him and how they had believed in him. He wanted to help them somehow in return.

I remember vividly how much Kurt's mom and dad loved him. It will always be an inspiration to me and remind me of God's love. When they adopted Kurt as an infant, they committed to loving him, and they never stopped. Even when he made it extremely difficult, they never gave up on him.

Kurt, in all his troubles, was amazingly resilient and still had a great time with those he was around. In the hospital, he was positive and grateful to be alive. Kurt tried to remain positive and hopeful for what was coming next, yet most of the possible paths in his life had somewhat bleak outcomes and seemed to telegraph struggle and despair.

We all struggle. We all are sinners. We all make mistakes. The question is: "Do you know what Kurt knew?" Jesus paid the price for his mistakes. Kurt knew who Jesus was and what Jesus did for him. Since Kurt knew Jesus, he was no longer a sinner; he was a saint. Jesus made him clean, and in the same way, he can make all of us clean. Mathew 8 reads:

After he came down from the mountain, large crowds followed him. And a leper approached, and bowed low before him, saying, "Lord, if you are willing, you can make me clean." He stretched out his hand and touched him saying, "I am willing. Be clean!" Immediately his leprosy was cleansed.

Matthew 8:1–3 (NET)

Lepers were so unclean that no one would dare to touch them. They were required to do the ancient equivalent of wearing a mask and social distancing. Cultures considered them not only cursed with sickness but also cursed with an evil, sinful life, as well. They were outcasts from society and left to die. Jesus reached down and touched the outcast and made him clean. The man went from sinner to saint with one touch.

Kurt told me he knew Jesus had saved him but that he still failed continually and made mistakes. Obviously, if he had a chance to do things over, he would have chosen a different path. He and I had a great talk about how God could use him to bless others from the experiences he had overcome, which was a challenging prospect to him. Although he could not overcome his struggle, he continued to grow as a believer. Weeks before his death, he completed five Bible study books, which gave his family great comfort in knowing his future.

John 5 says:

Very truly I tell you, whoever hears my word and believes him who sent me has eternal life and will not be judged but has crossed over from death to life.

John 5:24 (NIV)

We know that physically Kurt passed from life to death on August 4th. We also know that when he believed in Jesus, he passed from death to life. He had eternal life in him at that very moment. He did not have to wait till his passing to be with Jesus, and neither do we. The person we knew as Kurt didn't actually die; he merely changed rooms. He's no longer sitting around in our living room; he's in God's living room, sitting in the presence of Jesus. Someday I'll be in God's living room relaxing there with Kurt. I'm there in spirit now, but someday I'll be there in the flesh.

Kurt was not and will not be judged for his wrongs because he is forgiven according to Christ's work on the cross. Christ took away all his sins and has smiled at all his goodness. Kurt believed in Jesus, and it was credited to him as righteousness. As you see all the wonderful pictures of Kurt up on the screen, you realize how blessed his life was, except for a few bad decisions. That is the same for all of us. We're not any better as far as failure goes. We all have a few bad decisions hidden in our lives. Believing in Jesus changes us all from sinner to saint despite our transgressions, as it did Kurt. All who have received the forgiveness and eternal life that Jesus gives will someday rejoin Kurt in God's living room to hang out with Jesus.

This understanding of how Kurt was saved, even though he had done so much wrong and in his best attempts could not correct his life, is an example of one of the main driving forces that leads me to challenge some of the traditional ideas about salvation and sanctification. If I ever venture back to believing in sanctification by works, I would have trouble explaining where that leaves Kurt and where that leaves me in terms of our salvation. Where does that leave all the great Christian men and women who served God with their lives yet committed horrific evils later in their lives? Where does that leave the thief on the cross?

I know that there will always be people that say they cannot let go of rules and cannot take what I am saying about the end of the law to be right. I sat with a seminary student who was twenty years younger than me to discuss Christianity. I must say he was more intelligent than I am, and his biblical and theological studies were fresh on his mind. He had great plans to write a book about the fall in Genesis. Sadly, we talked past each other for four long hours. In the fifth hour, I began to listen and understand what he was saying, and he understood some of what I was saying. He did not agree with how I presented sanctification, but he looked directly at me and made this amazing statement: "I really want what you're saying to be true, but I don't believe it is." I hope that you, as a dedicated reader, are close to understanding what I am writing after reading this far in the book. I want to write to you what I said to him: "It is true! God is that good, and he loves us so much that he died to set us free." If you can get a glimpse of the freedom He has given us, me writing and you reading this book have all been worth it.

CHAPTER 25

HOW DOES THE CROSS CHANGE THE WAY WE PRAY?

Pray without ceasing.

1 Thessalonians 5:17 (NKJV)

So far, I have written about God's love for us and the love between humans, but what about our love for God. The image of the Savior on the cross and the image of God as our Father demonstrates and describes what it means for God to love us, but what demonstrates our love for Him?

There are many ways to direct our love to God. I feel loving towards Him when I experience curiosity and admiration for all of His creation and a reverence for the mysteries I do not understand or like. Loving God can be shown in the acts of praising and worshiping His greatness, acknowledging His love for me, sincerely wanting to know Him, and being willing to follow Him wherever He leads. It also entails being purposefully and steadfastly devoted to not turn away but to seek Him with all my heart. I love God, especially, by studying His message given to humanity through the ancient Jewish prophets and the New Testament writers. In addition, I demonstrate my love for God when I love my fellow humans who were created in His image, knowing that He loved them so much that He died for them.

The most prevalent act of love for God is to talk to God in prayer.

As we learn about and experience God, we are encouraged and inspired to increasingly pray. Loving the Father is done in a relationship with Him. As we believe in and follow the Son, we are comforted and guided by the Spirit, and this closeness is enhanced by our prayer. When we pray, we are simply talking to God as we would our earthly father, we are talking to Jesus as we would our brother, and we are talking to the Spirit as we would our mother; it can be any of these and much more. As Adam walked with God in the cool of the day, so should we do the same, now that we have the Spirit restored in us.[275] God does not force us to pray. He desires us to pray as a spouse desires the presence of his or her mate, as a father and mother desire conservation with their child, as a friend desires the companionship of a kindred spirit, and as a brother or sister desires to be with a sibling. Oh, how much better our relationships are when we communicate and spend time with each other. Prayer echoes that sentiment.

The most common question about prayer from a younger Christian is, "How does God talk to us?" God has spoken clearly in His Word, and yet He has more to say in subtle ways in His answers to prayers. We experience His answers in His inner nudges, in His gentle whisper, in the moments of awakenings He gives us, in the circumstances He brings in our lives, in our realizations of His goodness and love, in our experiences of the image of God in others, and in seeing God through our acts of love and service. He speaks in innumerable untold ways to us.

As we pray, simply talking to God in our own way is a great way to get started. The Lord's prayer is also of benefit in guiding our prayers:

After this manner therefore pray ye: Our Father which art in

---

275 Genesis 3:8

heaven, Hallowed be thy name. Thy kingdom come. Thy will be done on earth, as it is in heaven. Give us this day our daily bread. And forgive us our debts, as we forgive our debtors. And lead us not into temptation, but deliver us from evil: For thine is the kingdom, and the power, and the glory, for ever. Amen.

Matthew 6:9–13 (KJV)

This prayer is not a "Lord give me" prayer; it is a "Lord thank You" and "Lord help me" prayer. It is full of amazing wisdom and depth and contains the guidance to pray for our foundational needs in life that will help make our life truly abundant. God is not a magician in the sky who does tricks when we pray; He is our Father who gives us what we need and even want with respect to His greater plan, which is to perfect us in His love.

The prayer begins with "Our Father." With these two words, the Lord institutes family as first importance. Being in His family and knowing the importance of ours and our church is foundational. This is a phrase of relationship designating our position as a child adopted into the family of God. We are allowed as believers to call Him "Abba," like "Dad" in English[276]. We can approach Him in any way, at any time, knowing we will get the response of a Father, sometimes listening, sometimes instructing, sometimes correcting, always loving.

Next, we speak to the truth of His glorious residence. "Who art in heaven." God has His majestic place in heaven, and He has also come to live inside of us. We need to know and live by His Spirit inside of us. His Spirit shows us how to love on a daily, moment-by-moment basis. As God led the Israelites with a cloud by day and fire by night, He now

---

276 Romans 8:15 (NIV)

resides in us and wants to lead us. As God's glory filled the temple in Jerusalem, so He is in us, comforting us, guiding us, protecting us, loving us, and filling us with His glory.

We then attribute to God the glory He deserves: "Hallowed be thy name." Love and respect for God put us in a state of humility, knowing that it is in His greatness and not our own that this life is lived. This is also the wow factor! We are talking to the creator of the universe, the author of all the beauty, the designer of these amazing, intricate, miraculous machines we call life, and the engineer of this planet and solar system, which is perfect for this life. Nothing we worship or serve compares to His unsurpassable greatness. From Him, we are given natural gifts beyond comprehension, and we are given special gifts, especially the gift of salvation, which is being in a relationship with Jesus. Many of the gifts we receive are experienced as a result of His power being unleashed by prayer.

In our worship of God, we are to have no other gods before Him, and we are to make no graven images of other gods and set them before us. We are commanded to make no effort to worship other gods. Humans have gone so far as to sacrifice other human beings, including babies and children, to images of their gods. They also have worshipped other gods in a way that includes sexual perversion, drugs, and horrible treatment of other human beings. These practices are reasons God has allowed the deserved destruction on people groups, including the Israelites, at times. We, as His children, walk in love, freedom, and grace, but we also walk in hallow for Him by honoring His name. We walk in a way that brings Him glory and not shame.

In saying the phrase "Thy kingdom come." We know to seek His kingdom of love, truth, and reconciliation first before our own. This principle applies to all aspects of our lives. It can be seen when we think of a loving marriage. A husband seeks the success of his wife over his own success, and the wife seeks success for her husband over her own as well. They seek each other's good over their own and seek God's kingdom first together.

For the longest time, I shied away from the phrase "Thy the kingdom come." I thought of the terrors of tyrannical, earthly, religious kingdoms that claimed to be from God yet committed so many atrocities. Often when someone refers to God's kingdom, they are referring to their idea of His kingdom and attribute it to God. I am no longer leery, and I can fully embrace the phrase "Thy kingdom come" because I know what it means. It means us sharing, with others around us, the love and truth that God places in our hearts. It means leading others to be reconciled to God so they can experience His truth and love.

God's kingdom has nothing to do with people's priorities of social justice, righteous altruisms, reducing suffering, or any religious practices promoted as bringing the kingdom of God. His kingdom is God pouring out His love in our hearts to such a level that it spills out of us uncontrollably. It has to do with all the blessings and love He has in store for us as we are reconciled to Him. While bringing God's kingdom of love and truth, we may join some of the earthly causes that others desire, but they are not what drives us. We are driven by the Spirit who manifests Himself in our lives by increasing our love for God, our neighbor, and ourselves. When one lives in this way, there are no rules or obligations that would make us better than what His love can do in us. We do not move by human ideas of good and evil, but we are moved by the Wind which is in us, at the beckoning of our King.

The phrase "Thy will be done" is sometimes comforting when we feel out of control and threatening when we believe that we control the reins of our lives. Is this a Buddhist prayer of subjugation of our entire wills? I think not. This is a prayer of knowledge that God has a beautiful destiny for each one of us, and we participate in the unfolding of that destiny. We join God in discovering this destiny and our purposes in this life. We have a heavenly call to bring His love and truth to every aspect of our lives, especially to our earthly purpose, whether a farmer, a lawyer, or a pastor. One of the most loving acts of service we can do for ourselves and others is to discover and live out our earthly purpose and performing it well.

Our will and decisions about this earthly purpose change and shape our future. God is not sitting idle while we try to get our lives right–sometimes succeeding and other times failing badly. He is participating with us, shaping our future into something better with each step we take. We choose to seek His will in this walk of life, knowing that He seeks our best and wants us to cultivate the love that is in our hearts. We can rest–knowing that our destiny is in His hands, and we can trust God to work it out with us in His time—knowing that He seeks what is best for us. Scripture says: "Seek ye first the kingdom of God, and his righteousness; and all these things shall be added unto you" (Matthew 6:33, KJV).

Our earthly purpose is extremely important to discover because it is a key component in our ability to love others. If the farmer did not plant the seed, everyone would starve. Even though it is highly valued, we still need to be willing to set aside our earthly purpose for the sake of loving others around us as He leads us. We balance our heavenly allegiance to God's kingdom purpose, to love, led by the Spirit, with our earthly purpose to love, led by our work.

We seek to see God's purposes fulfilled "[o]n earth as it is in heaven." This is an understanding that we are walking with eternal life in us from the very moment we accept Christ, and we are bringing eternal life to our lives and to those around us. We are being perfected in His love so that, when we go to be with Him, we will have succeeded in becoming the same loving person on earth that we are pre-destined to be in heaven. Bringing God's love to this world through our actions is bringing His kingdom of love to our lives and to the world around us, as it is in heaven.

I love the phrase, "Give us this day our daily bread." How much do we pray that our future needs are met? We desire that the Lord gives us more than enough so we will have a certain future. When our prayers are about tomorrow, how do we even know God is answering our prayers? Praying for little things each day is an amazing test of faith, and it puts us in a position where we are depending on God and looking for His immediate answers—answers that build our faith each day as He provides our daily needs. Why do we need safety and comfort in the future when we have a God who provides our needs for us each day?

Greed, comfort, future security, and pride in our success all take us away from simply being content with our daily bread. In a perfect world, we would only keep what we need and give all else away. Clearly, we have obligations to love others—like family—in our lives, so we have to respond with a balanced love for all, a love with them in mind. Oftentimes it is only by the Spirit that we find that balance. I imagine our relationship with God to be more fulfilling if, moment by moment, we walked with God by faith, living each day trusting God to provide for our needs.

"Forgive us our debts as we have forgiven our debtors" calls us to walk in forgiveness. Unforgiveness will destroy our lives. Seek to give and receive forgiveness as much as you can. Forgiveness and graciousness are key to having a joyful life. We have complete forgiveness in Christ. There is no condemnation for the believers because we have already passed from death to life and are given eternal life at salvation.

Christ forgave us; He took on the consequences of our sin for us. In fact, Christ forgave everyone and died for everyone. Each individual you meet is someone Christ died for.[277] We are all equal in God's love. Knowing the forgiveness and grace Jesus extended to us, we ought to extend the same to others. Jesus took on our suffering, so we should be willing to take on another's suffering. When you forgive someone, you are taking on the consequences of their sin. The evil they committed broke something, and you will either avoid the brokenness or embrace it. Avoiding the suffering hurts us, and embracing it hurts as well. There is no way not to suffer from sin because evil just plain hurts. Forgiveness can take that hurt and make the best of it. As Christ forgave our debts, let us forgive others and also pray that others would forgive us.

We pray that God would "[l]ead us not into temptation but deliver us from evil." Of course, a good God is not going to lead us into evil, but this is a great reminder and plea for us to avoid evil in our lives and not to do evil to others. Evil, either way, will quickly destroy us. Do not be the doer of evil towards others, and pray that God would shield you from being the recipient of others' evil deeds. As believers, we cannot sin in the sense of being separated from God or by breaking the law of Israel, but we can do evil and great harm to ourselves and others. As the verse implies, great harm can also be done to us. When one gets older, we learn to avoid potentially dangerous situations and highly tempting ones, as well. But for some, engaging in their life demands vulnerability, and they need this prayer even more so. Still, in the sanctuary of our private room, all sorts of evil can be committed, so are we ever actually safe? Evil can come from anywhere. This is a serious prayer for treacherous times. We need to be delivered from evil.

Keeping us from temptation and delivering us from evil is not solely

---

3

about how we treat ourselves and one another but also, and maybe more importantly, how we treat God. While we love and respect others and their beliefs, one must not let themselves be put in situations where they revere other gods. This can be a vicarious road to walk. The Old Testament is full of catastrophe as a result of the Israelite's reverence and worship of other gods.

I had a dream about a friend making a garden in my backyard that was peaceful in every way. Then one day, he began drawing strange circles and burning incense in them, which I felt was odd. Finally, he began bowing prostrate in worship, and I had to speak up about his idolatry in my garden. The reverence for other gods needs to be removed from our lives.

I find it tremendously hard to walk the line of respect for other beliefs, knowing that there are some truths in their religions while not revering and possibly worshiping their god or gods. The Spirit has led me not to have symbols in my house that show reverence for other gods, like statues and dream catchers. Maybe I do not fully understand why or am not able to easily explain it well to those around me, but the uncomfortable feeling I feel is real. I do not want to give wrongful worship a foothold in my life through an image or representation of another god or another spirituality. I also do not want to give others that temptation either, especially my children.

At the end of the prayer, we are reminded, "For thine is the kingdom, and the power, and the glory, for ever. Amen." Know that God is in charge of all things. He understands and sees all things and is working out our destiny in His love. I am in His hands, and although life's circumstances may put me on top of a mountain or in the depths of the sea, I rest in the love He has for me.

We need to get our lives in perspective. Although we matter greatly

257

to God, we are small, and He is great. It is rewarding to know He still cares for us and is extremely interested in a relationship and what we think and do. He is the creator of the universe and holds esteem that we cannot fathom. Knowing that we are loved by the king of the universe, the most powerful and glorious being that exists, where else can we go for something more? In John's Gospel, Jesus asks the disciples if they want to turn away, and Peter gives a deeply passionate plea: "Lord, to whom shall we go? You have the words of eternal life. We have come to believe and to know that you are the Holy One of God" (John 6:68–69, NIV). We know that God is in control, and He holds us in His hands. He is sovereign over not just us but everything. We have nothing to worry about. He will work all things out for good.[278] This is how all prayer should end, with the peace in knowing that our Father is in control.

(See Appendix E for a summary list of key elements, in addition to prayer, for daily walking with Jesus.)

---

278 Romans 8:28

CHAPTER 26

HOW DOES SANCTIFICATION BY THE LOVE OF THE CROSS END JUDGEMENT AND ANGER?

The more one judges, the less one loves.[279]

All of the human "works of the flesh,"[2] like power, lust, pride, greed, anger, lack of self-control, idolatry, coveting, and others, will block our ability to love with the love of Christ. Judgment and anger, which include condemnation, are significantly worse in blocking love because they seem immediately destructive in nature as affronts directly against the nature of a person. Harmful attacks against someone make it almost impossible to love them at the same time as attacking them. Because of the destructiveness, I find it necessary that judgment and anger be specifically addressed if we are going to be perfected in the love of the cross. These are self-evident indicators in our lives that something is not right.

Judgment

Condemning judgment of an individual, pertaining to their motives and

---

279 Popova, Maria, Honoré de Balzac, Physiologie Du Mariage, "What is Love? Famous Definitions from 400 Years of Literary History," May 28th, 2020, https://www.brainpickings.org/2013/01/01/what-is-love/

280 Galatians 5:19

what is wrong with them, is not only a great hindrance to love, it is also a great hindrance to change. Jesus said to "judge not, that you be not judged" (Matthew 7:1, NKJV). He admonished us to "first remove the plank from your own eye, and then you will see clearly to remove the speck that is in your brother's eye" (Luke 6:42, NKJV). Jesus warned us that we would be judged by the same measure we judge others[281]. He told us to "do to others as you would have them do to you" (Luke 6:31, NIV), which implies not negatively judging our neighbor since it appears that no one likes to be negatively judged. The judgment of others will quickly deteriorate our relationships. Looking at others with contempt changes our approach and invokes anger in the receiver of judgment. It is the opposite of considering others better than ourselves[282]. Judgment of ourselves destroys our ability to love ourselves. Judgment aimed at God prevents us from receiving His gift of love. Our separation from Him happens entirely in our hearts and minds on our end, for we know that God does not stop loving us as His children even if we judge Him.[283]

The commandment not to judge can be confusing because it is completely normal for people to observe and judge behavior. In fact, we judge when we give praise for desired behavior, and we also admire those who have good judgment. However, that is different from negative judgment of one's motives and offensive behaviors. We cannot live without some type of discerning judgment. We not only naturally judge our own behavior but also that of others. We constantly make judgments about truth, safety, efficiency, enjoyment, and how to love those around us. We function by judgment. How can we not judge?

First, to clarify things, let us distinguish between two types of

---

281 Mark 4:24
282 Philippians 2:3
283 Romans 8:39

judgment, information input and negative judgment of another's behavior. In information input, I have three categories:

1. Observation: We notice the things around us with our senses and make observations about them.

2. Assessment: We assess how the observed phenomena will affect us.

3. Movement or passivity: We decide if we need to react or merely observe.

Information input was not the judgment Jesus was talking about. The judgment He mentioned was concerning pointing out the sin or destruction of another and assigning motives.

Concerning judgment of another's perceived offensive behaviors and motives, I have three categories as well:

1. Observation of the "sin" or destructive behavior: It is unavoidable for us to do as humans not to observe destructive behavior.

2. Pointing out the behavior to the person or others around them. (Speaking your judgment is almost always going to cause hurt, even when done in love.)

3. Exacting punishment for the behavior.

The first category is pointing out the fact that everyone, including Jesus, observes negative behavior. Christians are not precluded from observing the effects of evil. So, the first one is a given and unavoidable.

One might contend that unconditional love sometimes means trying our best not to notice offensive things, even though they may strain our senses. It is also sad that we often make uninformed assumptions and judgments about the cause, motives, and circumstances of one's behavior. This may lead us to fail to empathize with the circumstances of the person who is doing the negative behavior. If the evil intentions are not self-evident, then thinking the best possible motive is the loving action to do.

The third category, exacting punishment, is the one I believe Christians should not be involved in unless they have been given a position of authority to do that. Condemnation is up to God, the government, and others who are in the place of authority to carry out that work on behalf of their appointed position. Even then, mercy is necessary and preferred. Leaders would be wise to remember the verse from the Prophet Micah: "He has shown you, O man, what is good; And what does the Lord require of you. But to do justly, To love mercy, And to walk humbly with your God?" (Micah 6:8, NKJV).

The second category is the tough one, and I believe Christians can do this only if it is done in love and grace, not with law and judgment. We especially need the Spirit's guidance in these tough situations and need to have the best interest of the person and the people around them in mind. Even with our best intentions and our best efforts, pointing out someone else's problem, which is harming others, can go extremely wrong. The one place we are compelled by Jesus to speak out is in our obligation to tell people about how to find life in Jesus. In carrying out this duty, we are better off telling people about the love of Jesus than a toxic judgment of their sin.

Unfortunately, sometimes we struggle with judging ourselves, telling ourselves bad messages. We can go as far as self-condemnation and punishment. It seems that some of us cannot stop comparing, being jealous, and coveting. Only God's love, overwhelming us constantly, can overcome judging in our hearts, so we can be perfected in His love and change how we think and act towards ourselves.

Even the world, without Jesus, can see how judgment hinders love, as demonstrated in the movie *Shallow Hal*. In it, Hal falls in love with a large, socially unattractive woman he thinks is skinny and beautiful because of a spell put on him. This is a woman he would have never liked if he were in a normal state of mind. When the spell is lifted, he must decide if he loves her as she actually is. It is easy to find ourselves relating to Hal's dilemma because we are so programmed to see the world as a place to meet our needs. Yet, we find ourselves immediately recognizing the wrongness of that type of judgment. A needs-based view of the world forces us to judge others on the basis of how they can fill our needs and desires. In Hal's world, that would mean finding someone that fits into certain beauty norms.

When God supplies all our needs, we now are empowered to fill others' needs and trust Him to fill ours. He enables in us a giving approach to the world and removes our taking approach as we are perfected in cross-type love. God supplies in us what the world truly desires, the power to see the person as who they are on the inside and not the outward appearance. "For the Lord does not see as man sees; for man looks at the outward appearance, but the Lord looks at the heart" (1 Samuel 16:7, NKJV). Shallow Hal, fortunately, ended up seeing past himself and saw the beautiful person he was dating. When we are not seeking others to meet our needs, outward appearance is not as important.

This ability to see the world differently is only achieved consistently and genuinely by a supernatural presence of God's Spirit in us, enabling us to live with the love of the cross. One way we submit to His presence to help us overcome our hurtful judgment is through prayer. Maybe this prayer will help:

I pray that I can remember that we all are on a journey, and I am just blessed enough to be a small part of the journey of the ones I touch. I pray that I will not use people to meet my needs. I want to be a giver and not a taker. I pray that I would not try to compare others to myself or try to make them into something I would want them to be. I pray that I can help them to see Jesus, His love, and who He wants them to be. Amen.

Anger

Closely related to judgment is anger, which is another major hindrance to love and change in people. It is a monster that is hard to control. I have seen the most loving and beautiful people corrupted by anger. I have witnessed anger as a way of life in my father and have struggled with it personally my whole life. At different times I thought that I had conquered anger and felt miserable when anger again got the best of me. It seems the better one does, the harder they fall when they fail because the expectations for them are now greater. Matthew recorded Jesus' words on anger:

> You have heard that it was said to our ancestors, Do not murder, and whoever murders will be subject to judgment. But I tell you, everyone who is angry with his brother will be subject to judgment. And whoever says to his brother, 'Fool!' will be subject to the Sanhedrin. But whoever says, 'You moron!' will be subject to hellfire.
>
> Matthew 5:21–22 (HCSB)

How can Jesus connect anger to murder? Have you ever been mad enough to kill someone? The Apostle John echoes Jesus, writing that "Everyone who hates his brother is a murderer" (1 John 3:15, NASB).

Our judgment of those around us empowers our human emotions, sometimes even to the point of hate, and possesses us with the desire to destroy the other person. When we judge an offense that we think was done with intent to harm, our anger steps in. When Woodland Hills' pastor Greg Boyd states that "when you judge you cannot love," he is definitely on to the truth[284]. Have you ever tried to love the object of your anger? Yet, we are called to love at all times. As believers, we are duplicitous and torn asunder when we are angry. Sometimes when I am angry at the ones I love, I feel as if I am stretched over the fires of hell with one foot in hell and one hand grasping on to the eternal life that is in my heart and mind, or at least I thought it was. Nothing destroys my hope in salvation as much as anger. Jesus says that if I call someone an idiot or fool, I am entering into that danger of hell. I would say that I agree with Him, for it tears me to pieces inside.

The core of the problem with harmful anger is judgment. (Although, at times, anger can be a misplaced emotion covering fear and hurt, hiding our weaknesses, or even revealing a chemical imbalance.) When I am angry, I am in complete disagreement with another's actions. I am judging their actions as foolish or even judging them as a fool and an idiot who deserves my wrath.

How can I love someone when I am angry and judging them? My anger at people who I perceive are wronging me is truly the opposite of love. Even if the person is a grave threat, if I were somehow able to love perfectly, I could allow them to destroy me for the sake of love. Jesus did. When approaching others, there is nothing left for me to judge

---

284 Greg Boyd, "Sociopath Religion," The Narrow Gate, June 3, 2013, https://you tu.be/-3sZr8IWbKs

because Jesus has taken away their sins by taking them upon Himself. Could it be that when I judge and condemn others in my anger, is it equivalent to judging and condemning Jesus? Or, when I am angry at another believer, am I, in a way, expressing anger at Jesus? My judgment and anger are contrary to living by the Spirit, and they prevent God's love from shining through me. He wants me to walk in love as He walked, knowing that He takes away the sin of the world, which should leave us with no reason to judge and be angry[285].

Prayer can also help us with our anger:

> I pray that I can see my fellow humans as better than myself. I pray that I can see each person as made in the image of God and deserving of Jesus' great love and sacrifice for them. I pray that I can love and enjoy each individual as God sees them and without my judgment resulting in anger.

As God is perfecting us in the love of the cross, His Spirit will daily and even moment by moment instruct us in His love. Anger and judgment are definitely signs that something is wrong. However, like all evil, focusing on it will not rid ourselves of it. It is living in God's love by the power of His Spirit that we overcome the flesh. Overcoming judgment and anger are the two areas that the Spirit has laid heavy on my heart in teaching me to love. Obviously, each one of us is different. As the Spirit teaches us to love more each day, in the process of overcoming our weaknesses, He will continue to build us up, growing us to love with sacrificial love. We must keep walking in His light with our minds focused on loving as Jesus loved, especially seeking His help with anger and judgment. We should flee the darkness and the distractions that take us off that path.

---

285 John 17:26

CHAPTER 27

HOW IS THE CROSS AN ANSWER
FOR SUFFERING AND EVIL?

For I consider that our present sufferings cannot even be
compared to the glory that will be revealed to us.

Romans 8:18 (NET)

With so much suffering in the world, one might ask, "How can
one believe in a good God or, even more, that He works out all
things for the good?"[286] Christians seem to persevere and survive their
personal suffering, great or small, and continue to hold on to their belief
in this idea of a good God. At their core, they believe that God is good,
and His ultimate desire is for all to have a relationship with Him. If God
were arbitrary or evil, suffering then would reflect the character of God,
and we would have no hope of anything different. If we do not believe
in God, when we look to nature, we see violence and death as much as
we see life. We cannot prove one better than the other without a defining
force. The Bible states that God does not begin with malice or ill intent
towards anyone; He loves everyone. John 3:16 (NIV) begins, "For God
so loved the world."

How do we account for God's love when He allows so many natural
evils? Diseases, earthquakes, fires, hurricanes, tornados, volcanos, and

---

286 Romans 8:28

accidents are all scary and able to paralyze us in fear. Still, I contend that in His love, it appears that God is restraining natural evil in the world. Think of all the natural disasters that could happen, yet it seems that we live in a relatively tame world, especially compared to other planets. Why does God allow these grave natural evils to occur in our lives if He loves us? Natural evil is part of a fallen world, and for God to step in and work a miracle in every case would be God imposing on our free will in such a way that we would have no choice but to believe in Him. This answer is obviously not that comforting when we are on the receiving end of a natural disaster or a plague. Still, for our humility and our sanity, it is extremely important to rest in knowing that God has a sovereign plan. This world is not all there is. The other option is humans playing God and micromanaging our lives to reach the desired results of the ones in charge. If no one ever drove a car, there would be no deaths by car wrecks, but we would go nowhere. I would much rather live a full, free life than live a life restricted by fear with no threat of disaster. God's love is seen in our freedom even though it is a dangerous freedom.

In addition, there is nothing stopping God from allowing what people call evil when they rebel against Him. He has, in the past, allowed natural and human destruction to fall upon people who have ceased to properly love their fellow humans. God has permitted what we call evil to facilitate justice, and it might have even been a necessary step in the restraining of a worse evil if He had not stepped in. This idea is repeated in the Bible as He rebuts the nations, including Israel, for their sins. Sometimes humanity, when allowed to suffer the horrific consequences of their actions, is able to see their error and make a correction.

While some may see God as the cause of evil and suffering, the events recorded in the Bible display a different picture; they show God's overwhelming love for mankind and how He has sought to have a personal relationship with us. Although God desires to help us in our suffering, He knows that we need to get to a point where we will accept a Savior and give up trying to fix ourselves on our own and building our own kingdom. Jesus, the Son of God, came at just that right time, in the form of a man, to be the one who would save us from our sin and rebellion and reconcile us to the Father. Even though reconciliation with God will not end suffering, living in His love is the solace for our suffering.

The majority of my suffering and the evil in my life has not been caused by natural causes but by my sins and the awful things done to me. Therefore, it is this personal turmoil I would like to focus most of my attention on.

I remember going to a Billy Graham crusade and being in awe of how he told us that God cares about our struggles and problems. He then communicated to the crowd that Jesus is the answer and that surrendering your life to Him will make your messy existence better. Oh, how right he was! But, each one of us woke up the next morning in the same predicament that we were in the night before. Our hearts had changed, but what had changed in our actual lives? Although I believe Jesus is the foundational answer we need to cope with suffering, one crusade usually does not have the lasting, life-changing effect we are looking for. It is the process God does in our hearts before and after the crusade that brings change.

When we come to Christ, it does not make our lives perfect. We will still: break up, lose friends, go bankrupt, be accused of crimes, be ostracized, be persecuted, have social problems, lose our minds, have a temper, commit crimes, fail to love, face times when no one loves us, and have friends and family die. Even children we know will suffer disease, injury, or and sometimes die. Christians do not seem to get a supernatural break in terms of difficulties, and they seem to suffer from all the same problems as those who do not follow Jesus. We have the same difficulty deciding on careers, friends, and a spouse. Even with Jesus, we can lack a sense of purpose, wellbeing, joy, and peace. We can still be plagued with inner problems and need psychological help with our broken minds or healing from sin, guilt, and shame. We still need to forgive others and ourselves and need to get and receive forgiveness from ourselves and others. It seems Christians are in the same boat of suffering and struggle because of what life throws at us, and we are equally likely to live with despair, angst, and boredom. Accepting Jesus does not prevent any of these experiences. Christ said, "In the world you have trouble and suffering, but take courage - I have conquered the world" (John 16:33, NET). He also said, "Take my yoke upon you and learn from me, for I am gentle and humble in heart, and you will find rest for your souls. For my yoke is easy and my burden is light" (Matthew 11:29–30, NIV). Jesus seemed to clearly understand the human condition of suffering and struggle. Instead of removing it from our lives, He demonstrated the idea of embracing our suffering for the sake of love, as He did on the cross.

When we think of personal suffering in an everyday sense, physical ailments can be at the top of the list. Why does not God step in and take care of these as He did in New Testament times? Would not that be the convincing miracle everybody needs to turn to Him? Actually, the best miracle God can do in one's life is not to heal their physical suffering but to bless them with the Holy Spirit and change their heart from death to life. This is much greater than physical healing. God changes someone from the deceptions of the flesh to a life of love and truth through the Spirit. This miraculous transformation is God changing us on the inside through Jesus abiding in us and we in Him. It is the change that we need the most. While physical healing is spectacular and sometimes used to manifest the power of Jesus, it only affects our flesh and is not necessary in most cases to bring His love into people's lives.

When Jesus healed me from my clotting disease, about a year after my hospital stay with two blood clots in my lungs, He impressed a verse upon my conscience: "My grace is sufficient for you, for My strength is made perfect in weakness" (2 Corinthians 12:9, NKJV). I truly felt Jesus saying to me, "I will heal you of clotting, but I am leaving you with symptoms of pain in your muscles so you will be weak and humble and learn that I am the source of your strength." That is exactly what happened. One year later, my clotting factor was reversed—a one in a million chance, according to my doctor. My pain was not gone, but I praise God all the same.

I could not disagree with God. I knew I could not slow myself down; there was too much to do. I believed I could do almost any task with my strength, intelligence, and determination. At work, instead of doing all the complicated tasks myself, I needed to slow down and teach others. At home, I definitely needed to slow down, value my family, and spend time with them. Intellectually, I was inspired to stop depending on my past learning and to take time to grow in new ways for Christ's ministry.

Still, I feel I have fallen short of His calling for me to love in the midst of my weakness. It also seems that my coworkers, my family, my friends, my own brain, and my attitudes are not always willing participants in God's calling to depend on Him for strength in my weakness. My health struggles are not bad events in my life because they resulted in my growth. As I approach my struggles, I understand that they are a necessary part of life to teach me to love, to be humble, and to sacrifice. I feel well-taught to depend on Him.

God can and does choose to heal us physically on occasion, but this healing is usually temporary because very few of us are getting out of this world alive. This body is dying as a result of Adam's curse on the world, and life can also be shortened by some of our own choices and others' actions. In salvation, when we know that our person (or self) is no longer cursed, the physical does seem less important. Yet, when we are wrought with pain and suffering, the situation can overtake us. For me, it seems freeing and challenging to know that physical healing is less important because my love for Jesus and for others can grow in the midst of my suffering. If God eliminated all of our struggles, is it possible that we would cease to grow in love for others?

Hopefully, we come to understand that struggle and sometimes even suffering are primary tools that God uses to expand our own ability to love and teach us His truths. Without any struggle, we might be tempted to disregard God, our friends, and possibly even our family if it meant a better life for ourselves. Hardships force us to evaluate and choose what is important. When we have it too easy, we sometimes begin to differentiate ourselves from others and judge those around us as lesser because our circumstances seem superficially better. The more success we achieve, the more pressure we put on others in our lives to perform. As our circumstances get more favorable, the higher the chance we will see ourselves as superior to those who are not performing up to our new standards. A person who completely avoids struggle may have no empathy for others who do struggle.

In fact, humans have an insatiable desire for our life circumstances to be better. We are constantly seeking to better ourselves, our house, or our jobs, yet it is hard to measure up to our own new demands we put on ourselves. Those demands seem to bleed over to people around us. When our best efforts fail to meet the new expectations that we have created for ourselves, we might blame it on others and even possibly ditch our current life in search of one that is more fulfilling. It is crazy how we can create our own suffering if we do not have enough. What a person considers to be suffering can become hard to nail down.

For some, suffering can lead to healthy growth, and for others, it leads to bitterness and possibly evil. For believers, how we respond to suffering is part of the eternal growth process God is doing in our lives. Struggle brings out the question, "Can we see God's work in our lives, despite all the evil?" It is challenging to answer this question if we do not believe in the providence of God. As believers, "we know that all things work together for good for those who love God, who are called according to his purpose" (Romans 8:28, NET). He is conforming us into "the image of his Son" that we might be glorified by showing the same love He showed us.[287]

This conforming of ourselves takes time. It is especially true when people first become Christians; they usually struggle with still living under rules, sin, and condemnation. Most people who are not believers are drowning in a cycle of sin, guilt, shame, suffering, and destruction, and they struggle to get on dry ground. They are what Paul calls "slaves to sin.[288]" Providentially, while we were still slaves to sin, Christ died for us.[289] At the cross, He redeemed our struggle from the clenches of sin and death through His great sacrifice and struggle. He demonstrated the change that loving sacrifice and submission to God can bring in the midst of our struggle, giving us hope in our lives and for those around us.[290]

---

287 Romans 8:29-30 (NET)
288 Romans 6:17 (NET)
289 Romans 5:8
290 Romans 8:18-30

For while we were still helpless, at the right time Christ died for the ungodly. (For rarely will anyone die for a righteous person, though for a good person perhaps someone might possibly dare to die.) But God demonstrates his own love for us, in that while we were still sinners, Christ died for us. Much more then, because we have now been declared righteous by his blood, we will be saved through him from God's wrath. For if while we were enemies we were reconciled to God through the death of his Son, how much more, since we have been reconciled, will we be saved by his life? Not only this, but we also rejoice in God through our Lord Jesus Christ, through whom we have now received this reconciliation.

Romans 5:6–11 (NET)

The willingness of Jesus to suffer for the sake of love and reconciliation models the way we should look at life. The good life is not about seeking the enticements and comforts of the world but seeking love and a relationship with God and others. The curse of the law that God put on this world is no longer upon us because God is for us[291]. The way of the flesh, the way of achieving results through strength, rules, coercion, and violence, is done away with, and the way of the Spirit, the way of achieving sanctification through sacrificial love, has come.

Paul goes so far as to say our struggle is good and not to be feared or avoided. Paul wrote in his letter to the Romans about how Jesus redeemed suffering on the cross:

Therefore, since we have been declared righteous by faith, we

---

291   Romans 8:31

have peace with God through our Lord Jesus Christ, through whom we have also obtained access by faith into this grace in which we stand, and we rejoice in the hope of God's glory. Not only this, but we also rejoice in sufferings, knowing that suffering produces endurance, and endurance, character, and character, hope. And hope does not disappoint, because the love of God has been poured out in our hearts through the Holy Spirit who was given to us.

Romans 5:1–5 (NET)

What a great miracle when Jesus uses suffering to begin to change the bad part of who we are, replacing it with endurance, character, and hope.

By faith, God gives us hope. He begins to modify behavior that contributes to our suffering, empowering us to change. It is almost like we are juxtaposing guilt, shame, depression, greed, anger, slander, violence, perversion, and manipulation with Jesus' offer of salvation and becoming a new creation, where God supplies our needs for love, kindness, peace, contentment, compassion, and concern. God begins our restoration in the midst of our suffering. God fulfills our needs by His presence in us and can quickly begin to heal our emotional and mental suffering. He directs us to build ourselves up instead of tearing ourselves down. He teaches us to build others up instead of taking from them. He produces in us ever-increasing endurance and character, bolstered with love because God pours out His love in our hearts through His Spirit. The transformation through suffering is demonstrated by ever-increasing love in our hearts. We have a hope knowing that when we live by the Spirit in His love, the worst of circumstances cannot destroy our inner self that is in relationship with God; instead, we experience growth by being taught to love in the midst of our suffering.

Because of our call to suffer for the sake of spreading His message of a loving relationship with God and others, we are not to shrink from suffering as we put on the love of Jesus. We gladly go through suffering if necessary for the sake of communicating the gospel of reconciliation of our relationship with God. His love poured out in our hearts gives us the source to grow through struggle and grow in love. Jesus is the greatest example. He suffered for us when we did not deserve it to reconcile us to Himself. When James said to think of it as good when you face suffering and struggle, he was saying, *Embrace it all for the sake of the cross. The hugs and the punches—they are all the gift of the new life* Jesus gives us.[292] Renewed by the Spirit and bathed in His love, I know I am worthy to receive the hugs and have the strength to endure the punches, and both are glorious and grow eternal life in me, perfecting me in the love of the cross.

A Christian may put too little emphasis on what God is doing in us through struggle and too much emphasis on avoiding struggle and gaining success by worldly standards through building their own kingdoms or what they think is God's kingdom. Jesus said that He did not come to bring peace but strife in families.[293] Jesus also said that we must take up our cross (carry our beam of suffering) and follow Him if we want to be His disciples[294]. Another time He proclaimed, "Whoever desires to save his life will lose it, but whoever loses his life for My sake will save it" (Luke 9:24, NKJV). It is essential not to see struggle as punishment from God; instead, struggle should be seen as growing experiences to be lived and loved through or at least survived with God's love and grace. Struggle is God's tool in this fallen world to grow us to eternity.[295]

---

292 James 1:2 (NKJV)
293 Luke 14:26 (NKJV)
294 Luke 14:27 (NKJV)
295 Romans 5:1-5

As we face our struggles with His spirit in us and the grace, love, truth, and hope He brings, we grow eternally in our souls. We become more like God intends us to be for eternity. We are participating in our eternal life right now as we grow in His love.

The Apostle Paul pontificates on suffering in chapter eight of his letter to the Romans:

> And if children, then heirs (namely, heirs of God and also fellow heirs with Christ) – if indeed we suffer with him so we may also be glorified with him. For I consider that our present sufferings cannot even be compared to the glory that will be revealed to us. For the creation eagerly waits for the revelation of the sons of God. For the creation was subjected to futility [violence] – not willingly but because of God who subjected it – in hope that the creation itself will also be set free from the bondage of decay into the glorious freedom of God's children. For we know that the whole creation groans and suffers together until now. Not only this, but we ourselves also, who have the firstfruits of the Spirit, groan inwardly as we eagerly await our adoption, the redemption of our bodies.
>
> Romans 8:17–23 (NET)

The violence in the world brings suffering to each person and creation as well. We all, including creation, wait for when love reigns again, and there is an end to the reign of evil and suffering.

The idea of conquering suffering and struggle in our own way, in our own strength, and by our knowledge of good and evil is similar thinking that led Cain to kill his brother Abel. This same self-righteousness is in all utopian ideas that depend on human wisdom and strength to reduce suffering and struggle. Eventually, they have to eliminate the ones that disagree with or condemn them, and as a result, it leads to greater suffering. Suffering can only end when we change our paradigm. We need the act of Jesus on the cross as the means to facilitate loving relationships in us. On the cross, He embraced and redeemed suffering, demonstrating a willingness to suffer and sacrifice for the sake of loving others. This model of sacrificial and unconditional love is what we build the kingdom of God with, not success based on the knowledge of good and evil and our own effort.[296]

Since suffering no longer produces death in us but now produces eternal life as we approach it with God's Spirit in His love, we are able to embrace all that this world has to offer without fear of loss or strife because it is all God's creation, and we live in His power. We are no longer managing our lives to alleviate suffering; we are navigating this new life of ultimate experience that God has given us, growing eternally through struggle. Suffering is not my enemy, nor are the people who cause it. Christ redeemed suffering and now uses it for His glory, teaching us to follow His example of being willing to suffer for the sake of sharing His love and in hopes of reconciling people to God.

---

296 2 Corinthians 4:8-10

CHAPTER 28

THE PERFECT LOVE OF THE CROSS

Beloved, if God so loved us, we also ought to love one another …if we love one another, God abides in us, and His love is perfected in us.

1 John 4:11–12 (NASB)

The infinite God invaded the kingdom of man not to take it over and set up a new earthly kingdom but to demonstrate perfect love by dying on a cross to reconcile humanity to Himself.[297] The throne of His new kingdom was not the throne of David or a throne of conquest but the humiliation of the cross, portraying a kingdom of unconditional love and sacrifice.[298] It was not a kingdom brought on by might or power but a kingdom realized by His Spirit pouring out His love in our hearts[299]. It is a kingdom where we know and love God, and He knows and loves us. In a similar way, we strive to know and love one another and ourselves. Our own kingdom begins to fade as our first priority, or maybe even a priority at all, as we embrace and experience this new kingdom of reconciliation to God, where we emulate the love Jesus demonstrated on the cross. We now seek His truth, love, and reconciliation first above our kingdom. As

---

297 2 Corinthians 5:19
298 1 Corinthians 1:23
299 Romans 5:5

we seek God's heavenly kingdom, we find earthly purposes for our lives that work hand in hand with His heavenly purpose of unconditional, sacrificial love, salvific truth, and the ministry of reconciliation[300].

It is important to know that salvation is not merely the forgiveness of sins; that is what makes our reconciliation with God possible. The good news is not that we are sinners, for that is not joyful news. The gospel is that God loves us and desires to restore a relationship with us. He was willing to suffer for that potential relationship, taking away our sin and guilt so that we could return to His family. We are saved when we choose to believe Jesus was God, that He died in our place, and rose from the dead, demonstrating His power over sin and death; we accept His death for the removal of our sins and choose to follow Him. When we make that decision, we join His family, we are given the Holy Spirit as our guide and comforter, and we immediately receive eternal life.

Eternal life means that you, as a person, will exist forever with Jesus where He dwells. We currently have a down payment of this eternal life living in us in the form of the Holy Spirit, and we will be with Him in a place, often referred to as heaven, when we die.[301] How does that change how we live? Today is important, but tomorrow is important as well. How much different will we live this life in light of the eternity we have entered? How much will our priorities change? We walk this world with new life principles shaped by the love shown on the cross. Whether we are kind and tell the truth is more important than whether we know or say the right things to get ahead, support the right cause, believe exactly the right way, or if we have lots of money and possessions. As Christians, we are on this journey of the beginning of eternity together with the very brothers and sisters we will spend it with. What we do and become

---

300 Matthew 6:33
301 2 Corinthians 5:1-5

here may be a large portion of who we will be in heaven. If there is no evil in heaven, how much of us will be in heaven with God when we get there?[302] Will it be merely a shell of ourselves, or will it be the loving person we have become in Christ? How we learn truth and demonstrate the love of the cross on earth forms us and changes us into God's new creation that we will be in heaven.

Jesus' sacrifice on the cross did more than take away our sins; it changed the paradigm of our sanctification, from following the law of Moses as the means to be holy to sanctification through following the Spirit who teaches us to love with sacrificial love. When He died to take away our sins, He took away the law. There is no longer any source of condemnation for the believer. We now live by the Spirit guiding us to love as He loved. No law can teach us how to love; that is learned through truths concerning love found in God's written Word, interacting with one another, and most of all, listening to His Spirit inside of us. This life in Christ Jesus is a life of continually being perfected in the love of the cross.

Along with those who do not yet follow Jesus, it is obvious that plenty of Christians are not on board with the end of sin as defined by the law. Whether one is outwardly effective at being legally righteous, ineffective at keeping laws, or somewhere in the middle, we all have plenty of hidden wrongs we are guilty of, and we all need our sins forgiven and, I would contend, taken away. Everyone needs to be freed from the destruction brought on by their evil and the pride brought on by their rule-keeping, setting both aside and entering into a humble, loving relationship with Jesus. The problem is demonstrable; there is just disagreement on how it is solved.

---

302   1 Corinthians 3:15

When confronted with our sin, it is normal to respond with a "look at the bad someone else did" and "look at the good I did" sentiment. The truth is that we all end up equal in humility at the foot of the cross because of God's great sacrifice and love for us. What we did or did not do is not the issue. Our greatness and our evil are fleeting moments in eternity and will not save us or condemn us. It is only our trust in Jesus that gives us eternal life, and only our rejection of Him that prevents us from having this life.

God's message is not a message of condemnation but a message of truth, forgiveness, freedom, love, and grace. My desire to tell people of all religions and all walks of life about God's message comes from a desire that they have a relationship with God through the forgiveness of their sins and the indwelling of the Holy Spirit. They, too, can step out of the old covenant of living under the condemnation of law and judgment and enter the new covenant of eternal life, a life of truth, love, and freedom in Christ. Faith and hope in the future promise of abundant life here on earth and thereafter bring great comfort. John professed he heard the angels proclaim:

> God's dwelling place is now among the people, and he will dwell with them. They will be his people, and God himself will be with them and be their God. 'He will wipe every tear from their eyes. There will be no more death' or mourning or crying or pain, for the old order of things has passed away.

> Revelation 21:3–4 (NIV)

Carnell sums it up eloquently when he says that in Christ, "all threats to happiness are forever banished …No longing of the heart will be left unsatisfied.[303]"

Those against this simple plan of Christ can be anyone—from someone who does not believe Jesus is God to someone who preaches the law and does not think Jesus' death was sufficient for righteousness. This righteousness does not come by confession, repentance, personal sacrifice, penance, good deeds, or any other religious act that is purported to bring a right relationship with God. Our worthiness to be in His presence comes only through our choice to follow Jesus and embrace His death on the cross as our means to remove our sins and as an example of a life lived by His love to replace the law.

The Apostle Paul admonishes us to "not be conformed to this world, but be transformed by the renewing of your mind, so that you may prove what the will of God is, that which is good and acceptable and perfect" (Romans 12:2, NASB). John says for us "not [to] love the world nor the things in the world. If anyone loves the world, the love of the Father is not in him" (1 John 2:15, NASB). This new mindset that God gives us is a completely different mindset and a completely different way of life. At salvation, we embrace Jesus' forgiveness and love in exchange for the world's vision of success. Our whole worldview is changed, and we enter a life of freedom in Christ. We are leaving the way of violence and entering the way of love; we are leaving the way of grief and entering the way of comfort; we are leaving the way of money and entering the way of charity; we are leaving the way of safety and entering a life of suffering; we are leaving the way of the familiar and entering a life of unknown. Jesus said, "The wind blows wherever it pleases. You hear its sound, but you cannot tell where it comes from or where it is going. So it is with everyone born of the Spirit" (John 3:8, NIV). People do not know who our Father is and who is guiding us, so they cannot predict or

---

303 Carnell, The Kingdom of Love, p. 155

control what we do and where we are going on this journey. When we follow Jesus, we are entering the way of the cross.

The restoration of the cross to the center of our lives is not a self-help system or steps on how to live well. It is a life that can only be lived consistently by the love and power we receive from Jesus and the Holy Spirit. It begins with our total forgiveness and His unconditional love and acceptance of us into His family. We begin to understand the humility and sacrifice Jesus made on the cross and how emulating that transforms our lives. Without knowing how much Jesus loves each person, including ourselves, and that He died a brutal death for us, it is hard to have a lasting, deep motivation to love and forgive each person we meet, unconditionally, equally, and sacrificially. Judgment of ourselves and others will get in the way of the Spirit teaching us to love as Jesus loved. When we consider others equal to or even better than ourselves and that they are worthy of our sacrifice for them, we set the Spirit free to transform our lives with God's love.

Even knowing all this will not fully transform us. Our deepest power to love comes from His Spirit in our lives, meeting our needs in His love and freeing us from the slavery of our own needs and desires. It is by the power of the Spirit that Jesus makes us a new creation and fills us with His love that overflows out of us.

As a new creation, we are being perfected in the love of the cross. It is a love that humbly thinks of others first. This love seeks the success of others before our own success. It is a willingness to set aside our life agenda and sacrifice for the call to love and meet others where they are. It is going through life communicating to others how important they are—so important that you would sacrifice for them. Love is seeing each person as someone Jesus loved and learning to have that intensity of love for others. By the Spirit, we can have unending, sacrificial, and unconditional love for our neighbors and even give it to ourselves. Most importantly, we can develop that type of love towards God the Father, Jesus His Son, and the Holy Spirit inside of us.

Living with the love of the cross as our calling does not take away our suffering in life; it gives us a comforter to go through suffering with us. In fact, sacrifice, struggle, and suffering in humility are what Christ did on the cross in His great act to unconditionally love us. We then should not avoid sacrifice, suffering, and struggle. Following Jesus is almost the exact opposite. In the power of the Spirit, we are to endure hardships, if necessary, in order to love those around us. We are to live the cross for the sake of loving others, whatever that demands.

Jesus walks with us on our journey through trials, tribulations, successes, and failures. He helps us grow in love through all of them. God is always on our side. He is not condemning us with struggle; instead, Jesus is loving us and moving us towards truth and love so we can experience this life the way He intended it. Jesus did not intend life to be lived with a list of dos and don'ts by which we can judge ourselves and our neighbors; He intended it to be a life of love and relationship resembling the one that exists in the trinity. He wants to free us from the destruction and violence that we once used to serve ourselves as a means to retain our wealth, power, safety, and comfort. Living in fear of loss is not how God intended us to live. He wants us to embrace life with all its turns and twists, struggling together with Jesus by our side to experience all that life has to offer. We are thriving with Him and the people around us, loving, caring deeply, and growing to expand, to learn, and to participate in all the amazing adventures He has in store for us.

Understanding and knowing the deep love of Jesus is key to experiencing this new life and freedom in Christ. Growing in our relationship with Christ is about Jesus setting us free to become what

He intended us to be. We will not experience this freedom if we are still living by rules and obligations. Living by the law of the Spirit is a life completely forgiven with no condemnation, without the law of sin and death enslaving us. As Christians, we literally could kill somebody and not be separated from the love of God. Obviously, there would be earthly consequences, but knowing that there is no condition in which God will take His love from us frees us to openly admit and work on any fault that we have. We are free to make any decision we want at any given point; we are not tethered by past failures, rules, obligations, guilt, or condemnation heaped upon us. We are also not hindered by a fear of mistakes or future consequences. We are completely free to do the best, right, and loving action, and we are instructed on how to do this as the Spirit leads us in His love. We are free to grow in truth, love, and the knowledge of Him, free to be perfected in God's love. John stated this when he wrote:

> Whoever confesses that Jesus is the Son of God, God abides in him, and he in God. We have come to know and have believed the love which God has for us. God is love, and the one who abides in love abides in God, and God abides in him. By this, love is perfected with us, so that we may have confidence in the day of judgment; because as He is, so also are we in this world. There is no fear in love; but perfect love casts out fear, because fear involves punishment, and the one who fears is not perfected in love. We love, because He first loved us.

> 1 John 4:15–19 (NASB)

When we live our lives dominated by the love of the cross, God begins to melt away our past in His complete forgiveness. His love and forgiveness free us to become someone that our past says we are not and someone that our negativity says we cannot be in the future. There is little limit on what we can aspire to when bathed in God's love and forgiveness and living by the power of His Spirit inside of us.

The gifts of salvation, mercy, and grace were executed on the cross and through the cross. We were made clean and enabled to partake of the "tree of life and eat, and live forever" with Jesus and His Spirit dwelling in us.[304] Salvation takes place at the moment one puts their faith in Jesus.[305] As we know His love, we are perfected in His love to share it with others.[306] As we know His forgiveness, we can extend the same mercy and forgiveness He has extended to us. He keeps no record of wrongs, not that we commit no wrongs, but He loves us through them to maturity.[307] God's love is poured out into our hearts when we become His children, and nothing can separate us from His love[308]. There is nothing you can do to make God love you more and nothing you can do to make God love you less. Sin between God and us is no more, and it is replaced by His love. You have all of His love, and it is not conditional on anything. With that kind of love behind us, in us, and before us, we are left with no other option but to walk in His deep love for us. In salvation in Jesus, you do not have to do anything, but you will want to do everything. His Spirit dwelling in you will transform your life if you let Him. When you believe in the Lord Jesus, you will be saved, and the love of the cross, lived by the power of the Spirit, will transform your existence and open up a whole new abundant life for you to live.

---

304 Genesis 3:22 (NIV)

305 John 5:24

306 1 John 4:12

307 1 Corinthians 13:5

308 Romans 5:5, 8

Appendix

APPENDIX A

——

CAN WE TRUST WHAT THE GOSPELS SAY ABOUT JESUS?
(A CONTINUATION OF CHAPTER 2)

Matthew, Mark, Luke, and John appear to be written as biographical narratives and purport to contain the eyewitness testimonies of Jesus' disciples,[309] but can we trust them to be accurate accounts? The gospel writers claim to be communicating some of Jesus' sermons and an account of the notable things that He did and spoke. Two of the writers, Matthew and John, were of the twelve original disciples and were eyewitnesses to and participants in Jesus' ministry[310]. Mark was also thought to be with Jesus as one of His other disciples and is believed to have written on behalf of Peter.[311] Luke was a doctor, historian, and companion of Paul who set out to write a historically accurate account of Jesus in his Gospel of Luke.[312]

---

309 Burridge, Richard, "What are the Gospels?," 1992/2004, p. 251, http://www.fondazioneratzinger.va/content/fondazioneratzinger/en/news/notizie/riman di-news/graeco-roman-biography-and-the-gospels-literary-genre.html

310 Baukham, Richard, "Jesus and the Eyewitnesses: The Gospels as Eyewitness Testimony," Second ed. Grand Rapids: Eerdmans, 2017, Summary given by Robert J Cara, "Reformed Faith & Practice," https://journal.rts.edu/review/jesus-and-the-eyewitnesses-the-gospels-as-eyewitness-testimony/

311 Wallace, J. Warner, "Good Reasons to Believe Peter Is the Source of Mark's Gospel," Cold Case Christianity, August 24th, 2018, https://coldcasechristianity.com/writings/good-reasons-to-believe-peter-is-the-source-of-marks-gospel/

312 Luke 1:1-4

As Luke was writing his historical biographical gospel, he found enough credible eyewitness accounts and written accounts that he was able to write an entire gospel, extremely similar to Mathew and Mark and agreeing with John. The Gospel of Luke is a researched document that confirms the message of the other three, taken from available source documents and eyewitnesses. We can know it was written fairly early since witnesses were still alive.[313] One could also assume a major part of the other gospels were already written as well when Luke was written because of the similarities.

In addition, after the resurrection, the disciples were able to question Jesus about all that had happened.[314] Between Jesus' ascension and the day of Pentecost, they had more than a week in the upper room to discuss the words He had spoken over the past three years. It was most likely all they could talk about. Imagine the process and the conversations. Imagine them discussing what Jesus had said to them after His resurrection and all that had happened. Their messages about Jesus would have started there, likely from the notes they had kept and their memories of the events and teaching they experienced with Christ.

Peter preached his first great sermon on the day of Pentecost, which some or one of the disciples obviously took notes on. Luke, when he wrote Acts, would have used the notes. Other disciples, as well, preached the message of Christ, and notes were taken on their sermons, such as the sad example when Stephen was martyred[315]. The disciples began teaching about Jesus immediately after His death, so material in the gospels was being remembered and written from the beginning of their ministry. Their sermons would have been not only spoken but also written and

---

313 Luke 1:1-4
314 Mark 16:12-20
315 Acts 7:54-60

rewritten. From the first sermon to the writing of the formal gospels, it appears the disciples set out to tell exactly what Jesus said and did. They must have felt a great obligation to Jesus to get it right since they were conveying the very words of God.

I wish it were easy to answer critical questions about Jesus, but there are different voices claiming who Jesus was and how we discover Him, or if we can know the truth about Him at all. I have included this chapter in the book because it is important that the reader knows that there was a real Jesus and that He can be known. Most of our ability to know Him is ultimately going to come down to what we believe about the accurateness of the gospels. Is one going to believe that they are eyewitness accounts of Jesus, rendering His actual words spoken, as proclaimed by disciples and attested to by Luke and the church fathers from the very beginning, or are we going to listen to modern critics who are contending that their sparse knowledge of the actual situation overrides the claims of the gospel writers and the other early Christians who accepted the gospels as truth?

When we are looking to critical theologians to help us learn about the historical Jesus, it must be remembered that some of them are making their conclusions with presuppositional disbelief in the supernatural. This propensity to disbelief often leads to bias in their assumptions and conclusions. Fairly recently, the Jesus Seminar, a meeting of mostly liberal scholars, stated that "of the 176 events cataloged [concerning Jesus], the members of the Jesus Seminar concluded that only 28 actually occurred with any historical probability.[316]" The accuracy of the words and acts of Jesus has been under attack for a long time. This attempt to

316 Rivera, John, "The historical Jesus and the Bible Scholars cast doubt on mir acles, Easter," The Baltimore Sun, September 7, 2020, https://www.baltimore sun.com/news/bs-xpm-1998-05-03-1998123040-story.html

delegitimize them makes them optional and without authority. One must ask how scholars, two thousand years removed, can make this kind of determination.

Amongst some who question the sources for the gospels, the early dates, and the actual authors, there is the question as to whether the authors got their material only from oral sources, using pure memory, written sources, or a combination of both. Quite a few critics contend that the gospels were not written until much later; that the stories are merely orally transmitted and elaborated upon until the gospel writers, who were not the original disciples, wrote them down. Consequently, we are getting a romanticized religious version of Christ and not the actual words and accounts of Jesus. The more conservative theologians promote the idea of oral transmission, early dates, and claimed authorship. The conservative arguments rest on the accuracy of oral transmission and the idea that God gave them a supernatural remembrance of details.[317] This hypothesis is plausible, but I find it hard to defend the accuracy if one holds to it solely. In making our conclusions about means, dates, and authors, we should embrace all of the evidence, yet for the sake of our faith, we should be aware of the negative conclusions about how and when the gospels were written that secular, and sometimes even Christian scholars come to, and the validity and reasons of their conclusions.

The belief that the twelve disciples wrote down notes on what Jesus said and did in real-time and that they began writing teachings about Jesus early after His ascension is as valid of an assertion as contending that they were only orally transmitted for several years. Are not the early recorded messages of Peter and Stephen evidence of a written message? How would Luke have included them in Acts if they were not written? Is it possible that their whole sermons were memorized that quickly?

317   John 14:26

While it is believed that oral transmission was important and purported to be accurate, it should not be assumed that it was the only means of communicating about Jesus. It is highly probable that Jesus picked some literate disciples, if not all literate disciples. It would have been beneficial to the future church if He did. Matthew, the tax collector, most likely carried a scroll and knew a shorthand writing method so he could work as a stenographer[318]. It also appears that Phillip knew how to read and interpret scripture to the Ethiopian eunuch[319]. They had motivation to write Jesus' words down since they thought they were following the "Son of God, ...the king of Israel" (John 1:49, NET), as Nathanael proclaimed about Him when he was given a miracle at their first meeting. They knew who they were following and how important His ministry was as a teacher, prophet, and Son of God.

Jewish scholar Saul Lieberman, an expert in Talmudic literature, offers a brief summary of the possible practice of Jesus' disciples. Lieberman writes:

Now the Jewish disciples of Jesus, in accordance with the

general rabbinic practice, wrote the sayings which their master pronounced not in a form of a book to be published, but as notes in their ...codices (which is like notes for a book in the form of private small scrolls), (he writes) we would naturally expect the logia [sayings] of Jesus to be originally copied in codices.[320]

---

318 Thiede, Carsten Peter, "A Testament Is Born," Christian History Institute, Issue #43, 1994. https://christianhistoryinstitute.org/magazine/article/a-testament-is-born

319 Acts 8:30-35

320 Arlandson, James M., "Historical Reliability of the Gospels," 8. Did Some Disciples Take Notes During Jesus' Ministry? Bible.org, 2020. https://Bible.org/seriespage/8-did-some-disciples-take-notes-during-jesus-ministry

Lieberman's view supports the idea that the sayings of Jesus in the gospel are not merely from memory, but actual noted sayings and sermons of Jesus as He said them.

An interesting side note is that one of the most prominent theories about the formulation of the gospels is called the source documentary hypothesis. This theory states that Mark was the first gospel to be written. Based on the amount of word-for-word Markian content in both Matthew and Luke, it is assumed that Matthew and Luke based their gospels off of Mark while also supplying their own material. However, there is enough word-for-word content shared between Matthew and Luke that is not from Mark that scholars have concluded there must be another written source that Matthew and Luke are both drawing from. Scholars have named this source "Q," which is an abbreviation of the German word for "source." This theory supports the idea that there were early sources, possibly written, that the gospel writers utilized in compiling their material.

Even if one believes in a late date for the official final versions of the gospels, that does not dictate when the sayings of Jesus were written. Even a doubter like Allan R. Millard has to conclude there were some notes:

> To imagine any of these people going out with papyrus roll, pen and ink to take down the words of a traveling preacher would be absurd. To imagine some of them opening note-books they carried for their day-to-day business, perhaps hung at the belt, and jotting down a few key striking sayings that they had heard, or writing a summary of what they had experienced while it was fresh in the memory is quite feasible[321].

---

321 Arlandson, "Historical Reliability"

It is a high probability that Jesus' disciples were literate and took notes during the time they were with Christ since it was traditional at that time for disciples to write down notes of their master's sayings, and they would have been derelict in their duties had they not.[322] If they were not writing down notes from His sermons and teachings, what were they doing for three years? Did they merely sit and stare at Him with starry eyes and amazed at His every word? Maybe His servants? Maybe His cheerleaders? No, I would contend that part of their job, as disciples, was to remember and record what Jesus said and did.

We can be somewhat confident that we do have the actual words of Jesus that were most likely written down in the form of notes as Jesus said them. His sermons may also have been repeated more than once; so, the disciples most likely repeatedly recorded His words slightly differently. Their notes possibly were from different sermons, so they would have had plenty of variations yet corresponding notes to draw from. Knowing that the gospels were written from notes and not only oral tradition makes a stronger case that the gospel accounts of Jesus' words and ministry can be fully trusted.

The conclusion is that the written gospels were started while Jesus was with the disciples and a work in progress up until the time they were written in their final form by the named authors. The gospels are not written works that change or make up the words and message to fit the new Christian religion but works to communicate what the Lord had actually said and did. It is not naive, unscholarly, or a faulty conclusion to believe that the words of Jesus in the gospels are the recorded words of Jesus, and I believe that we can fully trust that they are. Jesus' words and actions, as recorded accurately in the gospels, are our greatest source for knowledge of Jesus, the incarnate God.

---

322 Arlandson, "Historical Reliability"

Appendix B

The Historical Jesus Outside the Gospels

(A Continuation of Chapter 2)

Jesus is not only mentioned in the Bible but outside the Bible as well. Josephus, a first-century Jewish historian, mentions Jesus:

> At this time there was a wise man who was called Jesus. And his conduct was good, and [he] was known to be virtuous. And many people from among the Jews and the other nations became his disciples. Pilate condemned him to be crucified and to die. And those who had become his disciples did not abandon his discipleship. They reported that he had appeared to them three days after his crucifixion and that he was alive. Accordingly, he was perhaps the Messiah concerning whom the prophets have recounted wonders.[323]

Roman documents also mention Jesus:

In chronicling the burning of Rome in 64 A.D., Tacitus mentions

---

323 Johnathan Marrow, "Helping a New Generation Build a Lasting Faith," What Did the Jewish Historian Josephus Really Say About Jesus? 2020, https://www.jonathanmorrow.org/?s=early+roman+documents+about+Jesus&submit=Search

that Emperor Nero falsely blamed "the persons commonly called Christians, who were hated for their enormities. Christus, the founder of the name, was put to death by Pontius Pilate, procurator of Judea in the reign of Tiberius[324].

Shortly before Tacitus penned his account of Jesus, Roman governor Pliny the Younger wrote to Emperor Trajan that early Christians would 'sing hymns to Christ as to a god[325].'

In addition to these Roman mentions, obviously, we have a tremendous number of early Christians writing about Jesus attesting to the authenticity of the gospels. These writings are corroborated to their authenticity by other writers after them. There is no widespread historical claim that the gospels are false or embellished in these early writings.

Jesus is also mentioned in the Jewish Talmud, which has been preserved and copied over the years. The Talmud is a document that recorded the goings-on and the history of the Jews. The Babylonian/Munich Talmud claims to have records from the time of Christ. It has a record of a figure who was hung and not stoned for deceiving the people with sorcery. It reads:

It was taught: On the Eve of Passover they hung accurate, the accurate. And the herald went out before him for forty days [saying]: 'Yeshu the Notzri [Jesus of Nazareth] will go out to be stoned for sorcery and misleading and enticing Israel [to

324 Christopher Klein, "The Bible Says Jesus Was Real. What Other Proof Exists?" history.com, April 16, 2019, https://www.history.com/news/was-jesus-real-historical-evidence
325 Christopher Klein, "The Bible Says Jesus Was Real. What Other Proof Exists?" history.com, April 16, 2019, https://www.history.com/news/was-jesus-real-historical-evidence

idolatry]. Any who knows [anything] in his defense must come and declare concerning him.' But no one came to his defense so they hung him on the Eve of Passover.[326]

This passage contains a close rendition of His name, "Yeshu the Notzri," almost definitely meaning Jesus of Nazareth. Claiming that He was doing "sorcery" proclaims that He was doing actions that appeared to be miracles, and it correlates to the Pharisee's claims in the Gospel of Luke that He was doing miracles by the power of the devil.[327] It is also stunning that it states He was "hung on the Eve of Passover" instead of stoned, which delineates the method and time of His death, which corresponds to the gospels. This document seems to proclaim eyewitness testimony of Jesus from the Jews at the time who were His enemies.

---

326 Instone-Brewer, David, "Jesus of Nazareth's Trial in the Uncensored Talmud, page 275, Tyndale Bulletin 62.2, 2011, http://legacy.tyndale.cam.ac.uk/Tyndale/staff/Instone-Brewer/prepub/07_Instone_Brewer.pdf
327 Luke 11:15

Appendix C

1 John 3, Law Versus Love

First John 3 is a chapter that is challenging for all who read it. If you are a person who follows the law, you will have to twist and turn your ideas to weave around John's words to keep your salvation. If you are like me, who believes there is no law for the believer, you have to assume motives behind John's words. Either way, one has to deal with this difficult passage.

John goes through an amazing argument. He at first reminds us of our position in Christ:

> See how great a love the Father has bestowed on us, that we would be called children of God; and such we are. For this reason, the world does not know us, because it did not know Him. Beloved, now we are children of God, and it has not appeared as yet what we will be. We know that when He appears, we will be like Him, because we will see Him just as He is.
>
> 1 John 3:1–2 (NASB)

We are His children, "co-heirs with Christ,"[328] and God's love is "bestowed on us." An amazing gift and transformation have taken place in us.

Next, John goes on to discuss what this new life implies in regard to

---

328 Romans 8:17 (NIV)

how one lives out their relationship to God and others.

And everyone who has this hope fixed on Him purifies himself, just as He is pure. [We want to be like Jesus, whose love was pure towards us.] Everyone who practices sin also practices lawlessness; and sin is lawlessness. [Although a believer cannot sin in breaking a law that separates them from God, they can "practice" sin in the form of unloving behavior. They can practice evil, even though they are not capable of sin according to the written law.] You know that He appeared in order to take away sins; and in Him there is no sin. [We cannot sin because He took away sin, and He is in us, "and in Him there is no sin." Although, to not live according to one's position and calling is definitely missing the mark.] No one who abides in Him sins; no one who sins has seen Him or knows Him. [There are two ways to look at this. First, if one is abiding in Jesus, they will not act in hate or unbelief, and the one who is hating is not living in the light of Jesus and the knowledge of our relationship with Him. The other is to understand that living in sin is living by the law; since the law does not apply to believers, they do not sin according to any law.] Little children, make sure no one deceives you; the one who practices righteousness is righteous, just as He is righteous; [We are only worthy to approach God because of what He has done for us, and we do not practice righteousness in the sense of obeying rules, but in terms of emulating the sacrificial love of Jesus.] the one who practices sin is of the devil; for the devil has sinned from the beginning. [The one who practices the idea of the knowledge of good and evil as the way to be righteous is "of the devil."] The Son of God appeared for this purpose, to destroy the works of the devil. [Jesus taking away sin has not only ended

302

the power of sin in our lives but also ended the destructive belief and practice of attempting to bring good, love, and relationship through law and striving. His purpose was to lead us, by faith, through His Spirit to sacrificially, unconditionally love as Jesus did.] No one who is born of God practices sin, because His seed abides in him; and he cannot sin, because he is born of God. [Sin has been uprooted, and the Holy Spirit has been planted in us. No matter what our actions are, we cannot participate in death, the old ritual of sin, judgment, condemnation, repentance, and maybe forgiveness. No one is made righteous by this practice, not you, not me, not a priest, not a madman, not someone with no cognitive ability, and not a child; the law only appears to work for very few. It has always been that our faith in God is what makes us righteous. It took Jesus to bring the understanding of the mystery out into the open.] By this the children of God and the children of the devil are obvious: anyone who does not practice righteousness is not of God, nor [namely] the one who does not love his brother. [The righteousness of God is believing in Jesus and loving each other, as John says at the end of the chapter. We again make ourselves acceptable before God by our faith and love, not following rules.] For this is the message which you have heard from the beginning, that we should love one another; not as Cain, who was of the evil one and slew his brother. And for what reason did he slay him? Because his deeds were evil, and his brother's were righteous. [Cain thought there were rules and procedures he could follow to earn God's favor. His recourse was to destroy the one who had earned God's favor without religion.] Do not be surprised, brethren, if the world hates you. We know that we have passed out of death into life, because we love the brethren. He who does not love abides in death. Everyone who hates his brother is a murderer; and you know that no murderer has eternal life abiding in him. [How often, when embellished in religion, did I hate those who threatened me. How my anger raged when someone threatened my world that I loved. At times I would get mad enough to murder someone, it seemed. It is not for no reason that John tells us not to love the world or the things in the world. All the things of the world, safety, pleasure, comfort, money, possessions, and influence, will lead us to sin to keep them. They will lead us to judgment, anger, and violence, and if we fail to achieve our desires, that touch us to the core, even murder. How convicting this is to the religious. They know what they are capable of, no matter what level of righteousness they achieve in their religious system. John paints such a contrast here between the one who abides in the love of Jesus and the one who abides in sin and religion.] We know love by this, that He laid down His life for us; and we ought to lay down our lives for the brethren. But whoever has the world's goods, and sees his brother in need and closes his heart against him, how does the love of God abide in him? Little children, let us not love with word or with tongue, but in deed and truth. [True transformation of one's life is action. When someone is given all the gifts the Lord has provided, there should be some eventual demonstration of them on a concrete level.] We will know by this that we are of the truth, and will assure our heart before Him in whatever our heart condemns us; for God is greater than our heart and knows all things. [The life of love, by the Spirit, is not easy to understand or even live out. The Spirit is in us, guiding us to love and good works. Sometimes we fail to listen or are unable to accomplish the love that we see possible. Our desire to love will become much bigger than this broken body in this fallen world. It would be easy to condemn ourselves, lest we forget that God is in control.] Beloved, if our heart does not condemn us, we have confidence before God; and whatever we ask we receive from Him, because we keep His commandments and do the things that are pleasing in His sight. [A knowledge of the Spirit and a close relationship with God can grow as we seek a relationship with Him and love for our fellow humans.] This is His commandment, that we believe in the name of His Son Jesus Christ, and love one another, just as He commanded us. The one who keeps His commandments abides in Him, and He in him. We know by this that He abides in us, by the Spirit whom He has given us. [John sums up the commandments one more time so that we do not get confused into thinking that he is talking about following the law. He lists the cores of the Christian life here; faith in Jesus, love for one another, a deep and growing relationship with God, and the transforming power of the Spirit in our lives. Following the law and confessing your sins are not listed.]

1 John 3:3–24 (NASB)

I have given my perspective on this passage which makes it clear to me the new freedom from sin we have in the Spirit. John is describing the great contrast from one who lives by sin, violence, repentance, confession, and temporary forgiveness to one who lives by the Spirit teaching them to love with their sins taken completely away. The mystery of how Jesus transformed the paradigm by which we achieve righteousness is a difficult one to grasp.

APPENDIX D

REMOVAL OF THE LAW VERSE LIST

Paul eloquently speaks of God's work on the cross and the mystery of this new life in Christ in his letter to the Colossians:

When you were dead in your transgressions and the uncircumcision of your flesh, He made you alive together with Him, having forgiven us all our transgressions, having canceled out the certificate of debt consisting of decrees against us, which was hostile to us; and He has taken it out of the way, having nailed it to the cross. When He had disarmed the rulers and authorities, He made a public display of them, having triumphed over them through Him. Therefore no one is to act as your judge in regard to food or drink or in respect to a festival or a new moon or a Sabbath day—things which are a mere shadow of what is to come; but the substance belongs to Christ. Let no one keep defrauding you of your prize by delighting in self-abasement and the worship of the angels, taking his stand on visions he has seen, inflated without cause by his fleshly mind, and not holding fast to the head, from whom the entire body, being supplied and held together by the joints and ligaments, grows with a growth which is from God. If you have died with Christ to the elementary principles of the world, why, as if you were living in the world, do you submit yourself to decrees, such as, "Do not handle, do not taste, do not touch!" (which all refer to things destined to perish with use)—in accordance with the commandments and teachings of men? These are matters which have, to be sure, the appearance of wisdom in self-made religion and self-abasement and severe treatment of the body, but are of no value against fleshly indulgence. Therefore, if you have been raised up with Christ, keep seeking the things above, where Christ is, seated at the right hand of God. Set your mind on the things above, not on the things that are on earth. For you have died and your life is hidden with Christ in God. When Christ, who is our life, is revealed, then you also will be revealed with Him in glory. Therefore, consider the members of your earthly body as dead to immorality, impurity, passion, evil desire, and greed, which amounts to idolatry.

Colossians 2:13–3:6 (NASB)

Paul paints almost the same picture that John paints of our new life in Jesus. Sin and the old law have no place in it; we are no longer bound by the law and are not judged. We have been set free from the old law and have a new calling to love as Jesus loved in the power of the Spirit in us. This revealed mystery is much more righteous and transforming than any worldly notion of law and sin, whether religious or secular.

Not only in Colossians but the end of the law is demonstrated in several other passages in the New Testament.

The next day he saw Jesus coming to him and said, "Behold, the

Lamb of God who takes away the sin of the world!"

John 1:29 (NASB)

Everyone who practices sin also practices lawlessness; and sin is lawlessness. You know that He appeared in order to take away sins; and in Him there is no sin. No one who abides in Him sins; no one who sins has seen Him or knows Him.

1 John 3:4–6 (NASB)

No one who is born of God practices sin, because His seed abides in him; and he cannot sin, because he is born of God.

1 John 3:9 (NASB)

And through Him everyone who believes is freed from all things, from which you could not be freed through the Law of Moses.

Acts 13:39 (NASB)

Now why do you delay? Get up and be baptized, and wash away your sins by calling on His name.

Acts 22:16 (NASB)

He has made us competent to be ministers of a new covenant, not of the letter, but of the Spirit. For the letter kills, but the Spirit produces life. Now if the ministry of death, chiseled in letters on stones, came with glory, so that the Israelites were not able to look directly at Moses' face because of the glory from his face — a fading glory — how will the ministry of the Spirit not be more glorious? For if the ministry of condemnation had glory, the ministry of righteousness overflows with even more glory.

2 Corinthians 3:6–9 (HCSB)

And you, being dead in your trespasses and the uncircumcision of your flesh, He has made alive together with Him, having forgiven you all trespasses, having wiped out the handwriting of requirements that was against us, which was contrary to us. And He has taken it out of the way, having nailed it to the cross. Having disarmed principalities and powers, He made a public spectacle of them, triumphing over them in it.

Colossians 2:13–15 (NKJV)

For sin will not rule over you, because you are not under law but under grace.

Romans 6:14 (HCSB)

Therefore, my brethren, you also have become dead to the law through the body of Christ, that you may be married to another— to Him who was raised from the dead, that we should bear fruit to God. For when we were in the flesh, the sinful passions which were aroused by the law were at work in our members to bear fruit to death. But now we have been delivered from the law, having died to what we were held by, so that we should serve in the newness of the Spirit and not in the oldness of the letter.

But sin, taking opportunity by the commandment, produced in

me all manner of evil desire. For apart from the law sin was dead. I was alive once without the law, but when the commandment came, sin revived and I died. And the commandment, which was to bring life, I found to bring death. For sin, taking occasion by the commandment, deceived me, and by it killed me.

Romans 7:8–11 (NKJV)

Knowing that a man is not justified by the works of the law but by faith in Jesus Christ, even we have believed in Christ Jesus, that we might be justified by faith in Christ and not by the works of the law; for by the works of the law no flesh shall be justified.

Galatians 2:16 (NKJV)

For I through the law died to the law that I might live to God. I have been crucified with Christ; it is no longer I who live, but Christ lives in me; and the life which I now live in the flesh I live by faith in the Son of God, who loved me and gave Himself for me. I do not set aside the grace of God; for if righteousness comes through the law, then Christ died in vain.

Galatians 2:19–21 (NKJV)

This only I want to learn from you: Did you receive the Spirit by the works of the law, or by the hearing of faith? Are you so foolish? Having begun in the Spirit, are you now being made perfect by the flesh?

Galatians 3:2–3 (NKJV)

For as many as are of the works of the law are under the curse;

for it is written, "Cursed is everyone who does not continue in all things which are written in the book of the law, to do them." But that no one is justified by the law in the sight of God is evident, for "the just shall live by faith." Yet the law is not of faith, but "the man who does them shall live by them." Christ has redeemed us from the curse of the law, having become a curse for us (for it is written, "Cursed is everyone who hangs on a tree"), that the blessing of Abraham might come upon the Gentiles in Christ Jesus, that we might receive the promise of the Spirit through faith.

Galatians 3:10–14 (NKJV)

Is the law then against the promises of God? Certainly not! For if there had been a law given which could have given life, truly righteousness would have been by the law. But the Scripture has confined all under sin, that the promise by faith in Jesus Christ might be given to those who believe. But before faith came, we were kept under guard by the law, kept for the faith which would afterward be revealed. Therefore, the law was our tutor to bring us to Christ, that we might be justified by faith. But after faith has come, we are no longer under a tutor.

Galatians 3:21–25 (NKJV)

Stand fast therefore in the liberty by which Christ has made us free, and do not be entangled again with a yoke of bondage. Indeed I, Paul, say to you that if you become circumcised, Christ will profit you nothing. And I testify again to every man who becomes circumcised that he is a debtor to keep the whole law.

You have become estranged from Christ, you who attempt to be justified by law; you have fallen from grace. For we through the Spirit eagerly wait for the hope of righteousness by faith. For in Christ Jesus neither circumcision nor uncircumcision avails anything, but faith working through love.

Galatians 5:1–6 (NKJV)

But if you are led by the Spirit, you are not under the law.

Now the works of the flesh are evident, which are: adultery, fornication, uncleanness, lewdness, idolatry, sorcery, hatred, contentions, jealousies, outbursts of wrath, selfish ambitions, dissensions, heresies, envy, murders, drunkenness, revelries, and the like; of which I tell you beforehand, just as I also told you in time past, that those who practice such things will not inherit the kingdom of God. But the fruit of the Spirit is love, joy, peace, longsuffering, kindness, goodness, faithfulness, gentleness, self-control. Against such there is no law. And those who are Christ's have crucified the flesh with its passions and desires. If we live in the Spirit, let us also walk in the Spirit. Let us not become conceited, provoking one another, envying one another.

Galatians 5:18–26 (NKJV)

But we know that the law is good if one uses it lawfully, knowing this: that the law is not made for a righteous person, but for the lawless and insubordinate, for the ungodly and for sinners, for the unholy and profane, for murderers of fathers and murderers of mothers, for manslayers, for fornicators, for sodomites, for kidnappers, for liars, for perjurers, and if there is any other thing that is contrary to sound doctrine.

1 Timothy 1:8–10 (NKJV)

For it is impossible for those who were once enlightened, and have tasted the heavenly gift, and have become partakers of the Holy Spirit, and have tasted the good word of God and the powers of the age to come, if they fall away, to renew them again to repentance, since they crucify again for themselves the Son of God, and put Him to an open shame.

Hebrews 6:4–6 (NKJV)

But this Man, after He had offered one sacrifice for sins forever, sat down at the right hand of God, from that time waiting till His enemies are made His footstool. For by one offering He has perfected forever those who are being sanctified.

Hebrews 10:12–14 (NKJV)

"And their sins and their lawless deeds I will remember no

more." Now where there is forgiveness of these things, there is no longer any offering for sin.

Hebrews 10:17–18 (NASB)

How much severer punishment do you think he will deserve who has trampled under foot the Son of God, and has regarded as unclean the blood of the covenant by which he was sanctified, and has insulted the Spirit of grace?

Appendix E

Hebrews 10:29 (NASB)

Daily Walking with Jesus

W hat are the keys to walking with Jesus? The most important key is to trust the Spirit to move you in the direction of truth and love, but the following list may be somewhat helpful for those who like lists. It is a descriptive list of places God has taken me.

1. **Receive Salvation in Jesus**. Deciding to become a follower of Jesus and baptized with His Spirit.[329]

2. **Live by the "Law of the Spirit" and Not the "Law of Sin and Death."** Transform oneself from living by the flesh (living by the law and violence, which is slavery to sin and death and includes the guilt, confession, and forgiveness cycle.) to one who lives by "law of the spirit of life in Christ Jesus" (practicing the righteousness of God, which is living out God's love in the truth of our complete forgiveness).[330]

3. **Knowing Righteousness Is by Faith and Not Works.** Understanding the righteousness of God, which is manifested in our love for God, our love for our neighbors, and our love for ourselves, through the power of the Spirit. It is not achieved through the enforcement of a code of ethics on ourselves and

---

329 1 John 4:15-16
330 Romans 8:2 (NASB)

others through condemnation[331].

4. **Receiving and Giving Love.** Receiving unconditional love and acceptance from God when we do not deserve it and giving that to others who are in the same undeserving state is our imitation of the cross. This is not only words but actions and deeds. It is generous to give of our time and treasure.[332]

5. **Receiving and Giving Forgiveness.** Receiving total undeserved forgiveness from God and then, in turn, forgiving others and ourselves, forgetting the evil done to us and hoping for grace for the evil we have done to others.[333]

6. **Knowing That It Is the Holy Spirit That Changes Us and Not Our Works.** Know that true and lasting change comes not by our power but only by the power of the Holy Spirit communing with us, guiding us, growing us, and pouring out His love in our hearts, producing the fruits of the Spirit in our lives[334].

7. **Living and Relating to Others by the Ethic of Love and Not Rules, Judgment, and Punishment.** We are called to love and serve others without judgment based on any code of ethics. Judging blocks love, hindering our love for ourselves and for our neighbor. The moment we make a law, we judge because laws demand judgment and violence to enforce.[335]

8. **Embrace the Suffering.** In this life, suffering and struggle are God's tools to grow love and eternity in our hearts. God, through His love, makes positive results out of our hard and/or negative

331 Romans 10:3-13
332 Philippians 2:1-10; 1 John 4:7-18
333 Colossians 3:13
334 Titus 3:4-7; Philippians 1:6; Galatians 5:1-5, 22-25
335 Luke 6:37-42

experiences[336]

9. **Seek Truth and Education.** Knowledge of great wisdom, starting with the gospel and God's Word, but also including all truth concerning God and the world around us, can facilitate change as we grow in the Spirit.[337]

10. **Living with Humility and Gratefulness.** In humility, God opens our minds to true wisdom (skill for living). Gratefulness helps us see the world from the eyes of others and God.[338]

11. **Embracing Friends, Family, and People in General.** God uses people in our lives as amazing catalysts for change. Oftentimes, people cause suffering, but whether suffering, encouragement, example, or love, they move us[339].

12. **Have Prayer, Praise, and Worship in Your Life.** Love God with all your heart, with all your soul, with all your mind, and with all your strength.[340]

---

336 Romans 5:1-5, 8:17-18; James 1:2-4
337 John 8:31-31, 14:6, 16:3; 2 Corinthians 13:8; 2 Timothy 3:16
338 Ephesians 4:2; Colossians 3:12; Proverbs 11:2; 1 Peter 5:5
339 Luke 6:27-36; Matthew 7:12
340 Mark 12:30; Psalm 150; Philippians 4:6; 1 Thessalonians. 5:16-18

BIBLIOGRAPHY

"Arlandson, James M., "Historical Reliability of the Gospels," 8. Did Some Disciples Take Notes During Jesus' Ministry? Bible.org, 2020. https://Bible.org/seriespage/8-did-some-disciples-take-notes-during-jesus-ministry.

Baukham, Richard, "Jesus and the Eyewitnesses: The Gospels as Eyewitness Testimony," Second ed. Grand Rapids: Eerdmans, 2017, Summary given by Robert J Cara, "Reformed Faith & Practice," https://journal.rts.edu/review/jesus-and-the-eyewitnesses-the-gospels-as-eyewitness-testimony/ .

BibleHub.com, "Strong's Concordance," https://www.Biblehub.com/greek/266.htm.

Boyd, Greg, "Sociopath Religion," The Narrow Gate, July 3, 2013, https://youtu.be/-3sZr8IWbKs.

Bromiley, Geoffrey W., The International Standard Bible Encyclopedia, Vol. 4, Q-Z, Eerdmans, 1988.

Budjen, Aaron, www.livinggodministries.net, 2020.

Budjen, Aaron, "Hebrews 6:1 Dead Works," Hebrews Message, Living God Ministries web site, https://www.livinggodministries. net/living_god_ministries/radio_archive/audio_files/hebrews_20_ ch6_1_dead_works.mp3

Budjen, Aaron, "Cloth and Wine," Living God Ministries, https:// www.livinggodministries.net/living_god_ministries/radio_archive/ audio_files/cloth_and_wine.mp3.

Burridge, Richard, "What are the Gospels?," 1992/2004, http:// www.fondazioneratzinger.va/content/fondazioneratzinger/en/ news/notizie/rimandi-news/graeco-roman-biography-and-the- gospels-literary-genre.html .

Carnell, Edward John, *The Kingdom of Love and the Pride of Life*, Grand Rapids, MI: Wm. B. Eerdmans, 1960.

Church of Jesus Christ official website (https://www.comeuntochrist. org/beliefs/book-of-mormon/who-wrote-the-book-of-mormon).

The Church of Jesus Christ of the Latter Day Saints, "Attributes of Christ," https://www.churchofjesuschrist.org/comeuntochrist/ believe/becoming-like-jesus/attributes-of-christ.

Crossway, "The Bible and Islam," https://www.crossway.org/

articles/the-Bible-and-islam/

Farley, Andrew, God Without Religion, book summary, Baker Books, Grand Rapids, 2011.

The First Presidency and Council of the Twelve Apostles of The Church of Jesus Christ of Latter-day Saints, "The Family: A Proclamation To The World," September 23, 1995, https://www.churchofjesuschrist.org/study/scriptures/the-family-a-proclamation-to-the-world/the-family-a-proclamation-to-the-world?lang=eng.

Fusselman, Midge, "What Blaise Pascal Saw In A November Night of Fire That Inaugurated A Year Of Grace," "The Federalist," 2020, https://thefederalist.com/2017/11/23/blaise-pascal-saw-november-night-fire-inaugurated-year-grace/.

Holloway, April, Accounts of Roman Infanticide and Sacrifice All Just Myth and Legend?, Ancient Origins, September 5, 2015, https://www.ancient-origins.net/news-history-archaeology/accounts-roman-infanticide-and-sacrifice-all-just-myth-and-legend-006591.

Instone-Brewer, David, "Jesus of Nazareth's Trial in the Uncensored Talmud, Tyndale Bulletin 62.2, 2011, http://legacy.tyndale.cam.ac.uk/Tyndale/staff/Instone-Brewer/prepub/07_Instone_Brewer.pdf.

Klein, Christopher, "The Bible Says Jesus Was Real. What Other Proof Exists?" history.com, April 16, 2019, https://www.history.com/news/was-jesus-real-historical-evidence.

Liddel-Scott-Jones Definitions, Entry for Strong's #863, Studylight.org, 2020, https://www.studylight.org/lexicons/greek/863.html .

Liddel-Scott-Jones Definitions, Entry for Strong's #2511, Studylight.org, 2020, https://www.studylight.org/lexicons/greek/2511.html .

Liddel-Scott-Jones Definitions, Entry for Strong's #93, Studylight.org, 2020, https://www.studylight.org/lexicons/greek/93.html.

Marrow, Johnathan, "Helping a New Generation Build a Lasting Faith," "What Did the Jewish Historian Josephus Really Say About Jesus?" 2020, https://www.jonathanmorrow.org/?s=early+roman+documents+about+Jesus&submit=Search.

The Metropolitan Museum of Art, "The Five Pillars of Islam," https://www.metmuseum.org/learn/educators/curriculum-resources/art-of-the-islamic-world/unit-one/the-five-pillars-of-islam.

Musumeci, Natalie, Man Shoots at wife and daughter over grilled cheese sandwich: cops, January 9, 2017, New York Post, nypost.com, https://nypost.com/2017/01/09/man-shoots-at-wife-and-daughter-over-grilled-cheese-sandwich-cops/.

Newsroom, "What Mormons Believe About Jesus Christ," Church of Jesus Christ and Latter Day Saints,https://newsroom. churchofjesuschrist.org/article/what-mormons-believe-about-jesus-christ.

Nyman, Monte S. "Why is the Book of Mormon the 'most correct book,' and how does it contain the fullness of the gospel?" Ensign 6, no. 9 (September 1976): 0-96. Accessed November 24, 2020. https://www.churchofjesuschrist.org/study/ensign/1976/09/i-have-a-question/why-is-the-book-of-mormon-the-most-correct-book?lang=eng).

Oxford English Dictionary, 2020, https://www.oed.com/viewdictionaryentry/Entry/110566.

Pascal, Blaise, Pensées, trans. Honor Levi (Oxford: Oxford University Press, 1995).

Popova, Maria, "What Is Love? Famous Definitions from 400 Years of Literary History," May 28th, 2020, https://www.brainpickings.org/2013/01/01/what-is-love/.

Rivera, John "The historical Jesus and the Bible Scholars cast doubt on miracles, Easter," The Baltimore Sun, September 7, 2020, https://www.baltimoresun.com/news/bs-xpm-1998-05-03-1998123040-story.html.

Sanders, John (14 May 1990). "The Perennial Debate." Christianity Today. Christianity Today International.

Stanley, Andy, *Irresistible: Reclaiming the New that Jesus Unleashed for the World*, Zondervan, Grand Rapids, 2018.

Studylight.org

Thiede, Carsten Peter, "A Testament Is Born," Christian History Institute, Issue #43, 1994. https://christianhistoryinstitute.org/magazine/article/a-testament-is-born.

Wallace, J. Warner, "Good Reasons to Believe Peter Is the Source of Mark's Gospel," Cold Case Christianity, August 24th, 2018, https://coldcasechristianity.com/writings/good-reasons-to-believe-peter-is-the-source-of-marks-gospel/.

Zacharias, Ravi, "How can we show that Christianity is the true religion?," Ravi Zacharias International Ministries April 2, 2012, https://www.youtube.com/watch?v=nWY-6xBA0Pk&feature=youtu.be.

CPSIA information can be obtained
at www.ICGtesting.com
Printed in the USA
BVHW042058020222
627761BV00017B/178

9 781685 560201